D1453566

"At the heart of Christian origins is a terrible act of violence, the crucifixion of Jesus. The death of Jesus meant many things to his followers, but the interpretation that took hold and perdured in story and ritual was the ancient myth of redemptive violence. This brave new book dares to ask, was that the right choice? In a world rife with violence, is there another way for followers of Jesus to bear witness to the meaning of his life, and death, that does not involve the breaking of bodies and the shedding of blood? In this remarkable book, Christopher Grundy offers a bold new vision for Christian ritual life that honors the past, but sets a new course for a future where remembered violence gives way to remembered community, resistance to oppression, and boundless hope."

—STEPHEN J. PATTERSON, Willamette University,
author of *Beyond the Passion* and *The Lost Way*

"How to celebrate Holy Communion without profiting from the violence done to Jesus? Christopher Grundy's book brings together deep engagement with recent scholarship on the biblical and historical roots of eucharistic meals, with a profound pastoral and social concern. It will speak powerfully to readers who have stumbled over the misuse of the Eucharist as a symbol of violence, as well as those simply open to finding fresh and engaging possibilities in their celebration of Holy Communion."

—ANDREW MCGOWAN, Yale Divinity School,
author of *Ancient Christian Worship*

"In recent years, I have longed for intelligent discourse about what kind of God is being 'performed' by the Eucharist. I just finished Christopher Grundy's *Recovering Communion in a Violent World,* and it is masterfully written, urgently needed, and theologically inspiring, and I believe it will be one of a handful of 'go-to' books on Eucharist and liturgy in general for decades to come."

—BRIAN D. MCLAREN, author of *The Great Spiritual Migration*

"With this book, Christopher Grundy asks Christians to re-think and change the practices they use for Communion. As they are traditionally enacted, Grundy argues, they lead congregations to participate in a re-enactment of an execution, the death of Jesus. Instead, he proposes practices that affirm love, solidarity, and agency, the heart of Jesus' witness. What at first seems shocking is, by the end of the book, exactly what is needed to contest what is seldom examined."

—JANET WALTON, Union Theological Seminary,
author of *Feminist Liturgy: A Matter of Justice*

"An eye-opener of a book. Grundy exposes the latent violence and de-personalization that characterize the rite of Holy Communion as most of us know it. Then he points the way toward a retrieval of ancient Communion practices that can bring churches closer to participation in the beloved community. The book asks the reader to stop and think and re-imagine."

—TOM F. DRIVER, Union Theological Seminary, author of *Liberating Rites*

Recovering Communion in a Violent World

Recovering Communion in a Violent World

RESISTANCE, RESILIENCE, AND RISK

Christopher Grundy

CASCADE *Books* · Eugene, Oregon

BV
825.3
.G78
2019

RECOVERING COMMUNION IN A VIOLENT WORLD
Resistance, Resilience, and Risk

Copyright © 2019 Christopher Grundy. All rights reserved. Except for brief quotations in critical publications or reviews, no part of this book may be reproduced in any manner without prior written permission from the publisher. Write: Permissions, Wipf & Stock Publishers, 199 W. 8th Ave., Suite 3, Eugene, OR 97401.

Cascade Books
An imprint of Wipf & Stock Publishers
199 W. 8th Ave., Suite 3
Eugene, OR 97401

www.wipfandstock.com

Paperback ISBN: 978-1-5326-6034-4
Hardback ISBN: 978-1-5326-6035-1
Ebook ISBN: 978-1-5326-6036-8

Cataloguing-in-Publication data:

Names: Grundy, Christopher, author.

Title: Recovering communion in a violent world : resistance, resilience, and risk / Christopher Grundy.

Description: Eugene, OR: Cascade Books, 2019. | Includes bibliographical references and indexes.

Identifiers: ISBN 978-1-5326-6034-4 (paperback). | ISBN 978-1-5326-6035-1 (hardback). | ISBN 978-1-5326-6036-8 (ebook).

Subjects: Lord's Supper. | Psychic trauma—Religious aspects—Christianity. | Suffering—Religious aspects—Christianity. | Human body—Religious aspects—Christianity.

Classification: BV825.3 G80 2019 (print). | BV825.3 (ebook).

Manufactured in the U.S.A.   NOVEMBER 13, 2019

Scripture quotations are from New Revised Standard Version Bible, copyright ©1989 National Council of the Churches of Christ in the United States of America. Used by permission. All rights reserved worldwide.

The author gratefully acknowledges permission to reprint the following:

Excerpt from "The Ones Who Walk Away from Omelas," copyright © 1973 by Ursula K. Le Guin. First appeared in "New Dimension 3" in 1973, and then in *The Wind's Twelve Quarters*, published by HarperCollins in 1975. Reprinted by permission of Curtis Brown, Ltd.

Excerpt from "And the Truth Will Make You Free" by Hope [pseudonym] in *Victim to Survivor: Women Recovering from Clergy Sexual Abuse,* edited by Nancy Werking Poling, copyright ©1999. Reprinted by permission of Pilgrim Press. All rights reserved.

Excerpt from "Try to Praise the Mutilated World" from *Without End: New and Selected Poems* by Adam Zagajewski. Copyright © 2002 by Adam Zagajewski. Used by permission of Farrar, Straus & Giroux.

Excerpt from *Sexual Violence and American Manhood* by T. Walter Herbert, Cambridge, Mass.: Harvard University Press, copyright © 2002 by the President and Fellows of Harvard College.

Excerpt from "Diving into the Wreck" by Adrienne Rich. Copyright ©2016 by the Adrienne Rich Literary Trust. Copyright © 1973 by W. W. Norton and Company. Used by permission of W. W. Norton and Company.

Excerpt from "Little Gidding" from *Four Quartets* by T. S. Eliot. Copyright 1942 by T. S. Eliot; copyright © renewed 1970 by Esme Valerie Eliot. Reprinted by permission of Houghton Mifflin Harcourt Publishing Company. All rights reserved.

If you do not transform your pain,
you will surely transmit it
to those around you and the next generation.

—RICHARD ROHR, *The Naked Now*

The discovery that the past might have gone another way
is simultaneously the discovery that the future can be different.

—JAMES CARROLL, *Constantine's Sword*

Just as the cross failed to silence his story,
for Jesus rose to live on in a religious movement that kept his memory alive,
so all the appropriations of him into constructions of ecclesial domination
through the centuries also have failed to silence the subversive power of his
    name.

—ROSEMARY RADFORD RUETHER, *Women and Redemption*

Contents

Acknowledgments

I'M GRATEFUL TO A great company of saints who have added their thoughts and support over a period of more than twenty years to bring this book to life. Tom Driver first drew my attention to ritual violence at Union Seminary back in the early 1990s. My uncle, Jack Noble, listened to my questions and sent me books on ritual and violence. John Krueger, then conference minister of the Kansas Oklahoma Conference of the United Church of Christ (UCC), convened a group of local pastors around a table to discuss their own discomfort with Holy Communion and my first, faltering, outlandish ideas. Ruth Duck, my doctoral advisor, guided an earlier stage of this work with a gentle wisdom and allowed me the room to develop my own views. The other members of my dissertation committee—Scott Haldeman, James Poling, and Marjorie Procter-Smith—gave me invaluable feedback. Numerous colleagues in both the liturgical theology seminar and the UCC scholars group of the North American Academy of Liturgy read excerpts and chapters over a span of twelve years. My colleagues at Eden Theological Seminary also read chapters, consulted when I became muddled, and encouraged me time and again. Stephen Patterson reviewed excerpts related to his own work. Students in my classes on Holy Communion wrestled with incredibly difficult issues, shared their own pain, and were patient when I struggled to articulate new, emerging concepts. Kaudie McLain provided invaluable insights for the shape of the project as a content editor. Jackie Gutschenritter and Moira Finley read through this work with an eye to the experience of survivors. K. C. Hanson provided important guidance through the publishing process. Carla Tellor Grundy prayed with me about starting this journey, believed in me when I felt unbelievable, supported me long after the project should have been done, and never gave up on this work.

There is one other group of people to whom I'm grateful, whose contributions to this work have come at great cost. They are the women and men who shared their stories of suffering and survival with me. They helped me begin to perceive things about Holy Communion that I sensed but could not see clearly, and, to be honest, didn't really want to see. I hope that this work is helpful, and worthy of their courage and trust.

PART ONE

1

Communion

An Invitation

A Showing Forth

Communion, really, is why we're here. That may sound trite, but it's what I've come to believe and to trust. We exist—you, I, all of us—both *in* and *for* communion. We exist *in* communion, in a broad sense, all the time—whether we are mindful of it or not. There isn't much that's surprising in that, perhaps, except that we forget. From subatomic particles to galaxies, from grizzly bears scooping at trout to complete strangers sitting next to us in worship, we are in this together, and the pulse of something deeply connected—even divine—runs through all of it. We are bound up with one another and with God far more than we are usually aware. In every moment we are caught up in the activity of the universe—solar winds, cells dividing, weather patterns. Today almost three hundred and seventy-two thousand of us humans will be born, while some one hundred and fifty-six thousand of us will die.[1] We are carried along together in the strong, swaying mystery of the Sacred.

There is also a particular sense in which we exist *for* communion as well, as a constant purpose and a way of life. We are drawn by instinct into the practices of relationship and community, cooperating with

1. Central Intelligence Agency, *World Factbook*.

others, more or less gracefully, in struggle and in song. This continues despite all of the damage that has been done. In the rubble of the last war we build schools and town halls. Though we can't take back things we've said in anger, we stand in small circles, holding hands. We pour out into the street with signs and banners and march together one more time. We seek out intimacy—at times almost in spite of ourselves—over cups of coffee, under bedcovers, or just out under the stars. In all of this we are joining in, swimming with the great tidal movement of the Holy.

Some of us respond consciously and intentionally to this holiness. Formed by the practices of faith or awakened by a sudden deer-in-the-landscape movement of grace in our lives, we try with mindfulness and purpose to move in sync with the divine in the world. We pray or meditate or listen to wind in the leaves. We look into the faces of those who are hungry, sick, or abused, searching for the trace of divinity. We study scriptures, news reports, and want ads for a sense of which path to follow next. We struggle to weave relationships that are right and just. We try to reconcile, and to forgive. These practices of drawing closer, this contemplative, activist collaboration with the Spirit's lead, wherever and in whomever it is found, is the communion *for* which, and *toward* which we live.

In the lives of those of us who are Christians, the practices of living in and for communion most often take the form of discipleship. That is, our practices are framed by the imitation of Jesus and participation in his ongoing ministry in the world. As best we can, we follow in the way of Jesus, who himself practiced a ministry of communion with God and with many different types of people—in spite of the risks.

When we come together to continue Jesus' ministry, and that ministry becomes a concrete, social, contemporary reality, then extraordinary things can happen. Our efforts, moving in time with the elegant dance of the divine, can help to clear away a kind of "thin place," in the language of Celtic spirituality, anywhere in the world. For a moment heaven and earth kiss—or perhaps righteousness and *shalom* kiss, as Psalm 85 says—and we may suddenly get the sense that we are on sacred ground. That's when the party really starts: when people are not just bored to tears or resigned to the idea that pious sign-acts are enough. It's when they are actually fed enough to sustain their bodies, when their needs and stories are actually listened to, when they have prayerful hands laid upon them, and they are drawn into collaboration with the work of the Holy Spirit. Friends and strangers bring their brokenness along with whatever resources they have. We try to look one another in the eye. We share food, and stories: the latest news, the good news. Confessions of regret, and testimonies of grace. Sometimes we manage to find dignity, strength, new friends, and real community with God and one another. Sometimes we find healing, and new purpose. There, said Jesus, the *basileia tou theou*, Beloved Community of God, has come near.[2] As liturgical theologian Robert Hovda said, that kind of worship "lifts us temporarily out of the cesspool of injustice we call home, and puts us in the promised and challenging reign of God, where we are treated like we have never been treated anywhere else."[3]

At its best, Holy Communion can be like that. Maybe not always: maybe not every week for every person, but far more than it usually is now. At its best, the Christian meal can be a social, political, economic, and spiritual reality that is not just a sign or a foretaste, but is a change-the-facts-on-the-ground kind of epiphany of God's ways in the world. It can be a kind of portable thin place, a showing forth of the great communion in which and for which we exist.

An Invitation

If you've ever had the prickly, nagging feeling that something is seriously wrong while taking the bread and grape of Holy Communion into your mouth, then you've come to the right place. Or if you've ever presided at the table with a sinking sense that the sacrament you are leading may be doing this congregation some harm as well as good, then chances are you will find language here for what you've always felt. The first part of this book examines the ritual logic of beneficial violence embedded in Holy

---

2. Here I am thinking of Luke 10:9 ("Say to them, 'The kingdom of God has come near to you.'"), but also Matt 11:4–5 ("Go and tell John what you hear and see"). I have chosen to translate the Greek *basileia tou theou* as "Beloved Community of God" through much of this book, a version of the "Beloved Community" coined by the philosopher Josiah Royce and popularized by Dr. Martin Luther King Jr. I will occasionally use the term "kin-dom" as well, a term meant to echo the language of "kingdom" without simply perpetuating the dominating (and male) structure of that concept. I understand that terms like "Empire of God" more directly challenge political structures, but one of the underlying theses of this book is that attempts to subvert oppressive structures by using the same language usually perpetuate the language they are challenging, and thus carry an inherent vulnerability to reappropriation by systems of domination.

3. Hovda, "Vesting," 220.

Communion—the way that we enact, again and again, a system in which we gain from what was done to Jesus.

If your congregation is one of a growing number of Christian communities already wondering what to do about the way that Holy Communion enacts and interprets violence, then you will find a helpful conversation here. Some congregations have found it easy to discuss the ethical and theological problems associated with substitutionary atonement ("Is it right that we benefit from Jesus' death? What kind of God would choose that?") but have been dancing around Holy Communion for years. If you sense that your church may already be moving away from the liturgical use of Jesus' body and blood, but you're not really sure where you're headed, you will find biblical, theological, and practical ideas here for where you might go next.

If you've given up on Holy Communion as hopelessly violent and patriarchal and have stopped participating in it altogether, then you may find some confirmation of your concerns here, but also some hope. I once asked ecofeminist theologian Ivone Gebara why she thought there were so few eucharistic prayers in feminist liturgical resources. She replied that it was too much work to try to rehabilitate the rite, burdened as it was with patriarchal violence, and that feminist worship leaders probably prefer to direct their energies toward other kinds of worship.[4] I understand that this is a necessary path for some people. Even so, I would invite you into this book, in the hope that the ideas here might help you to find a way back toward the sacrament. If nothing else, you'll be able to see ways that others are continuing the struggle.

Last, if you've always held out the hope that it is possible to celebrate Holy Communion without profiting from the violence done to Jesus, you'll find that hope confirmed in these pages. That is the second part of this book. Other ways of enacting Holy Communion *are* possible: faithful, challenging, awe-inspiring ways. There are tremendous possibilities emerging from new theological and historical perspectives. Biblical and liturgical scholars are beginning to show us how the now dominant form of Holy Communion—or the Eucharist, or the Lord's Supper—emerged from a variety of local meal practices in the early church. Contemporary theologians are rethinking the meaning of atonement in astonishing ways. Local churches and worship renewal movements are exploring ways to reappropriate the ancient Christian meals. A variety of cultural

4. Ivone Gebara, conversation with author at Garrett-Evangelical Theological Seminary, spring 2002.

and historical factors have come together to make this particular moment a good time for a deep reconsideration of Holy Communion. If you are looking for ways to renew your congregation's Communion practices, or if you are longing to find your way back to the table, then this is a good place to begin.

But then, maybe you've never had the slightest misgiving about Holy Communion. Maybe you're fine with it, and you just picked up this book because in an era when religion seems to be so easily hijacked by extremism, you're concerned about the role of religion in violence. Or maybe you just opened it thinking, "Good grief! What on earth have they found to complain about now?" That's okay too. Whatever has brought you to this book, most likely there will be something in it to surprise you or to ponder—or to argue with, if nothing else. You may even find, whether you end up agreeing or not, that this exploration helps you to rediscover Holy Communion as an important spiritual practice in your life, influencing all your meals and feeding your creativity and passion more broadly for a life of courageous discipleship. That's certainly my hope.

Now, especially if you are part of the latter group, those stalwart faithful who have always loved Holy Communion without reservation and who harbor no discontent about it, I feel that I owe you a candid word up front. Even if you *do* harbor some discontent, actually, I think a few words are in order. As you may suspect already, some of this work is rough going. When I speak on this topic in local congregations, it's usually only a few minutes into the conversation before someone asks, "So, what are you proposing we do instead?" Over time I've come to detect a certain urgency in these cut-to-the-chase reactions. I suspect they surface because of discomfort. It's difficult to sit for long with the idea that Communion can form us negatively in relation to violence. Yet, as we'll see, it's crucial that we not look away too quickly.

It's sort of like the *Series of Unfortunate Events* novels for children. On long van rides our family will sometimes listen to audiobooks from this series. (We have three lively boys, so this listening is in itself a practice meant to reduce violence.) The books invariably begin with a dire warning from the author, Lemony Snicket, contrasting typical children's books with the calamity, misery, and general wretchedness of the one you are about to begin. The warning is overstated, since they're children's books after all, but the analogy still seems apt. I wish I could say that this book will lead you into beautiful new Communion practices that will help you to commune more deeply with God, creation, and other people, all without ever having to examine the pain of contemporary practices of violence—or of Jesus' death. I wish I could promise to skip quickly to the good part, the "less violent practices" part, without ever having to talk about Communion in connection with real, actual violence—like rape or torture or lynching. But I can't do either of those things, because just the opposite is true: In order to get anywhere, to see the problem clearly and make the particular changes that will really help, we will need to start by looking squarely at how our practices of Holy Communion form us, or fail to form us, in relation to concrete acts of violence. So, if you find yourself partway through the book with a voice in your head grumbling, "Get to the good part already!" know that I've been there too. All I can say is that if we're going to get anywhere, we will need a fairly nuanced understanding of the collusion between the violent ritual logic of our Communion practices and other practices of violence. Until we can acknowledge the particular ways we both benefit from and suffer because of that collusion, we will just continue finding new theological explanations for why our current Communion practices are okay, instead of changing what we do.

I wouldn't even invite you to begin, though, if I didn't think it was worth it. It's worth reading the whole book, too, not skimming the un-comfortable parts or starting with the last couple chapters. This is partly because the trouble with Holy Communion that we'll uncover first doesn't hinge upon the suggestions that come later. That is, you might disagree with the alternatives that the later chapters offer, but the problems with our current practices will still be there. More than that, though, the early chapters will help you to see more clearly why we really need practices of Holy Communion that no longer enact a violent ritual logic, but that re-main grounded in Scripture and liturgical tradition, still speaking clearly of the life, death, and resurrection of Jesus. You'll have a better sense of how alternate ways of doing Communion can help to form people like us as agents and communities of nonviolent resistance. And you'll be able to see why it matters that these renewed practices seek to more clearly embody and enact the kind of risky, resilient ministry that Jesus and his disciples undertook, collaborating with the fragile but resurgent *basileia* of God.

Walking Off the Map

In her short story "The Ones Who Walk Away from Omelas," Ursula K. Le Guin describes a beautiful, idyllic city. The city of Omelas, "bright-towered, by the sea," is a place where few laws are needed, the farmer's market is magnificent, and guilt is unheard of. The people there are not naïve children or bland utopians, Le Guin says. They have some well-chosen technology, such as central heat and railways, but no soldiers, no clergy, no advertising, no atomic bomb. They are mature and cultured... and happy.

The thing is, all happiness and prosperity in Omelas, all creativity and peaceableness, depend upon the misery of a single, small child. The child is locked permanently in a dank, windowless broom closet in the basement of one of the city's public buildings. The child suffers horribly from malnutrition and neglect. It is naked, debilitated, and covered in sores from sitting in its own excrement.

All the residents of Omelas know the child is there. Some even go to see it, though they agree not to speak to it or be kind in any way. They go home in tears, says Le Guin, or in a tearless rage, but eventually come to accept that "it is the existence of the child, and their knowledge of its existence that makes possible the nobility of their architecture, the poignancy of their music, the profundity of their science."[5]

They all accept this arrangement as given, as the way things are. All, that is, except for a few. Le Guin writes:

> At times, one of the adolescent girls or boys who go to see the child does not go home to weep or rage, does not, in fact, go home at all. Sometimes also a man or woman much older falls silent for a day or two, and then leaves home . . . They leave Omelas, they walk ahead into the darkness, and they do not come back. The place they go towards is a place that is even less imaginable to most of us than the city of happiness. I cannot describe it at all. It is possible that it does not exist. But they seem to know where they are going, the ones who walk away from Omelas.[6]

In some ways, to even suggest that Holy Communion is possible without a ritual logic that enacts this kind of beneficial violence is to leave a city of seeming happiness and "walk ahead into the darkness," off the edge of the map. To seek out alternative Communion practices is to set

5. Le Guin, "Ones," 30.
6. Le Guin, Ones," 31–32.

out toward a place that is, as Le Guin says, even less imaginable to most of us than Omelas.

Of course, the parallels between our examination of Communion practices and this story have their limits. Unlike Le Guin's story, the point of our exploration is precisely *not* to leave, but in some ways to stay—with the church, and with the Christian meal. Also, whereas the story presents the possibility of a clean departure from all violent systems, we will pursue habits of patient, ongoing resistance to those systems as being more practical and realistic.[7]

Even so, there is a kind of journey to this work, and an unavoidable element of departure from the necessity of beneficial violence. Trying to find our way out of Communion's violent ritual logic can be like trying to find our way out of a city whose vast network of twisting streets has been paved haphazardly over the course of many centuries. It can take a while for us to find our way out of the landscape we've always known, and get our bearings.

We'll begin by gathering some resources for our trek, outlining a theology of resilience—ours, creation's, and even God's own resilience—as a starting point. Why do people heal at all? What can we learn by leaning in close to pay attention to the stubborn dandelion or the baby whose arm is broken during childbirth? How can this theological perspective help us as we examine Holy Communion, beyond fostering a sort of naïve hopefulness? This groundwork will help to point us in the right direction as we begin, and perhaps allow us to regain our footing along the way.

Then we will set out in earnest. The critique of feminist and womanist theologians, along with insights from the field of ritual studies, will help us begin to see more clearly the ritualized practices of beneficial violence in Holy Communion. We will map out a ritual process of objectification, violence, and benefit within the sacrament, and see how our participation inscribes on us certain instincts for beneficial violence in our daily lives.

---

7. The assumption here is that we can't disentangle ourselves from violence completely, any more than the French philosopher Derrida could avoid allowing other cats in the world to starve by feeding his own. As he famously wrote in *The Gift of Death* (71): "How would you ever justify the fact that you sacrifice all the cats in the world to the cat you feed at home every morning for years, whereas other cats die of hunger at every instant? Not to mention other people?"

At this point we'll take a deep breath, walk outside to look at something beautiful, and then start trying to figure out what to do about all this. The second half of the book begins with an examination of trauma theory and its implications for Holy Communion. We'll draw upon the work of people who have studied both trauma and the difficult journey of recovery from it, asking what the impact of trauma might have been upon early followers of Jesus and their meal practices.

The next stage will be a recovery mission of sorts, as we begin to unpack some of the biblical resources that will be useful if we are actually going to change what we do in worship. We will see how biblical and liturgical scholars have challenged the tradition that Holy Communion flows narrowly from a single upper room story. We'll search out evidence of struggle between multiple local meal traditions. We'll look for sites within the biblical text where we might begin to see the variety of Communion practices that were eventually overshadowed by a dominant form.

Finally, a chapter called "Resistance, Resilience, and Risk" will bring together many of the insights we've gained along the way in order to outline some general suggestions for sacramental meal practices in your community of faith. These practical guidelines are meant to help you to recover and reimagine sacramental meals in your own context, in ways that form us to participate in the Beloved Community of God rather than in the ways of beneficial violence. These suggestions will also begin to develop a sacramental theology that fits with this new terrain. A brief concluding chapter will reflect on practical sacramentality and the Beloved Community of God so as to clarify these two concepts as they are developed in this work.

Is It True for Us?

Naturally, it will be up to each of us to decide how much the ideas developed here are "true for us" in our own context.[8] (Believe me, you wouldn't be the first person to read or hear these ideas and say, "For a minute there I thought you were talking about *all* eucharistic practices, and not just your own—because *our* practices are just fine.") Like everyone else,

---

8. Marjorie Procter-Smith (*In Her Own Rite*, 13), quoting poet Adrienne Rich, suggests that women need to ask of Christian worship and its claims to truth, "Is it true for us?"

I bring my own history and commitments to this work. So, for example, you will see me tend to focus on the practices of Holy Communion that I know best: the practices of White, upper-middle-class, Midwestern, liberal Protestantism in the United States. This doesn't mean that nothing here applies to those in other social locations, but it does mean that context matters.[9] I don't presume that my perspective fits with your walk of faith, and I think it will help for you to know some of my background and commitments as you begin to sort through these ideas.

First, you'll notice that, early on, this book gives more attention to the experience of women who are survivors of male violence than to other kinds of violence. This is a natural outcome of the path by which I came to this work, and not an indication that Holy Communion is more closely tied to this particular kind of violence. Over the years, as my concerns about Holy Communion and violence grew, I found conversation partners not only among pastors and feminist liturgical scholars, but also among people who were survivors of sexualized violence. They were friends, members of the churches I served, or seminary students. Not all survivors are uncomfortable with Holy Communion, of course. Some find great comfort in it. Some, though, are deeply troubled by it, and some have stopped participating altogether. As I listened to the concerns some of these survivors had about Holy Communion—how it glorified suffering, how it made the experience of enduring violence seem automatically virtuous, how it felt unsafe, how it seemed to be trying to get us to go along with something violent—I began to make connections with my own discomfort, as well as with my study of ritual.

As we will see as the book continues, male violence against women isn't the only form of violence related to Holy Communion. For many of us, the experience of violence based on gender is bound up together with violence based on ethnicity, race, religion, class, sexual orientation, or colonial exploitation.[10] Male violence against women isn't the only form of

---

9. "As [Linda Alcoff] so clearly states, to retreat from all practices of speaking for others assumes that one *can* retreat into one's discrete location and make claims entirely and singularly within that location that do not range over others, that one can disentangle oneself from the implicating networks between one's discursive practices and others' locations, situations, and practices. . . . There is no neutral place to stand free and clear in which one's words do not prescriptively affect or mediate the experience of others, nor is there a way to decisively demarcate a boundary between one's location and others.'" Isasi-Diaz, *En La Lucha*, 7.

10. Ada María Isasi-Díaz says of Latina experience, "We do not suffer two or three different kinds of oppression, each stemming from different prejudices, each one at

sexualized or domestic violence, either. It's just the form of violence that has confronted me most often as a straight White American Christian male from the suburbs. Though I didn't grow up in a violent household, for me it has been the violence closest to home. The approach taken here, then, is in part an attempt to begin with my own experience. We will make connections with other kinds of violence along the way.

As part of my commitment to empowering survivors and reducing male violence against women, you will occasionally find trigger warnings in this book, indicated by a superscripted exclamation point: [!]. These markers will appear before stories and descriptions that I consider to be likely triggers for survivors of traumatic violence. I understand that anything can be a trigger: a smell, an image, a common phrase. I also understand the debate surrounding such warnings. Because of the topics we will cover, and because I know there will be survivors who read this book, I believe it is responsible to label passages that have a greater likelihood of being triggers.[11]

Second, the path we will follow reflects my commitments as an ordained minister and a practicing Christian. It will hardly be surprising, then, that the process both begins and ends with Christian worship, rather than leaving church behind. It relies upon the current worship practices of churches (some churches, at least) and assumes that we can get back to some kind of Holy Communion by the end. You may love the result, or condemn it as heretical and unfaithful, or dismiss it as one more pathetic attempt to rescue practices that are hopelessly violent and sexist. I get that. My approach here reflects a commitment to not simply surrender this central and often staunchly guarded Christian practice to those who, wittingly or unwittingly, would continue to use it in ways that collude too easily with various kinds of violence.[12]

---

different moments or circumstances. Rather, the different modes of oppression are compounded into one multilayered burden which touches every aspect of our lives in an ongoing way. None of these modes of oppression, therefore, comes before the other or is more intrinsic to our subordination" (Isasi-Diaz, *En La Lucha*, 17).

11. For perspective on why trigger warnings are useful, see Shaw-Thornburg, "This." If, while reading this book, you need someone to talk to about your own experience of rape or abuse, please contact the Rape Abuse and Incest National Network at www.rainn.org.

12. Although she and I might have slightly different ideas of what is meant by this, I agree with and have been inspired by Marjorie Procter-Smith when she says, "We must disrupt these processes of marginalization, claim the central prayers of the church as our prayers, and thereby transform them from the language of the rulers to

Along the same lines, we will use a hermeneutic of suspicion in our search, but also a hermeneutic of confidence.[13] That is, we'll approach early liturgical documents with some healthy skepticism because they are ambiguous by nature and are steeped in the biases of the communities that produced them.[14] Similarly, our critique of current worship practices will assume that Communion rites are at least partly human constructs and are therefore "subject to the usual human flaws and manipulations," as ritual theorist Ronald Grimes says.[15] At the same time, though, we will keep sight of the fact that Holy Communion is not *only* flawed, but has also been in some ways a liberating practice for many women and men across the centuries. We'll proceed with a confidence that there is more to Holy Communion than just human construction, and that the Holy Spirit is still able to coax us toward practices that will help to bring the Kin-dom near in our contexts.

Third, our approach will be more about what we *do* in Holy Communion than what we think or say about what we do. It's an approach that can throw some of us off at first, especially if we're used to focusing mostly or solely on what we believe about a particular worship practice. A good motto for this project might be: *In worship, how we do what we do matters more than what we say we do.*[16] How and where do we sit? Who gets to say and do particular things? How are we shaped by what we are doing? It's not that our theological reflections on Communion don't matter here. It's just that, for our purposes, attention to how we're doing

the language of the whole, free people of God" (Procter-Smith, *Praying,* 13).

13. For discussion of the hermeneutics of suspicion, faith, and confidence, see David Power's examination of Jean Grondin (Power, *Sacrament,* 10–11).

14. In his *Search for the Origins of Christian Worship,* Paul Bradshaw points out numerous reasons for suspicion of early liturgical documents, among them the fact that early liturgical documents do not necessarily provide complete descriptions of actual practices, do not provide evidence of uniform practice in other locations, and may contain more interpretive strata than they purport to contain. See Bradshaw, *Search,* 14–20.

15. "Ritual criticism is the interpretation of a rite or ritual system with a view to implicating its practice. Such criticism is possible only if we consider rites to be human artifacts subject to the usual human flaws and manipulations. Ritual criticism is not always negative, but it is based on the premise that rites—however noble in intention or sacred in origin—are imperfect" (Grimes, *Deeply,* 293).

16. This is an elaboration of liturgical theologian Scott Haldeman's assertion ("Welcome," 5) that "in the event of worship itself, it matters more what we do than what we say."

what we're actually doing matters more than what we tell ourselves we're doing.[17]

In keeping with this emphasis on practice, the end goal here is to encourage you to *actually do something different* and see where the Spirit leads. As Millard Fuller, the founder of the organization Habitat for Humanity, was fond of saying, "More people act themselves into a new way of thinking than think themselves into a new way of acting."[18] Some of the ideas here won't begin to have much impact on your journey of discipleship until you can get past the book group discussion or the paper for class and actually risk eating and praying with people in new ways.

A Gracious Persistence

Just so we're really clear at the start, participation in current forms of Holy Communion doesn't make people more violent or less resistant to violence all by itself. I'm not suggesting that people are going to finish taking Communion and run right out to hold up the nearest convenience store. It's just not that simple. The sacramental meal is only one factor that shapes our behavior, colluding in certain ways with a broader culture of violence. It shapes us in concert with many other practices, from social activities to media consumption to interaction with role models.[19] Sometimes it reinforces these other practices, and sometimes it resists them. Sometimes it does both, but in different ways. The results play out differently in different contexts with different people. As we will see, a lot depends on how often one participates, and on how important the sacrament is in one's life.

17. This approach also reflects my position that theological reflection doesn't necessarily precede or provide the foundation for worship—that instead the relationship between theological reflection and ritualizing is mutual. Besides, as Catherine Bell suggests, such a way of thinking may impose an artificial distinction between action and reflection that doesn't actually exist in our practice. See Bell, *Ritual*, 19–25.

18. Quoted in Maudlin, "God's Contractor."

19. Ritual theorist Catherine Bell follows Mary Douglas in suggesting that "despite its importance in particular types of societies, ritual has no intrinsic priority as a social strategy in establishing and maintaining such a society. Rather it works in concert with many other forms of activity and types of attitude. Hence, ritualization is not a single-handed method or method of social control; it is one of several ways of reproducing and manipulating the basic cultural order of a society as it is experienced by, embodied in, and reproduced by persons" (Bell, *Ritual*, 180).

Because they are only one factor shaping how we live, the renewed practices of Holy Communion we will be working toward here are not by themselves going to make Christians less violent or more resistant to violence, either. They are only one piece of the puzzle. They will not fix everything, and their impact will be relatively small unless we allow them to influence many of our other practices as well, both within and beyond worship. Unless we engage in a variety of practices that build countercultures within and between particular communities, the meal practices suggested here may well end up being yet another ideological smokescreen.[20] They will allow us to go on telling ourselves that we are communing deeply with God and our neighbors, engaging deeply in the ministry of Jesus, without our having to actually *do* anything close to that.

All that being said, Holy Communion can do more—and *has done* more, historically—to help us resist violence. It can be more transformative and more central than it is for most of us—and more *frequent* than it is in the worship life of most Protestant congregations. Much of what is best about Holy Communion has been overshadowed by a narrow focus on beneficial violence. Fortunately, as we will see, there are other aspects of Christian meal practices that remain. The approach of this book is meant to nurture the natural resilience of the meal—to make room for some of those subjugated practices to flourish again in our worship.

So, if you've always suspected that Holy Communion could be less grounded in violence and *still be Communion*, you're right. From the potent but flawed logic of beneficial violence, it is possible for us to find our way toward meals that collaborate more fully with the gracious persistence of God's steadfast love, *in spite* of violence and death. From the habit-memory of Jesus' execution, a sort of repetition compulsion of the violence done to him, we can find our way toward meal practices that more clearly reenact and rehearse the resilient resistance of Jesus and his community. From a preoccupation with sacred objects and objectifying violence, we can find our way toward acts of mutual generosity and risk that can in small and fleeting ways become epiphanies of and collaborations with the Beloved Community of God coming near.

---

20. For broader discussion of the ways that churches can develop local cultures resistant to male violence, see Cooper-White, *Cry*; Coleman, *Dinah*; Fortune and Poling, "Calling"; and Min, "Beginning."

2

Provisioning

A Theology of Resilience

A Trace of the Divine

Hope has a new appreciation for dandelions.[1] For many of us who stoop and sweat out in the yard, the flowers are a bright yellow bother, a blight of perky, pesky little suns rising again and again from an otherwise tranquil carpet of green. Hope, though, has come to see them differently. For her, they are an unfurling banner of her own resilience. They keep coming back.

Hope is not an abstract concept in this case, not a hypothetical, but an actual person. Hope is not her real name. It's a pseudonym, but a well-chosen one, because Hope continues to struggle for a life that is more than just the damage that was done. Her struggle to live is like a burning bush that is not consumed. It is a trace of the divine in the world.[2]

Hope was abused emotionally and sexually by a youth pastor she trusted and admired, starting when she was a sophomore in high school. The abuse continued for years, through high school and into the early years of her marriage. When the abuse ended but the trauma didn't, a

1. Hope [pseud.], "And the Truth."

2. 'Trigger warning: the following passage may be a trigger for survivors of sexualized violence.

friend suggested that she go to another pastor in her hometown for help. After this pastor heard her story, the first words from his mouth were, "Well, you will not believe this, but I've been attracted to you since you were a freshman in high school."[3] He took her to a local park, moved in close to her, and it started all over again, for another three years.

Though she felt like it at times, Hope did not give up on living. She wrestled with depression, anorexia, and other self-destructive behaviors. Still, she persisted. She read self-help books. She tried several counselors, but without much change.

Then one day she went to a conference, a gathering for abuse survivors sponsored in part by some local churches. From there she began to build a network of support and eventually was able to confront both of her abusers. She faced each of them in the context of worship services that she had designed herself. She told the truth of her story, to them and to all who would listen. She even shared it in print, in Nancy Werking Poling's book *Victim to Survivor: Women Recovering from Clergy Sexual Abuse.*

None of this was easy. There was no straight path to recovery, no clear or tidy conclusion. Hope writes, "I can honestly say I now live as a thriver and not just a survivor,"[4] but her thriving looks a bit different from the illustrations in the book of happily ever after. As with any traumatic experience, the lingering effects do not simply disappear. Theologian Shelly Rambo quotes Deacon Julius Lee, a survivor of Hurricane Katrina, saying, "The storm is gone, but 'after the storm' is always here."[5] Hope's thriving is bound up together with the irreversible shatteredness of what came before. Her persistent blossoming includes the ongoing dialectic of damage and recovery that is the legacy of trauma. Things will never be the same, and if we're being honest, it's not all for the good. *And yet, by her own estimation, she is thriving nonetheless.* It's that part that fills me with awe.

"Daniel would tell me I was his special flower," Hope says of her second abuser:

> I was his bud that he had put in his treasure chest, and now it was time for me to come out and become a beautiful blossom. Thinking about his metaphor today, I know that before he and

3. Hope [pseud.], "And the Truth," 67.

4. Hope [pseud.], "And the Truth," 77–78.

5. Quoted in Rambo, *Spirit,* 1.

Jacob got their hold on me, I *was* a blossom, so fresh and new.
They turned me into a dandelion, but today I'm proud to be
one: firmly rooted, persistent. No matter how often people try
to chop me off, I just keep coming back. Sometimes I wonder
why we dandelions aren't valued more.[6]

For Hope, the dandelion has become an emblem of her own resilience. It speaks of a personal characteristic, a quality within her that she
has come to recognize and honor. This resilience, and the broader, more
profound resilience in the world to which it points, is the glimmer of
hope, the spark of inspiration and restless energy, that will get us on our
way.

It may seem odd to talk about resilience before we've even begun.
More logical, perhaps, when starting a book about recovering less violent
practices of Holy Communion, would be to focus on the problems. After
all, it's the troubling, wounding experiences that tend to throw some people's relationship with Communion out of joint and start them searching.

There will be plenty of time for that, and plenty of attention given
to the trouble. For a moment before we depart, though, it may help us to
consider resilience, both as a lived experience and as a way of thinking
about God. For, as we'll see, resilience is woven into the universe in a
way that actually precedes all our struggle and critique. Just as important,
the theme of resilience is a wellspring to which we can return when the
going gets hard. So, we'll pause to gather up this theme as a resource and
then get on our way. Think of it as the packing of provisions before we
go: water bottle, dried fruit, matches, tarp, GPS, extra socks, and a robust
theology of resilience.

The Grace of Resilience

There has been an outpouring of research on resilience in recent years,
particularly in the field of psychology. Much of this research has focused
on the role that helping professionals can play in fostering resilience in
individuals and helping them to rebuild their resilience following a traumatic experience. Part of what we learn from this research trend is that
resilience is an extremely complex phenomenon, involving a wide variety
of historical, cultural, relational, and individual factors. We also learn the
benefits of widening our focus from trauma and its effects to include the

6. Hope [pseud.], "And the Truth," 67–68.

resources that survivors themselves bring. For example, we might ask why 90 percent of trauma survivors *don't* develop post-traumatic stress disorder, and investigate more thoroughly the tremendous perseverance and resilience of those who do.[7]

In the majority of this research, however, resilience is seen primarily as a set of manageable qualities or assets that helping professionals can improve or instill. This is hardly a negative, but given the secular framework of much of this research, the inclusion of faith perspectives is largely limited to the assessed spirituality or religiosity of individuals— their practices and beliefs. The possibility that there might be any transcendent source of resilience with which practitioners and their subjects might collaborate tends to be muted.

That deeper possibility is precisely where I would like to draw our attention. The following pages focus on a more inherent or given dimension of resilience. It is a basic resilience that occurs—in different ways, and to differing extents—in all living things, and perhaps all of creation. This aspect of resilience is less manageable, calling more for reverence, humility, and wise study of that which exceeds our control.

In my experience, the concrete, lived examples of resilience we find around us in the world exist by more than just happy circumstance, and by more than just environmental factors; they are traces of the divine.[8] Hope, who survived clergy abuse, labors to rebuild a life for herself out of the wreckage. Divorced parents strain to build a new relationship as they continue to raise their children. A community or region begins reconstruction in the wake of a natural disaster. A persecuted ethnic group struggles to avoid handing down to its children the genocidal violence inflicted upon it. Within an ecosystem, new shoots spring up after the forest fire, or the water quality continues to rebound despite the dumping of endless barges of garbage. Every day, and across centuries of time, spectacular and mundane examples abound of how resilience has been woven into the fabric of creation.

---

7. Peres et al., "Spirituality," 46.

8. I am using the word *trace* here not in any way that tries to rigorously follow Derrida or Levinas, but in the limited sense of a mark or phenomenon that points to an absence (in this case, the absence of God as verifiable phenomenon) and thus points beyond itself (in this case, to the possibility of God's graciousness permeating creation). Derrida says of *trace*, "The trace is not a presence but is rather the simulacrum of a presence that dislocates, displaces, and refers beyond itself" (Derrida, "Form," 156).

None of this has to be this way. There is nothing that says healing has to exist at all. When a gecko drops its tail in order to escape attack, there's no law, no handbook of evolutionary biology that says it *has* to grow back, though we might easily speculate on why such evolution happens. When we get sick with the flu, there's nothing to say we have to get better, though often we do. In his book *The Abuse of Power: A Theological Problem,* James Poling describes a young sex offender who was arrested just as he was making the transition from being sexually abused as a teenager to abusing others. When told by a counselor that his chances of recovery were one in a thousand, he replied, "I don't plan to be a statistic." Poling reflects on this, saying, "The resiliency of his spirit cannot be explained by any theory."[9] Viewed in this way, the fact that we are resilient at all is nothing short of miraculous. "For me," says theologian Flora Keshgegian, "the miracle, the divine mystery, is in the resilience of the human spirit that is able to choose life again and again in the midst of death."[10]

By its very existence, I would suggest, resilience as an attribute of creation points beyond itself. It points to something greater, something that I would name as divine. It is a trace, in that we can't simply point to examples of resilience and say, "Look! There's God!" Yet such examples of resilience seem to be marks of something greater, of some larger possibility. Because such examples of resilience seem to be intimations, subtle hints of the divine, I would also say they are sacramental.

Certainly all of creation can be said to be sacramental, in that it bears traces of God. Theologians from Bonaventure to Teillard de Chardin have reminded us of that, not to mention Psalm 19. Resilience, though, as an ongoing process in the cosmos, does more than point beyond itself. When it occurs, it brings a certain graciousness to our existence: the easing of pain, the fading of loneliness, even the unexpected strength of persistence. In trying to understand it, we might say that resilience speaks not just of God but of a character of graciousness. The grace of resilience, we might say, is a trace of God's steadfast love.

Now, at this point some of us are yawning. After all, what's particularly new about this? We've always associated restoration and recovery with God's love. Healing is practically synonymous with Jesus' ministry. So, what's so remarkable about resilience as a sacramental trace?

9. Poling, *Abuse*, 52.

10. Keshgegian, *Redeeming,* 156.

What's remarkable, actually, is what happens when you take resilience in your hands and begin to look carefully at its peculiar grace. To begin with, it is in some ways remarkably unreliable. While it is constant in a general way, resilience is inconsistent from moment to moment and person to person. Five different people break their wrists playing basketball, and they may have five slightly or dramatically different outcomes. The same kind of chest cold that slowed you down for a day and a half last year may put you in the hospital with pneumonia today. The harder, deeper truth is that sometimes people don't bounce back. Sometimes a teenager simply gives up, or a hospitalized grandmother doesn't recover. Today, as I write this, a friend's mother has learned that the cancer is back and has spread to her lungs, and possibly her brain. Sometimes whole tribes or communities are wiped out. Species disappear. Resilience seems to be all around us, but when we consider how vulnerable it still is—and thus, how vulnerable we are—then words like *consistent* or *steadfast* are probably not the first ones that come to mind. What kind of grace is that?

Resilience can be ambiguous as well. The body's drive to survive and to heal can prolong excruciating pain before the end. The brain's healing after a stroke is rarely as complete as we would wish, sometimes leaving us with difficult questions about what is a reasonable quality of life and whether it's good or not that our loved one survived. Anyone who is in recovery from addiction can tell you that often even the good days are a mixture. And when a traumatized person or group's survival is marked by perseverance bound up together with the abuse of a younger generation, it's not clear sometimes whether resilience is happening or not.

Perhaps all that unreliability and ambiguity are why we tend to prefer theological frameworks like victory and protection and a perfect world at the end of time. Even though victory is always messier and less complete than we say it is, it offers a sense of resolution. Even when the vanquishing or destruction of our enemies creates moral and theological dissonance with Jesus' teachings about loving our enemies, victory offers a sense of security. We may try to soften our position by directing our sense of victory toward powers and principalities more than people. We may claim victory now but say that it will only be apparent in the coming age, when death and crying and pain will be no more. Still, the point is to *win*. Game over. That has a lot of appeal.

Protection, though many of us would hem and haw if asked directly, has a strong pull as well. Some of us pray for safe travel. Some pray for soldiers and firefighters. We may say that we understand, that we're not naïve, that we know there are no guarantees. We've read the story of Jesus' temptation and his response to the passage from the psalms that says, "On their hands they will bear you up, so that you will not dash your foot against a stone" (Ps 91:12). He says, "Do not put the [HOLY ONE] your God to the test" (Matt 4:7). Even so, when it's my child in the back seat as we drive to the emergency room, the prayer wells up: Intervene. Protect. Please.

Compared with these, resilience is far less flashy. It offers no exemption from vulnerability. It does little to reduce the fragility of our lives. Even resilience itself is fragile: survivors of trauma sometimes have less resilience in facing future events. There is no promise of happily ever after, only the slow, halting, nonlinear process of growth and regeneration, moving uncertainly toward fullness of life. And even this movement remains shot through with brokenness—the "after the storm." Instead of fire from heaven consuming all fifty of Elijah's adversaries and Jesus coming on the clouds of glory, all we get is maybe the stump of Jesse with a single, small shoot sprouting up and a few frightened disciples who dare to gather in spite of Jesus' execution.

And yet . . . and yet. In recent years the insights of those who study trauma have begun to pose a serious challenge to theological themes like victory and protection, and even to the central Christian narrative of death and resurrection. In this context the linear movement from Jesus' life to the cross to resurrection becomes overlaid with the testimony of those for whom the event of trauma returns again and again. Even when things are getting better, a dislocation remains, a blurring of the boundaries between life and death. Trauma messes with any simple, straightforward sense of redemption, with the easy assumption that we are moving on inexorably toward perfection. Even the witness of Scripture is reconsidered as we try to gauge the impact of trauma on the New Testament writers and their communities. As Shelly Rambo says, "Trauma becomes not simply a detour on the map of faith, but, rather, a significant reworking of the entire map."[11] In light of trauma theory, theological claims like victory, protection, and a perfect world can seem brittle at best and cruel at worst—just an attempt to cover over a deep wound of unexamined trauma.[12]

11. Rambo, *Spirit*, 9.

12. Rambo (*Spirit*, 16) says, "Insofar as theology ascribes to a certain governing logic of the passion and resurrection, theology is complicit in covering over suffering, in offering a redemptive gloss over its deep wound."

This is where inherent resilience, with its peculiar grace, can provide some help. Precisely in its ambiguity and fragility, a theology of resilience can hold together both the ongoing shatteredness of post-traumatic experience and the tenuous, tenacious possibilities for abundant life. Resilience does not preclude the traumatic return: the flashbacks, the bouts of depression, the lingering failure of language. It doesn't rule out woundedness. There isn't the pressure to sing as if death is swallowed up in victory on those days when the specter of death lingers as a faint shadow in the land of the living. There is no guaranteed outcome, either, no foregone conclusion.

But neither are we completely bereft, left with nothing but the trauma itself. Yes, at times traumatic events come to dominate the whole landscape of our lives, and a shadow comes over the whole land at noon. But even then, resilience has a way of going on unnoticed. Sometimes the stubborn heart keeps beating, even when God seems absent and the pain is intense, or when the will to get out of bed is gone. Sometimes friends arrive, and like Job's friends they mostly offer cold comfort and bad advice, but at least they've got coffee and they distract us from our self-destructive plans. Sometimes we are able to look back and honor what we did to survive a crash injury or a battering relationship even though we felt completely helpless and overwhelmed at the time. Resilience has been there, growing up through the cracks. It points not only to something within ourselves, not only to something persistent at the heart of trauma,[13] but in a sacramental way, to something that is very subtle and very basic—as foundational as the blessedness of creation. It may even point to God's own resilience, time and time again.[14]

---

13. While I would affirm the importance of a theology willing to face the traumatic return, approaches that focus only there carry with them the risk of focusing less on the practical, pastoral needs and theological implications of recovery. The approach I am using here attempts to incorporate the traumatic return, but I am concerned to theologize from the phenomena of recovery at least as much, if not more. Thus, where Rambo, and perhaps Caruth, seek to find a gracious element of survival and witness within the trauma itself, I will focus more on the dialectic of trauma and recovery, and upon the sacramental or referential (pointing-beyond-itself) aspect of that dialectic, pointing toward the divine. In this view, even the traumatic return itself (whether it comes unbidden for the sake of reintegration, or to witness its own unspeakable truth) can be seen as a sign of resilience. See Rambo, *Spirit*; and Caruth, *Unclaimed*.

14. I'm grateful to James Poling for introducing me to the theme of God's resilience in coursework and conversation.

Provisions

As a theological perspective, resilience will provide a number of provisions as we set out to explore Holy Communion. First, it can offer a sense of holding or accompaniment, a kind of floor beneath our feet as we try to look squarely at the relationship between Holy Communion and broader cultural practices of violence. It can pull us back onto the path and give us some sense of direction if the heavy topics start to weigh us down.

Also, a theology of resilience will provide us with a hermeneutical key: a new way of looking at the biblical stories, the ministry of Jesus, and our own sense of discipleship. It can unburden us of the blinding need to make the violence done to Jesus into something meaningful and necessary—something good as well as bad. A theology of resilience can allow us to face Jesus' death and the persecution of the early Christians as traumatic and to honor what his early followers did to survive while at the same time allowing us to claim the peculiar grace of letting go the habitual rehearsal of that trauma.

Finally, it will help us to see how meal practices of Jesus and his community are themselves resilient. Some of those early meal practices have been abandoned or dis-integrated from one another over time. Other practices were suppressed but have persisted, subtly, despite the damage to bodies, habits, and communities. By focusing on the resilience of the meal, we can begin to imagine how we might assist in nurturing those practices, helping them to send out new, yellow-green shoots in our communities today.

The bad news is that practices of kindness and compassion are inherently fragile. To be kind to someone is to be vulnerable, and the efforts of those who are gentle in this world are broken easily and often. Thus, the God-grounded practices of compassion, right relationship, and sharing that are central to God's Beloved Community are easily damaged or effaced by violence. Furthermore, the legacy of trauma can continue to haunt those practices across time.

There is, thanks be to God, also good news. The good news is that because the universe is the particular way it is—I would say because God's love is steadfast—resilience is also part of the way things are. Not in all ways, of course. Sometimes kind people are killed and don't come back. Sometimes the efforts of the compassionate are washed away in a tide of blood. Still, the fact of resilience remains. Despite the ways that Christian meal practices have been distorted by violence across the centuries, there are still ways in which they persist. There are still places, moments, when the reemergence or flowering of what is best in Holy Communion occurs and the Beloved Community of God comes near, like a bush bursting into flame. It's astonishing, really. With Hope to guide us, let's be on our way.

> Praise the mutilated world
> and the gray feather a thrush lost
> and the gentle light that strays and vanishes
> and returns.
> –Adam Zagajewski[15]

---

15. Excerpt from "Try to Praise the Mutilated World" from *Without End: New and Selected Poems* by Adam Zagajewski. Copyright © 2002 by Adam Zagajewski. Reprinted by permission of Farrar, Straus and Giroux.

3

Departure

A Logic of Beneficial Violence

I Had to Get Out of the Sanctuary[1]

"Even before I began to recover memories of being sexually molested I had decided to stop taking communion," writes Rebecca Parker in *Proverbs of Ashes.*

> I remember one Sunday sitting in the back of the church when the words of the communion liturgy were being read. An overwhelming feeling came over me that I had to get out of the sanctuary. The place felt dangerous. The idea that the sacrifice of somebody was a good idea, to be praised, suddenly felt directly threatening to me.[2]

It took several years for Parker to fully understand the connection between the circumstances in her own life and the practice of Holy Communion. After she had recovered memories of being molested by a neighbor when she was a child, she realized that she had been treated as a sacrifice herself. She had been made to suffer for his sake. The words and actions of Holy Communion, which responded to the sacrifice of Jesus

---

1. [1]Possible trigger for survivors of violence.

2. Brock and Parker, *Proverbs*, 213.

for the sake of others with gratitude and praise, felt dangerous because they drew her into the idea that such sacrifice was a good thing. She had to stop taking Communion for a while, just to clear a space in her head to face her own life story in a different way.

In the same book, Parker recounts the story of a Lutheran clergy-woman who raised her hand at a conference to describe a recent dream. In the dream, she was presiding at a Communion table that turned into a coffin. "I love the liturgy in all its beauty," she said. "At the same time, I feel that something is dreadfully wrong." She described her reservations about presiding, wondering aloud whether the images and ideas she was reenacting were life-giving or not. "Now when I pray in the church before the congregation arrives," she said, "I ask God to forgive me for perform-ing the eucharistic rite."[3]

How could Holy Communion be so directly threatening, so pain-fully problematic? For those of us who have felt nourished and comforted by the Christian meal for as long as we can remember, the idea can seem bewildering. We can see how the rite calls us to deeper discipleship per-haps, and discipleship has its risks. What is usually harder to see is how a rite that offers hope, builds community, draws us closer to God, and at times even seems to work *against* violence could somehow be a problem as well.

"Maybe it's just a personal thing," we might say. If our experience of Holy Communion has never been disrupted by the legacy of violence, then it's easy to assume that it's not really a problem for us. Even if we *have* experienced violence, but our relationship with the sacrament has never been thrown out of joint, we may be sympathetic, but inclined to see the problem in the way the meal is perceived rather than in the way it is practiced. After all, plenty of survivors find great comfort in Holy Com-munion. We can see how the rite might be troubling for some of those who have experienced violence, but not how that makes it problematic for everyone. Maybe the problem isn't really with Holy Communion, if you know what I mean. Maybe the meal is fundamentally liberating for most of us and a few people take it the wrong way.

I understand this impulse, and I shared it at one time, but it misses a crucial point. An analogy may help: if you draw attention to the fact that most TV shows use only White characters, your friends who are White may respond with sympathy for people of color who feel excluded or

3. Brock and Parker, *Proverbs of Ashes*, 19–20.

invisible. That sympathy is a start, since these White friends have gained some awareness of the issue of racial bias in the media. But it misses the deeper truth that the problem isn't somehow attached to people of color. Rather, a media culture steeped in White supremacy shapes all of us negatively in ways that matter. That media culture skews all of our worldviews and warps all of our expectations. Similarly, with Holy Communion, it's not enough for those who have not experienced sexualized violence to feel sympathy for survivors who struggle with the meal, to wonder if we need to tone it down for them, or help them to understand it better. At some point, the problems experienced by others should prod us to ask whether there are deeper, structural issues that shape us all.

Once you've seen those deeper issues, it's hard to go back. At least it has been for me. Once the critique of feminist and womanist liturgical theologians and the insights of ritual studies are allowed to illuminate the scaffolding of problematic practices that have gradually built up around the meals of Jesus' ministry, it's hard to unsee them. It's hard to continue, just like it's hard to continue using sexist or racist or homophobic language once you've begun to glimpse the damage it can do to everyone involved. To use the metaphor of the city of Omelas from chapter 1, it's hard to stay in town once you know what's going on in the basement. It's hard to just go back home and continue your daily routines and comforts, washing the dishes and walking the dog, knowing what you know.

In this chapter we will do our best to look unblinkingly at how practices of Holy Communion draw us into a ritual logic of beneficial violence.[4] We will examine three basic ritual schemes, or organizing prin-

---

4. Here I am adapting Pierre Bourdieu's concept of a practical logic (see Bourdieu, *Outline*) and George Lakoff's ideas of both embodied logic and conceptual embodiment (see Lakoff, *Women*, xiv–xv). Catherine Bell also speaks of "the natural logic of ritual, a logic embodied in the physical movements of the body and thereby lodged beyond the grasp of consciousness and articulation" (Bell, *Ritual*, 99). By "ritual logic" I mean a certain logical or structural consistency of practice, a coherence of principle that is exercised in ritualized practices. In one sense, drawing upon Catherine Bell's discussion of Lakoff and Victor Turner, this logic is rooted in a preconceptual structuring of experience, tied closely to the orientation of the body (up, down, behind, in front, and so forth). In another crucial way, however, it is tied to the broad range of embodied practices that are particular to a given culture. The logic of how we eat at a particular instance of Holy Communion, for example, is tied to the embodied logic of how we eat elsewhere. The significance of a ritual action is partly dependent upon what similar, less ritualized actions it echoes or inverts. How we do what we do sacramentally *in relation to how we do other, similar things* makes a difference. This logic is very difficult to make explicit. It consists largely of aspects of acts within the ritual environment that we take for granted. We are not inclined to conceptualize this

ciples, that function together to form that logic: objectification, violence, and benefit.

It may seem in both this chapter and the next that I am being unfair, that I'm not giving a balanced view of Christian sacramental meal practices. They may be imperfect, you may think, but there's so much about our eucharistic practices that is really good and is being glossed over. What about the beauty of prayers and all the brokenness of the world the rite is able to hold? What about the community? What about the embodied sense of grace?

To be sure, there are many positive aspects of Holy Communion as it is practiced in today's churches. That is part of the meal's continuing resilience and a driving force behind this project. At their best, our current eucharistic practices can ground us in concrete sensory experiences of connection with God and each other. At their best, they can reach out with more than words and welcome us when we feel unlovely and unlovable. They can draw us into the habits of gratitude. To some extent, they already embody and enact God's resilient love in spite of failure, violence, and even death. I'm sure you can think of other aspects of the sacrament in your context, or other language for what Communion does best.

For a while, though, we need to give our attention to some difficult issues and try not to look away. So I hope you will keep in mind as we proceed that it's both/and: there are some significant problems with the way we do Communion, but many aspects are worth continuing.

---

logic any more than we would be likely to conceptualize the experience of reaching out a hand as we approach a door. It is minimalist, and embedded. The very act of making it explicit is artificial, involving a translation into words and concepts that alter its character and ability to function. This logic is also labyrinthine in nature. Bell speaks of "an endlessly circular run of oppositions that come to be loosely homologized to each other, deferring their significance to other oppositions so that the meaning of any one set of symbols or references depends upon the significance of others" (Bell, *Ritual,* 207). The moment we touch or jostle one specific act, our interference ripples through a hundred related issues. Thus, even as we begin to focus on particular acts, it will be important to keep in mind that, in part, it is the very appearance of symbolic coherence, drawing upon endless chains of biblical and theological images and concepts, that lends legitimacy to these practices of Holy Communion. The performance of the sacrament itself "generates a 'sense' of logical systematicity" (Bell, *Ritual,* 104).

Objectification

A friend of mine recounts her childhood experience of visiting the shop where her father worked as a diesel mechanic. He would sometimes take her with him on Saturday mornings. She would sit on a stool, out of the way, while her father and the other men worked. On the walls of the shop were pictures of naked women, draped over cars or posing provocatively. The bathroom walls were plastered with them. She remembers that sometimes the men would talk about the women in the pictures. Sitting so near the photos, my friend sometimes felt like maybe she was the one they were talking about. Already, she felt that she was not thin enough or beautiful enough in comparison. She could sense that this mattered, perhaps more than how she felt, sitting there in the shop. So she would go home and practice the same poses she had seen there. She was ten years old.[5]

Objectification is the opposite of communion. As the opening of this book suggested, we exist both *in* and *for* communion. We exist *in* it because we are far more connected to God, to one another, and to all creation than most of us realize from day to day. We exist *for* it because we all carry deep innate longings for relationship, community, and a spiritual sense of a greater whole. We generally keep searching for deeper communion doggedly, despite the mess that we can sometimes make of our efforts.

Objectification is a denial of all that. It's an attempt to obscure the deeper communion that we all share. In the early 1920s, theologian Martin Buber talked about objectification as a shift from an I-Thou relationship to something closer to I-it.[6] In her book *The Cry of Tamar: Violence against Women and the Church's Response,* Pamela Cooper-White follows Buber, describing objectification as "the annihilation of connectivity, the dulling and erasure of human relationality."[7] When we objectify someone, we stop experiencing them as a Thou. We stop thinking about their interior lives, or we invent one for them that better suits our purposes. In this way we lose track of the real, deeper connection with them. We lose sight of the small, bright flame of the Holy flickering inside the ribcage of the fashion model or the undocumented worker or the younger kid we are inclined to bully. We no longer treat them as a sacred other in whom

5. Gutschenritter, personal correspondence with the author.
6. Buber, *I and Thou,* 59, 63–64.
7. Cooper-White, *Cry,* 41.

the eternal Thou resides.[8] Though we may not notice it, we experience a kind of spiritual impoverishment in the process. Objectifying others robs us of our experience of communion with them.

If you've ever been objectified in ways that stand out in your memory, then you know how difficult the experience can be. In addition to the pain experienced in the moment, such treatment can also shape us over time. This is particularly true if we are children or adolescents. We may start to think and act as if our ideas and actions really are less important than our appearance, or that we have less agency than others do. Worse yet, we may feel isolated, cut off from a deeper sense of communion, and we may no longer notice our own inviolable spark, at the core of what novelist Toni Morrison calls our "deeply loved flesh."[9]

The damage and spiritual impoverishment caused by objectification are bad enough in themselves. What makes them much, much worse is that objectification is a crucial step in the process that leads into concrete acts of interpersonal violence.[10] As Cooper-White says:

> In a battering relationship, just before the actual physical violence occurs, the batterer calls his partner a name. There is a moment of decision, when the man consciously crosses the line and hits (or kicks or chokes): "You ____." . . . The epithet he hurls at her becomes the key that opens a passage for him into a violence that in his mind at that moment seems justifiable.[11]

In this case, the expletive is needed to try to efface the victim as subject, to shield one's eyes from the light of the other as Thou. In similar ways, soldiers in basic training learn dehumanizing epithets and stereotypes for their enemies as part of a military training program's overall effort to break down new recruits' inhibitions against killing.[12] Language and images preceding violent acts based on race or ethnicity, sexual

8. Buber, *I and Thou*, 123.

9. Morrison, *Beloved*, 105.

10 The following section may be a trigger for survivors of violence.

11. Cooper-White, *Cry*, 42.

12. "Killing another human being is not a natural act. To make it easier it is often necessary to dehumanize the enemy, make them something less than human. In our own Civil War, terms like Blue Belly and Johnny Reb were used for this purpose. In World War I it was the Hun, in World War II it was Kraut and Nip, in Korea it was Commies or Reds, and in Vietnam it was Gooks. In Iraq and Afghanistan it is Rag Heads or Hajis" (Evangelical Lutheran Church in America, "Care for Returning Veterans"; see embedded notes to slide 29).

orientation, or class also dehumanize the other. Analogies can even be found between language or images used to objectify human beings and language used to exploit the natural world.[13]

Objectifying practices also play an important role in normalizing certain types of violence within our society. This will be particularly important when we begin to look at the impact of Holy Communion practices beyond the context of worship. The objectifying images in movies and magazines, the lewd jokes and crude names that seek to obscure the sacredness of the other, the endlessly repeated scripts and relentless male gaze of pornography—all of these provide a mediating structure that opens a way for the kinds of violent acts that help to maintain privilege for some of us at the expense of others.[14]

A Body for Us

Most of us don't generally associate Holy Communion with the kind of objectification I've been describing. When we come to the sacramental meal, some things we can easily see about the rite, such as the community of faith coming together. We may easily perceive a certain grace in receiving food that is a gift. We can see a meal connected through story and prayer to the meals of Jesus' ministry, and particularly to the upper room. What we do not generally see, because we haven't been formed to see it, and maybe we don't really want to see it, is that we also help to produce an objectified human body each time we gather. That is, we engage in a ritual process by which an objectified body that was not present becomes present.

Now, we may understand that body to be either symbolic, or actual (real) under the sign of bread and grape, or something more ambiguous.[15] We may believe that the production of this body in our worship is primarily an act of the Holy Spirit, with only a bit of liturgical help from us, or we may believe that it is more of a human act, tied to remembrance

13. See, for example, Mallory, "Acts," 59–89.

14. For discussion of the male gaze, see Mulvey, "Visual." For the concept of a mediating structure, see Cooper-White, *Cry*, 65.

15. This ambiguity or liminality of the elements may well be part of the functioning of the ritual process: they're not *just* symbols, but they're not *just* a regular human body and blood. It's quite possible that this helps to obscure the ritual process of objectification, thus allowing it to go forward.

and the use of symbol. Either way, a body of some kind becomes present in a way that it wasn't before.[16]

There is a process here in which we are all involved. We participate in the Communion prayer, listening or sometimes speaking or singing parts of it. If we are the one presiding, we repeat the words of institution: "On the night in which he was betrayed . . . Jesus took the bread . . . saying, 'This is my body, which is broken for you,'" or something similar. What is obvious to us is that these are words of remembrance. They help to render present (*anamnesis*) the long-ago meal that Jesus and his disciples shared in the upper room, and they focus our attention on that. They also serve to locate the authority (and thus the responsibility) for the designation of bread and cup as flesh and blood beyond the immediate environment. Jesus, after all, was the one we remember as saying, "Do this." The structuring of our liturgical environment is thus understood to come from Jesus himself. In our view, we are simply receiving what has been handed down to us.

What is less obvious to us, however, is the ritual process happening in the room. It's less obvious that our acts of repeating these words and gestures here and now in this worship, in relation to the ritual objects of bread and grape, actually accomplish something. "*This* (indicating and thus designating the bread in our worship) is my body," the presider says, quoting Jesus. *This* bread is *that*. *This* cup *here*, and not just that other cup way back then in the upper room, is a cup of blood. Whatever we believe about the agency of the Holy Spirit and its effects, the words and gestures *and all of our participation* have a role in accomplishing the production of a symbolic body and blood, whether we notice or not.

Another clear example of this is the epiclesis, that part of the Communion prayer that asks the Holy Spirit to change the bread and cup (in

16. It is true that especially in congregations influenced by the liturgical movement, multiple meanings are often assigned to the elements: bread of life, bread of heaven, bread of the eschatological feast, and so on. But most often these symbols are arranged or invoked in ways that actually reinforce the privileging of body and blood over other meanings, as the dominant meanings are reiterated at key points in the rite (words of institution, epiclesis, fraction, serving) and in conjunction with specific actions. It's possible to leave out the meaning of bread as manna, for example, and still have a "legitimate" Holy Communion. The coding of body and blood, however, is rarely, if ever, omitted completely—even if it is reduced, or camouflaged, as in more progressive Protestant circles. Efforts to "thicken" the meaning of the elements by adding additional meanings are generally systematized *in relation to each other* in ways that ultimately serve to shore up the dominance of the privileged symbols, even if the latter are mentioned rarely. Thus, the result is largely the same.

substance or signification) into the body and blood of Jesus. An epiclesis in the Book of Common Prayer (used in worship by the Episcopal Church and other Anglican churches) says, "Bless and sanctify these gifts of bread and wine, that they may be unto us the Body and Blood of thy dearly-beloved Son Jesus Christ."[17] *The United Methodist Book of Worship* says, "Make them (indicating the bread and grape) be for us the body and blood of Christ."[18] These acts are performative as well as declarative in function.[19] That is, they accomplish something, in the same way that saying, "I now pronounce you partners in marriage" accomplishes something. They help to make present bread-as-body and grape-as-blood within this particular instance of the meal. They project that scheme, that way of understanding and structuring what is happening, onto the liturgical environment. By participating, we *choose* to help produce this body each time we come to the table.

Significantly, we choose to produce a body rather than a symbolic or real person. In the rest of our worship, in prayers, litanies, readings, and sermons, Jesus is most often remembered, interpreted, and even invoked in prayer as a subject, a *Thou*. In the Communion service, however, the language of a body is suddenly introduced as well.

And it's not just any kind of body. It's a body that is for us. It's a body that has been produced specifically as human-body-as-ritual-object.[20] This body carries only limited intrinsic resistance to being used as we desire. Certainly, it is treated with respect, but it can be carried around, covered with a fine linen, or displayed publicly on a table. It is a body without agency or autonomy: we don't have to worry about what this body wants at the moment. It lacks subjectivity: we don't spend a lot of time worrying about what this body is experiencing or feeling. ("What is it like being broken and poured out right now?") Perhaps most crucially, it is a body from which the ordinary moral constraints against interpersonal violence have been removed. We specifically produce a type of body we can destroy.

---

17. Episcopal Church, *Book*, 342.

18. "Service of Word and Table I," *United Methodist*, 8.

19. For discussion of the declarative and performative poles of language, as well as the illocutionary and perlocutionary functions, in relation to liturgical language, see Chauvet, *Symbol and Sacrament*, 131–35.

20. For discussion of what constitutes the objectification of people, see Nussbaum, "Objectification."

Seeing and Not Seeing

But what about real presence? That is, what about the liturgical language that indicates Jesus himself is present in the elements, or in the Communion service in some way? What about the words of the Agnus Dei, and sometimes the Memorial Acclamation, which are directed to Jesus himself?[21] What about the common reference to the Emmaus story during the rite, which says that the disciples' eyes were opened and they recognized the risen Jesus himself in the breaking of the bread? Don't these and similar acts structure the liturgical environment as well? Don't they point to Jesus' presence as a subject in our worship?

The answer is, yes, they may well structure an environment that points us toward belief in or experience of Jesus' presence as subject. The problem, however, and perhaps the key to understanding how the process of objectification functions in Holy Communion, is that this language of Jesus as subject does not find its way into the embodied logic of the rite. That is, it doesn't change the character of the bread and cup as an objectified body, *as produced by the way that we treat them.* The use of language that refers to Jesus as a subject may heighten the importance of the elements, leading us to treat them with even greater deference and respect, but it doesn't stop us from using them. This is not the deference and respect accorded to a person with autonomy and subjectivity; this is the respect accorded to a sacred object, such as a relic or a Bible.

That very discrepancy, between the way that we experience Jesus' presence in Holy Communion and the way that we use the bread and cup as an objectified body, points us toward the heart of the ritual logic we are trying to see more clearly. Speech acts that deploy the language of Jesus-as-subject combine with actions that produce elements-as-objectified-body in a way that plays a crucial role in our misrecognition of what the sacrament is doing. We ourselves structure the liturgical environment in such a way that our attention is deflected: directed toward an experience of the presence of Christ as subject, and not to the ways that our actions are producing an objectified body and its blood.[22] The use of lan-

21. The words of the Agnus Dei, sung during the breaking of the bread in some traditions, are addressed directly to Jesus: "Lamb of God who takes away the sins of the world, have mercy on us." In the Roman Mass, some versions of the Memorial Acclamation are addressed directly to Jesus as well: "We proclaim your death, O Lord, and profess your resurrection until you come again." It is significant that these occur after the words of institution and in the case of the Roman Mass, after the epiclesis.

22. One of the particularly thorny questions here is whether the actions of

guage about Jesus as subject actually helps us to *not see* the objectifying practices of the sacrament. This "not seeing" is a central factor enabling participants to participate in the structuring of activities that would otherwise give them pause.

Two analogies that have stayed with me through the years will help to clarify the ritual strategies at work. The first is just a passing reference in anthropologist Mary Douglas's book *Purity and Danger.* She briefly describes a ritual of the Lele people of what is now the Democratic Republic of the Congo, in which an animal called a pangolin, or scaly anteater, is hunted in the forest and brought back to the village. There, initiates in the tribe's religion are allowed to eat the otherwise forbidden animal in a solemn ceremony. What is striking about Douglas's description is that it includes two particular details. First, "It is a kingly victim: the village treats its corpse as a living chief and requires the behavior of respect for a chief."[23] The second is that the carcass of the animal is carried around the village by men who sing songs that put words on the dead animal's lips: "Now I will enter the house of my affliction . . ." Douglas remarks that the songs seem to describe how the pangolin was not captured but came willingly into the camp to be killed. A combination of ritual strategies that is difficult to see in our own rites is easier to wonder about here. Why would the Lele people combine ritual acts that treat the pangolin's body as a living, kingly, and willing victim, with ritual acts that use that body as an object that can be eaten?

The second analogy is more disturbing but has stayed with me because of the searing insight it provided.[24] In T. Walter Herbert's *Sexual Violence and American Manhood,* he describes the activities by which 'organized' rapists try to get to know their intended victims:

> 'Organized' rapists sometimes elaborate their fantasies through precursory activities as well. Ann Burgess and her associates discuss a multiple offender who saw one of his victims out shopping some months after the assault and recognized her plaid dress. She had not been wearing the dress at the time of

---

participants produce ritual objects treated as a living body or a dead one. I argue that, while in many ways the actions of Holy Communion bear more resemblance to broader practices of handling a corpse, the verbal emphasis upon Christ's living presence at Holy Communion helps to structure an environment in which we produce a living body that is simultaneously treated as a ritual object—and an object of violence.

23. Douglas, *Purity and Danger,* 199.

24. The following section may be a trigger for survivors of violence.

the attack, but it appeared in family photographs that he had examined on the numerous occasions when he had entered her apartment and familiarized himself with her belongings. He had embellished his fantasy with details drawn from the victim's life, said the rapist, so she would not be "a stranger."

Yet the victim was all the more a stranger because of the information the rapist had collected. His knowledge of her may have been accurate, but it was organized exclusively by his own need. The feminist critique of male perspectives in business, politics, and academic research can be applied without revision to his investigations. The victim's daily life was known to him, but told him nothing of her personal reality. . . . The woman ceased to exist as a person in her own right, even as the man lavished attention on her.[25]

Here the rapist believes that he has come to know his intended victim. The details he acquires may be accurate. But even so, the process by which he "gets to know her" is the very same process by which her status as a person in her own right, as a *Thou,* is effaced, mapped over. The rapist may convince himself that she is present to him as a subject, but his actions objectify her nonetheless, because they are organized around his preparation for the violence that will follow.

A chilling thread in these analogies has remained with me. It's not only the objectification involved and its close relationship with violence. It's also the way people in these examples construct subjectivities for their victims.[26] In both cases what surprised me was the kind of willful self-deception that allowed both the tribe and the rapist to enact violence while experiencing a kind of fantasized relationship, a false sense of communion even, with those they were objectifying. The constructed subjectivities create an imagined quality of relationship for the one committing the violence while deflecting attention from the process of objectification itself.

For me, the parallels with Holy Communion were, and still are, striking. We who participate come seeking Jesus as subject—in mystical presence or in memory. The information that we have about him from Scripture may be accurate. Yet, even as we structure a worship environment in which we are open to him as a subject, even as we believe that

25. Herbert, *Sexual,* 31.

26. For a helpful discussion of some of the problems associated with constructing subjectivities for the bodies of others, see Fitzpatrick, "Movement"; and Fitzpatrick, "Reconsidering."

we are helping to render him present as a *Thou,* our actions are organized around the production of his body and blood as usable, violable ritual objects. Thus, even the very acts of remembrance and adoration can contribute to the objectification of Jesus, because they are organized around our need to structure an environment in which we can go forward with what happens next.

Violence

The lynching tree, says James Cone, is the quintessential symbol of Black oppression in America.[27] The book *Without Sanctuary: Lynching Photography in America* is a catalog drawn from newspapers, personal photographs, and postcards (yes, postcards), accompanied by historical commentary from the book's authors. As you can imagine, it is a difficult book, but in its sickening repetition of detail it accomplishes a particular kind of cumulative instruction that any brief lesson about lynching cannot. Working through the book, page after page, I was first horrified by the nature of the violence itself. Increasingly, though, I was also horrified by the many faces of the White folks who stood around the tortured bodies of African Americans, smiling into the camera as if they were out at a Halloween bonfire. As Leon Litwack, one of the authors, writes:

> What is most disturbing about these scenes is the discovery that the perpetrators of the crimes were ordinary people, not so different from ourselves—merchants, farmers, laborers, machine operators, teachers, doctors, lawyers, policemen, students; they were family men and women, good churchgoing folk who came to believe that keeping black people in their place was nothing less than pest control.[28]

Looking into the eyes of the ordinary men, women, and even some children in the photographs, I tried to fathom what it had been like for them. These people were participants, whether they engaged actively in the violence or not. How could those who stood by not be shaped by what they had witnessed and, in a sense, done? I wondered about the impact, years into the future, upon those who came to watch and pose for pictures. A reporter commenting on a lynching in Howard, Texas, in 1905 described the scene and then concluded: "That five minutes of a

27. Cone, *Cross,* xiii.

28. Allen et al., *Without Sanctuary,* 34.

return to primal savagery cannot be wiped out within the course of one brief lifetime. Five thousand Texans are irremediably debased."[29]

I couldn't help thinking about Holy Communion as well. Sooner or later, in most of our services of Holy Communion, the bread is broken and the wine is poured out. Someone—ordained clergy in most traditions—takes that bread/body and tears it apart. Often, someone spills that wine/blood out of a pitcher and into a chalice. In many congregations these actions occur together as words attributed to Jesus are spoken— words that clarify what is happening: "This is my body, which is given for you." "My blood of the covenant, poured out for you and for many." In a few congregations the entire congregation actually participates in these acts, receiving wafers, which they hold until all have received. Then, on cue, they all break their own little hosts (from the Latin *hostia*, meaning "victim") at the same time, in a rush of little snapping noises.

In one sense there is nothing new or startling about this. The scandal of the violence of the Christian meal is as old as the sixth chapter of John's Gospel, where Jesus is said to have lost some followers because of his reported insistence that they eat his body and drink his blood. (More about that will come in a later chapter.) We ourselves may have experienced some revulsion at the thought of participating in the dismembering of Jesus' body. Like the citizens of Omelas in Ursula Le Guin's story, though, most of us generally come to accept that this is the way things must be. We become inured to the acts themselves. Mostly, we see the breaking of the bread as an act of remembrance. We see our actions as responses to the liturgical environment, or to Scripture, or to Jesus' own request: "Do this."

What is really startling is what we don't see: ourselves regularly constructing an exercise in collective violence. In the same way that we do not see clearly the process of objectifying Jesus, producing an objectified body in our worship, so also we don't see ourselves engaging in a violent act, in imitation of those who crucified Jesus. Merchants, farmers, and laborers, family men and women, good churchgoing folk, we both generate the necessary ritual environment and enact the ritualized violence itself. Over and over, each time we celebrate Holy Communion, we rehearse this, repeating particular actions again and again. We provide ourselves with the opportunity to do so.

29. Quoted in Allen et al., *Without Sanctuary*, 18.

It's true that a good number of Protestant churches have taken steps to try to deemphasize this logic in their Communion services. You may worship in a church where the fraction, the actual breaking and pouring, has been moved away from the words of institution to a point after the Communion prayer, in the belief that this restoration of earlier practice will avoid the acting out of Jesus' words about breaking and pouring out.[30] Your congregation may, as in the United Church of Christ *Book of Worship,* remove from the epiclesis all language asking the Holy Spirit to make the bread and cup into body and blood, saying only, "We ask you to send your Holy Spirit on this bread and wine, on our gifts, and on us."[31] Your church may pile a variety of metaphors upon the elements (bread of life, bread of heaven, bread for the journey, and so forth) in the hope that they will bury the privileged and deeply ingrained meaning of body and blood in the process. Some denominations have added a resurrection acclamation after the Communion prayer in an attempt to move beyond a morose liturgical preoccupation with Jesus' death. A few congregations even substitute words such as "the bread of life" and "the cup of salvation" for the traditional words "The body of Christ, broken for you" as the elements are distributed. Taken together, these changes appear to signal some discomfort with the enactment of ritual violence and a desire to address the problem.

Unfortunately, none of these changes goes far enough to alter the basic ritual logic of enacted violence. The words of institution are still considered to be *the* crucial words, without which the meal is not really Holy Communion. Also, in many congregations, the naming of bread and cup as body and blood is often retained at the moment when worshipers receive the elements, reinforcing that scheme at a crucial point. In addition, a more general sacrificial interpretation of Jesus' death remains present in the prayer and preaching of most congregations. These factors, along with the impact of two millennia of eucharistic practice, help to

30. Arguments that the fraction is altered as an action because of its location at the end of the Great Thanksgiving fail primarily because the language of the revised (some would say "restored") fraction itself still privileges the images of body and blood. The Presbyterian *Book of Common Worship,* for example quotes 1 Cor 10:16 after the prayer, as the eucharistic actions are performed: "When we break the bread, is it not a sharing in the body of Christ? When we give thanks over the cup, is it not a sharing in the blood of Christ?" (Presbyterian Church [U.S.A.], *Book,* 74). The symbol system of the body/blood tradition is thus reinvoked and reinforced.

31. United Church of Christ, *Book,* 48.

ensure that the basic embodied logic of interpersonal violence remains, albeit in more subtle ways.

Benefit

The third scheme in this logic is both economic and organic. It is economic in that it engages participants in a system of transfer of benefit. It is organic in that the benefit is experienced most fundamentally at the level of the body: the eating of bread and the drinking of grape juice or wine.

As we take and eat the bread and drink the grape, we can see clearly our consumption of the body and blood of Jesus. We may also see ourselves receiving spiritual benefits from that consumption (an organic oneness with Jesus, deeper communion with the gathered community, forgiveness of sin, and so forth). We may notice a vague spiritual connection between that benefit and the unfortunate violence done by others— by those who crucified Jesus. We are likely to see the commands of Jesus himself as the authority needed to breach taboos against cannibalism and to see ourselves as merely responding to the traditions handed down to us.[32]

We are much less likely to see clearly the basic semiconscious connection between our physical consumption of the food and our participation in the ritualized objectification and violence that preceded it. We don't see ourselves generating a liturgical environment that permits us to consume a human body and thus to benefit directly from our own collective violence. Each time we come to the table, we produce the

---

32. Attentive readers might well ask at this point, "If the basic schemes of Holy Communion are so formative, why has cannibalism never been a major social problem in cultures where Holy Communion is an influential practice? After all, the destruction *and consumption* of a symbolic human body seems very basic to the sacrament." The answer lies, I believe, in the interaction between the schemes of the sacrament and the schemes of the broader culture, which either reinforce or compete with one another. Where the powerful taboos against cannibalism break down, we might expect to see a greater degree of collusion, Holy Communion being only one influencing factor. In December 2002, for example, Armin Miewes was arrested in Rotenburg, Germany, for killing and eating forty-three-year-old Bernd-Jürgen Brandes. From time to time, Miewes would defrost a bag of flesh from the freezer, and eat it. "With every piece of flesh I ate, I remembered him," he reportedly said. "It was like taking Communion." Miewes was found by court psychiatrists to show no signs mental illness, and was sentenced to eight and a half years in prison. See Landler, "Eating." The only part of this originally German-language movie still available in English is here: https://www. youtube.com/watch?v=WKzf-rG9JBs.

conditions necessary for this organic bodily transfer of benefit. It is not merely communicated to us or signified for us. We all enact it. Even more than the other schemes it is something that we all rehearse together, time and again.

Three lenses, three ways of looking more carefully at what is going on, will help us to see the problematic economic character of this benefit. The first is the lens of surrogacy. Delores Williams, in her book *Sisters in the Wilderness*, draws upon the pre- and postbellum experience of African American women to develop the concept of surrogacy. She maps a social mechanism by which one person is made to labor, suffer, or die as a surrogate, in place of another, for that other person's benefit. Williams describes how African American women were forced as slaves and then coerced after emancipation to be surrogates: to stand in for White women in the roles of housekeeper, mother, or sexual partner. They were also forced to stand in for men, both White and Black, in certain forms of manual labor. African American women's experience of social role surrogacy, she asserts, should make them and all of us wary of social systems that are arranged so that one person is made to suffer in order to transfer benefit to others. More pointedly, she critiques the portrayal of Jesus as a kind of "ultimate surrogate figure" and the sacred aura that this portrayal gives to surrogacy—making it harder for Christian African American women to resist.[33]

While we see clearly the violence done to Jesus, it is much harder for us to see the way that Holy Communion subtly assumes and normalizes surrogacy as a relationship.[34] Even less do we see ourselves structuring our worship so that we can enact this kind of relationship during the meal. Our focus on gratitude or sorrow or even indignation at what was done to Jesus deflects our attention from how we ourselves are participating in a ritualized reiteration of surrogacy. We are also distracted from the possibility that *it might not be okay for us to benefit from the suffering of others*, including Jesus.

The second lens is that of commodification. Commodification is the process of assigning something a market value and categorizing it as available for exchange. It happens when economic (usually monetary)

33. Williams, *Sisters*, 162.

34. Liturgical theologian Marjorie Procter-Smith has helpfully applied Williams's surrogacy critique to Holy Communion, arguing that the redemptive interpretation of Jesus' suffering in Communion prayers and elsewhere suggests the mechanism of surrogacy (Procter-Smith, "Whole," 473).

value is assigned to something that wasn't previously understood or treated in that way—like teenagers, for example. For eight years prior to this writing, Operation Cross Country has brought together local law enforcement in more than a hundred U.S. cities, the National Center for Missing and Exploited Children, and the Federal Bureau of Investigation for an annual, weeklong action. The goal is to remove children and teens from sex trafficking and to place them in protective services. Over the years they have removed literally thousands of teens, mostly girls aged thirteen to seventeen, from the control of their pimps. And we're not just talking about Las Vegas or New York City here. We're talking about Cleveland; about Seattle; about Downers Grove, Illinois, a Chicago suburb near where I grew up. And while this operation is some cause for rejoicing, the number of teens recovered is probably modest in comparison to the vast numbers who are still out there. As Michael B. Ward, Special Agent in charge of the FBI's Newark division, said after the operation in 2010, "In this world, children are bartered and sold like products on a store shelf with no regard to their well-being or the physical and mental damage done to them."[35]

The commodification of people and their bodies occurs in a variety of ways in our culture. Human trafficking (sex trafficking, slavery) provides the clearest example, but commodification of the body also occurs through images in various media. Think of the commodification of Native American culture through high-priced sweatshirts bearing trademarked sports logos, or Indian princess Halloween costumes. Not only native dress, but also images of native people are objectified and introduced to the marketplace, divorced from the lived reality and circumstances of native peoples.

The point here is not that we somehow exchange Jesus for money in Holy Communion (although worship services that are not careful about juxtaposing the collection of the offering with the serving of the elements run this risk). The point is that we do not see ourselves structuring a ritual process of commodification through which Jesus becomes available as a valuable item of exchange.

Plenty of people would object strongly to this notion, insisting that Jesus' body and blood are gifts given by Jesus himself, not commodities. And for what would this commodity be exchanged, anyway? This leads us to the third lens, which focuses our attention on the economic

---

35. Quoted in *Star-Ledger*, "FBI."

character of distribution and deference. Whereas the rhetoric of our Holy Communion services often seeks to minimize difference and dominance and to emphasize unity, equality, and sharing, our eucharistic practices actually accomplish something more complex.[36] They may indeed foster some unity, and even some equality among those who receive. Even so, in almost all instances, the elements are not shared in any mutual sense but are rather controlled and distributed to the congregation by a few authorized individuals, or even by a single person who is usually ordained and usually male. Our attention may be directed toward the biblical paradigm of an abundant meal where all share and Jesus is the gracious host, but the actual logistics of our sacramental meals reveal the use of Jesus' body as a closely guarded (and scarce) commodity distributed by those in power. This not only signifies but also constructs relationships of dominance and deference. It also constructs an economy of scarcity rather than the manna economy of Jesus' ministry (Luke 6:31–44 and parallels).

In exchange for receiving the elements, we who participate display our deference to those who lead us (regardless of how we understand our relationship with them) and our assent to the rite as it is performed. We enact our acceptance of the authority of clergy or deacons. We receive the elements in ways that are nonreciprocal: we only receive without getting to share. We stand in line before our leaders, or we wait in our pews to receive the trays passed to us, while they speak and move about. In some cases we kneel to receive, or we bow, or we hold out our hands to have the elements placed in them by another. In some cases we even receive the elements directly into our mouths. In these ways and others, we rehearse relationships of deference to those who distribute the elements.[37]

---

36. Here I am drawing upon Marjorie Procter-Smith's previous work on the topic: "Although the rhetoric that surrounds the celebration of the Christian meal appears to emphasize spirituality and unity, and minimize difference and dominance," she suggests, "the politics of Eucharistic community influence a set of feminist critiques against traditional Eucharistic prayer and practice" (Procter-Smith, *Praying*, 118).

37. Procter-Smith reminds us that nonreciprocal postures of submission or vulnerability, such as kneeling, bowing, or prostration, have roots and echoes in the power relationships between monarchs and masters on the one hand, and subjects and slaves on the other (Procter-Smith, *Praying*, 78.) I would not deny that, as John Leonard and Nathan Mitchell say (*Postures*, 21), "Any particular gesture or posture can have many different, even contradictory, meanings; postures and gestures always have to be interpreted from within their contexts." Kneeling, for example, does not always automatically carry only a meaning of subordination. I am suggesting, however, that liturgical scholars are often unable or unwilling to see the influence of historically persistent cultural and liturgical contexts of male dominance when they speak freely

On some level we may understand ourselves as kneeling or bowing our heads in deference to God, but concretely the rite trains us to kneel and bow before God's representatives in worship.[38] The actions themselves map power in relationship, shoring up the authority of those who lead us in exchange for benefits associated with the body and blood of Jesus.

Taking these lenses together, we can begin to see the outlines of a very basic ritualized economy of the meal as it is currently practiced, and of the ritual scheme of benefit in particular. It is an economy of distribution, in which an objectified and broken body is received and eaten in exchange for ritual displays of deference to those who are simultaneously being authorized to control and distribute the valued commodity. It is also an economy of scarcity, in which control of a rare and valuable commodity becomes a way of constructing power-in-relationship. We may believe that the extraordinary, sacred character of this commodity makes our actions not only permissible, but also faithful. We may believe that divine intention renders the relationship of surrogacy morally and spiritually acceptable. Even so, all of us reconstitute and enact a ritual process that moves through objectification (and commodification) through violence and then to the distribution of benefit in exchange for our deference, both to those who lead us and also to the liturgical environment we have helped to reconstruct.

Strategic Misrecognition, Negotiated Appropriation

The ritual schemes we have been discerning here hang together to create a kind of logic, a sense of coherence and natural progression that helps to frame and permit our ritualized collective violence. In this way, we tend to experience the rite as given, as simply the way things are, or even as the reality that God intends, rather than as something we are reconstituting in particular ways each time.

But why don't we see it? Why don't we see the way that we create for ourselves a context in which to behave like this? Why isn't all this

about the multiple meanings of such postures.

38. Astute readers might object here that submission to God is altogether different from submission to male, human authority, and that the former may, in fact, subvert the latter. Procter-Smith acknowledges that such subversion is possible but doubts the "ultimate subversiveness" of this language because the historical ties between God and human males in positions of authority mean that the same discourse can continue to be used in diametrically opposed ways. See Procter-Smith, *Praying,* 78–79.

obvious to us when we participate in Holy Communion? Ritual theorist Catherine Bell calls this strategic misrecognition.[39] The *misrecognition* part is the dynamic that we have been describing: we don't see the way that we ourselves generate the very liturgical environment that shapes us. We don't see ourselves projecting organizing schemes on that environment through the very actions of our participation.[40] Instead, we tend to see ourselves as responding—to the tradition, to Scripture, to Jesus, or to the worship environment. We tend to see our actions as "the natural and appropriate thing to do under the circumstances."[41] The *strategic* part is not a conniving, conscious choice to ignore the basic practices through which the rite accomplishes its ends, but rather a largely unconscious selective attention, directed toward the rite's sources of authority and its more explicit, promised results.

This brings us to the issue of what Bell calls "negotiated appropriation" or "negotiated compliance."[42] It's not that we who participate in Holy Communion are simply duped by its duplicitous rhetoric, willingly participating in something that is wholly disempowering and morally objectionable for us. If that were true, if there were truly nothing beneficial in our practices of Holy Communion, it would be difficult to get us to keep coming back.[43] Rather, we who participate tend to negotiate our participation, our show of compliance, because we perceive some

---

39. Bell, *Ritual,* 108–10.

40. Here it may be easy for us to fall into a sort of bourgeois, existentialist notion of the autonomous individual who possesses absolute freedom to structure the liturgical environment. While I would suggest that a combination of social formation and individual choice is more the case, my emphasis on how we choose to structure the liturgical environment is necessary here in order to bring to the surface the dynamics of misrecognition at work.

41. Bell, *Ritual,* 109.

42. Bell, *Ritual,* 215.

43. This argument does not assume that participation in the sacraments is always freely chosen in some individual-as-autonomous-free-agent sense. Practices such as infant baptism, confirmation of young teens, and first Communion all provide limiting examples. We also need to take into account the formative influence of sacramental practices, influencing choices about participation. Further, we should acknowledge that in high-group, high-grid communities (à la Mary Douglas), non-participation is much more difficult than in low-grid, low-group communities such as liberal Protestant churches in the U.S. Despite all these complicating factors, I would still argue that compliant participation would be harder to secure in an ongoing way, or would result in more noticeable forms of resistance (attempts to nuance the liturgical environment), if participants received no benefits whatsoever.

potential for personal or group empowerment or the resolution of a problem. We hope for healing or forgiveness, for the benefits of belonging, or for eternal life.

Such negotiated participation may include minimal forms of resistance. We may engage in internal resistance, bringing our own meanings to the sacrament without acting upon them.[44] We may take the bread while telling ourselves that it's okay because it isn't *really* a human body (is it?). Or, we may drink the wine or grape juice while objecting inwardly, thinking, "I don't really approve of this whole thing," but not wanting to be rude.[45] We may even enact our resistance in minute ways, attempting to nuance the ritual environment. For example, we might refuse to say "Amen" to the server's words, "The body of Christ, broken for you."

Even when our participation includes internal resistance, however, or even though our activities within the liturgical environment include minute acts of resistance, the overall show of compliance we give still contributes to the construction of the liturgical environment. What's more, this "complicity to the point of public consent"[46] that the sacrament asks of us contributes to the demonstration of a relatively unified corporate body. Thus, ironically, our negotiated compliance still helps to structure an environment that "leads all to mistake the minimal consent of its participants for an underlying consensus or lack of conflict."[47] We help to create the impression that we all agree, when in fact the gathered group is actively reformulating itself as unified despite its lack of consensus.

Even more unsettling is the reality that we do not generally see the ways we are being shaped by our acts of compliance, even as we resist. As Bell says, "One might retain one's limited and negotiated involvement in the activities of ritual, but bowing or singing in unison imperceptibly schools the social body in the pleasures of and schemes for

---

44. "On another level of the strategies of ritualization, such an act may in fact set up a bifurcation between the external show of subordination and an internal act of resistance." Bell, *Ritual Theory, Ritual Practice,* 100.

45. Here Bell follows Maurice Bloch and others, saying that the ritual context "catches people up in its own terms, asking little more than a mere consent to the forms, while relegating anything but the most concerted challenge to the non-threat of rudeness." Even when we disagree, that is, we tend to go along simply because to do otherwise would seem inappropriate or impolite. Bell, *Ritual Theory, Ritual Practice,* 214.

46. Bell, *Ritual,* 218.

47. Bell, *Ritual,* 210.

acting in accordance with assumptions that remain far from conscious or articulate."[48] We may well experience our participation as relatively empowering. We may view our compliance not as conditioned or molded,[49] but as negotiated, or even resistant. Even so, our repeated acts of compliance with the ritual logic of the sacrament gradually shape us over time.

Theological Explanations

Before we conclude this stage of the trek, I want to take a moment to address some of the theological explanations that normally occupy our thoughts, quieting or deflecting our anxieties about the way violence is interpreted and practiced in Holy Communion. In some ways I hesitate to draw our attention to them here, out of concern that they may divert our focus from the meal's enacted logic of beneficial violence (which is part of their function). Even so, I think it's important to outline some of these theological explanations in order to explain why they don't really solve the issues being raised in this chapter.

The theological explanation most likely to be familiar to you suggests that neither the sacrament nor the cross is a grim transaction required by God, but that both are rather acts of self-giving, offered by Jesus, God, or both. Liturgical theologians such as David Power and Louis-Marie Chauvet argue that both Holy Communion and the death of Jesus are better understood as an antisacrificial economy of gift. That self-giving, in their view, is actually able to short-circuit the machinery of sacrifice in human culture by refusing to participate in cycles of violent retribution.[50]

The main flaw in this framework is that it already takes place in a narrative space where Jesus has been construed as dying willingly, or even intentionally. That is, this theological explanation relies upon biblical and liturgical narratives that describe Jesus (and by extension, God) as choosing to suffer and die, or that conflate faithfulness to the Beloved Community of God with a willingness to die (as in "faithfulness even unto death"). The problem here is the tendency of those of us who survive (perhaps including some of the New Testament writers) to cast the victims of violence as having "given" their lives. The living always have the prerogative of drawing a veil of willingness over the faces of the dead,

48. Bell, *Ritual,* 215.
49. Bell, *Ritual,* 221.
50. See Chauvet, *Symbol,* 287–309. See also Power, *Sacrament,* 276.

who can no longer resist this means of coping with our guilt and grief. This veil of willingness covers more ambiguous circumstances that often include an unwillingness to die. Think of the Lele ritual described earlier, in which the body of a pangolin is processed with songs that express the animal's willingness to be killed. This is similar to the shift we sometimes hear in discourse about soldiers killed in action—from the soldier who is killed against his or her will while trying to prevail and survive and get home, to the memory of that soldier as having simply given his or her life for God and country. The shift moves from the soldier's altruistic willingness to *risk* for the sake of some greater good, while still retaining the goal of survival, to a mythologized space, constructed by those who survive, in which the soldier gives his or her life freely. It's the same shift Jesse Jackson was working against in a speech he gave at Northwestern University in January 2001 when I was a student at Garrett-Evangelical Theological Seminary on the same campus. Jackson reminded the crowd that "Martin Luther King, Jr. did not give his life for the cause. His life was *taken from* him."[51] Of course, Dr. King knew his assassination was likely. You only need to listen to the last speech he gave to know that.[52] He chose to continue speaking and marching in spite of the threats, but even so, he did not give his life in order to remain true to his principles, or for the sake of future generations. That interpretation may be empowering in some ways, granting him a degree of control over his own death, but it obscures the truth, and all but removes James Earl Ray from the equation.[53]

Relying upon their understanding of the crucifixion as gift economy, theologians like Power and Chauvet slip too easily back into the language of sacrifice, confident that our understanding of Jesus' death as gift can neutralize the formative impact of the rite.[54] In doing so, Power

51. Jackson, Keynote for Dr. Martin Luther King Jr. Day observance (speech, Northwestern University, Evanston, IL, January 15, 2001).

52. "Well, I don't know what will happen now. We've got some difficult days ahead. But it really doesn't matter with me now, because I've been to the mountaintop. And I don't mind. Like anybody, I would like to live a long life. Longevity has its place. But I'm not concerned about that now. I just want to do God's will. And He's allowed me to go up to the mountain. And I've looked over. And I've seen the promised land. I may not get there with you. But I want you to know tonight, that we, as a people, will get to the promised land!" King, "I've Been."

53. I should add here that even if Jesus *did* intentionally seek death, that doesn't change the problematic ways we are formed by reenacting the violence done to him.

54. Chauvet is aware that the church, "is always in danger of sliding back into the

and Chauvet not only underestimate the tenacious and resurgent nature of our scapegoating tendencies in history but also overestimate their ability to subvert the violent embodied logic of Holy Communion in a permanent way. The move to an economy of gift by itself cannot in an ongoing way counter the powerfully structuring effects of violent sacramental practices and their mutually reinforcing relationship with broader cultural practices of violence. At its best, the move to a gift economy can only help to illuminate the matrix of sacrificial, transactional logic at work. At its worst, this move obscures the responsibility of the perpetrators of Jesus' execution, placing the responsibility fully on Jesus and his supposedly generous choice. Eventually, it collapses back into the same basic scheme of beneficial violence: Jesus' choice to be faithful to God or to serve humanity becomes "death-for others" as a function of "life-for others" and by extension the death itself becomes gift to others.

A second theological explanation, popular among some liturgical theologians follows the work of René Girard, who suggests that Holy Communion is actually antisacrificial because we experience it from Jesus' perspective. In Girard's view, the story of the crucifixion, told from the perspective of the victim (he misses the distance between Jesus' own experience and how his memory is deployed), reveals a culturally universal scapegoating mechanism by which societies maintain themselves. He also suggests that by applying what he calls a nonsacrificial reading of Scripture we can avoid participating in that cultural mechanism.[55]

Girard's theories are useful to the extent that they help us to see how groups use scapegoating to resolve conflict and build community. He also helps us to see how a kind of misrecognition allows us to avoid seeing the strategic, arbitrary nature of our own objectification and violence. The great irony of Girard's work, however, is that despite his skill at unveiling the human tendency to use mythology to justify the death of the scapegoat, he comes full circle in the end, casting the violence done to Jesus as both necessary and beneficial. He argues that the Gospels reveal the workings of mimetic contagion and a single victim mechanism in a unique way, and thus, Jesus' death was *necessary* because we could not

---

sacrificial" (Chauvet, *Symbol*, 308). Yet, he and Power, and even René Girard, return to the language not only of sacrifice but also of giving and receiving Jesus' body, and even of Christ as "object" (albeit in quotes) of exchange. Chauvet says, "We must remind ourselves that the 'object' placed into circulation in the exchange is Christ himself and that he comes to us in his threefold body, through the Spirit" (Chauvet, *Symbol*, 289).

55. See Girard, *Things*, 180–223.

have been delivered from the sin of scapegoating without it.[56] Jesus' death is seen as beneficial because his suffering and *death*, in particular, reveal this great truth. In this new mythology we are once again invited to attach positive value to the violence of Jesus' execution because of what it reveals to us.

Even more important, and parallel to the gift economy explanation, the intellectualist fallacy of Girard's position is the presumption that because we have recognized the scapegoating dynamics at work, our knowledge of it will somehow inoculate us permanently against the structuring effects of the sacrament. We can return to the traditional sacrificial language and violent practices of Holy Communion without being adversely affected. The idea that we can successfully apply Girard's nonsacrificial reading of Scripture to our beliefs about Holy Communion while leaving the embodied logic of the sacrament intact (and relatively unexamined) misunderstands the ways ritualized practices shape us. As mentioned earlier, Catherine Bell explains that our participation in a given ritual can shape us even as we resist the ritual's dominant schemes internally. Thus, the "revelation" provided by Girard's antisacrificial reading of the Gospels simply can't neutralize indefinitely the structuring effects of our ongoing reenactment of the violence done to Jesus, and his reading may even fool us into allowing the rite to form us precisely because we think it doesn't affect us. A helpful analogy might be the way that we allow ourselves to be shown the same TV advertisement literally hundreds of times, because we tell ourselves that we know what they're up to, and therefore we are immune to being manipulated.

A third explanation says that Holy Communion isn't really a reiteration of the violence done to Jesus because his sacrifice was once and for all. We see this most clearly in the insistence of the Protestant Reformers that the Eucharist is not a sacrifice. One of the great ironies of the reformation is that despite the Reformers' grave concerns about the sacrament as a sacrificial act, they did not alter the embodied logic of the meal. In fact, they narrowed its focus upon a sacrificial interpretation of Jesus' death through their dramatic reduction of the rite and their emphasis on the words of institution.[57] This minimalist tendency has continued

56. See, for example, Girard, "Uniqueness."

57. For related discussion see Goudey, *Feast,* 76–84. Also, see Procter-Smith, who writes, "It would be a mistake to assume that the historic Protestant aversion to referring to the Eucharistic rite as a sacrifice means that sacrificial language and symbolism is not present in Protestant worship. Nothing could be further from the truth.

historically to the point that in a good number of Protestant churches today, the entire Communion prayer has been reduced to the words of institution, combined with a fraction that acts out Jesus' words. Thus, changes that were intended to move Holy Communion away from the reiteration of violence, have not only retained the ritual enactment of beneficial violence, but have ended up focusing more specifically upon it.

Conclusion

If the violent ritual logic of Holy Communion outlined here has emerged with any clarity, we can draw a few tentative conclusions. First, it appears that there are deep theological and ethical problems with Communion practices that rehearse us in the objectification of Jesus, producing him as an objectified body in our midst. At its best, the meal should work in the opposite direction, engaging us in practices that lead us away from the tendency to treat other people as objects for our own use and toward deeper, authentic communion with the other. Bluntly put, if Christ is risen, not just as a body (mystical or not) but rather as a person, as a subject and a *Thou,* and we want to remember and treat him that way in our faith practices, then his body and blood are simply not available for us to use, or even *to be.* We in the church cannot even claim to be the body of Christ (1 Cor 12:27; Eph 1:22–23) without treating his body as something that is available for us to occupy or constitute ourselves, distinct from him as an integrated subject.[58] This has tremendous liturgical and theological implications.

Second, we do not honor Jesus or help the Beloved Community of God to come near by engaging in a mimetic repetition of the violence done to him, basically imitating those who killed him. Holy Communion cannot provide a true alternate politics, a clear alternative to the violent, dominating ways of exercising power exemplified by the crucifixion, if

Resistance to the use of sacrificial language to understand the Eucharist does not mean refusal to use sacrificial language to understand the death of Jesus, which is memorialized in the Communion rite" (Procter-Smith, *Praying,* 126).

58. Along the same lines, I also find myself wondering about our tendency to create images of Jesus that portray him as different races and ethnicities, rather than allowing him to retain the particularities of his sociohistorical location. While I support challenging the hegemony of Caucasian images of Jesus with the images from others cultures and understand the importance of doing so, a risk arises with any image that treats Jesus as a floating signifier unmoored from his identity as a brown-skinned, Middle Eastern person.

it continues to engage us in rehearsing that violence. What are needed instead are practices that counter the terrorizing and atomizing effects of violent power. We need a meal that includes clearer, more intentional practices of nonviolent solidarity and reconciliation, a meal that celebrates *in spite* of the violence that has been done, acknowledging and grieving that violence but continuing practices that help the resilient Kindom of God to come near. Meals like this would be more in keeping with the resilient nature of Jesus, of his community, and of God.

Finally, we cannot pretend that Holy Communion is a practice of sharing food so long as it continues to ingrain in us an economy of scarcity rather than of abundance, organized around the distribution of a rare and valuable commodity in exchange for our acts of deference toward clergy. Quite simply, sharing should look (and act) like sharing—and not the sharing of Jesus in ways that objectify him and treat him as a commodity. We cannot continue to pretend that abstract theological explanations are sufficient to inoculate us against ongoing, embodied, ritualized practices that habituate us toward benefitting from surrogacy and the commodification of another human being. Rather, our sacramental meal should and *can* draw us into faith practices that enact a truly alternate economy. That alternate economy can focus on actual sharing and community more than a scarce commodity. It can refuse the exploitation of persons—and perhaps even the earth—in keeping with the resilient ministry of Jesus and the Beloved Community of justice and compassion he proclaimed.

A major question that remains, though, is how or even whether the ritual logic of beneficial violence actually shapes us. In the next chapter we will take up that question, examining how the particular schemes of objectification, violence, and benefit gradually inscribe certain *habitus*, or structures of agency, on us. We will also look at the relationship between the ritualized practices of the sacrament and the broader cultural practices of objectification and violence in order to understand how they interact.

4

Walking Away

Eucharistic Formation and the Formative Power of Violence

Away from Omelas

In this chapter we will address the likely objection of some readers that even if Holy Communion *does* enact a ritual scheme of objectification, violence, and benefit, it doesn't really affect us negatively. We'll focus our attention on the subtle ways we are formed by our participation in Holy Communion, as well as the powerful ways violence can structure our behavior. At a minimum, our participation in the sacrament often fails to contribute to the formation of our resistance to broader practices of violence. At its worst, the structuring influence of the rite can actually collude with the ways we are formed by violence, drawing us into behaviors that have contributed to Christianity's often violent history. At some point, to work against that collusion, it becomes necessary to leave Omelas, as Le Guin says, to walk ahead into the darkness, and not come back.

Game Instincts

If you have ever learned to play a musical instrument, then you know how awkward it can be at first. You concentrate on each finger, trying to get it where it's supposed to be, watching as it slowly bends into position. You are focused intently on the moment, trying to get it right, hoping the instrument won't sound like an indignant cat if you are learning the violin, or a belching walrus if you are learning the trombone. Over time, though, your hands begin to take on a life of their own. You don't have to think about *exactly* what they are doing, and eventually your mind can run on ahead, thinking about your musical expressiveness or reading the next several measures. It's as if the music, or the instincts for it, have become lodged in your hands.

Just as learning to play an instrument takes concentration at first, so does learning to play a sport. At first your eyes are always on the ball (if there is one), whether you're dribbling with your hands or your feet. You have to think about how your elbows are positioned or where the racquet or the bat is in relation to your body. With hours of practice, though, with lots of repetition, these movements and stances become second nature. After a while you can focus on where the other players are on the field instead. You can focus your attention on the flow of the play, or on an opening between opponents. Meanwhile, almost on its own, your body is following the patterns that have become ingrained.

Rituals like Holy Communion function in similar ways. We dip in a common cup, or drink from one, or pass little cups down the pew. Once a week, or once a month, or a few times a year we look into the smiling eyes of the worship leader who serves us—or maybe we don't look, keeping our eyes cast down or focused on the food. We say certain things: "Amen," or "Thanks be to God," or we say nothing at all. If we do it often enough, we get used to it. If we use the same words and gestures—if the prayers evoke the same stories, the same memories handed down, if the same people play the same roles—then the practice forms us over time. It shapes us in a way that is holistic. Only by thinking about it analytically do we separate out the domains: physical, mental, or spiritual formation. Without all of that scrutiny, we just do it. It becomes something we step into naturally, without having to think about it.

In the simplest, most immediate sense, one of the main functions of ritual is to form us as people who can enact a particular ritual well. No big shock there: in the way that the cellist gets better at Bach's unaccompanied suites and the volleyball player gets better at setting up the spike, the participant in Holy Communion gets good at the rhythm of the responses, or at saying or singing the Sanctus ("Holy, Holy, Holy . . .") if there is one. You need only visit a church where Communion is done in a significantly different way to sense how you've been formed. While we may not think about it often, this kind of formation is generally obvious to us.

What is less obvious but more important for our purposes is the way that the structures of the liturgical environment shape our perception and our instincts for behavior beyond worship as well as within it. By "liturgical environment" I mean everything about our weekly worship, from the height of the chancel to the heavy ceramic or shining silver of the chalice to the gestures and format of our eating: dipping torn pieces, passing trays of cubes, or receiving wafers in our cupped hands. Social scientists use the concept of *habitus* to describe how our environments, particularly ritualized environments, shape our behavior. *Habitus* (plural) are structures—dispositions or principles of improvisation—instilled in individuals by a particular environment.[1] These structures don't rigidly determine our behavior, but they influence our improvisation, often causing us to reproduce the structures of one environment in other contexts. So the inmate who is paroled after many years is surprised to find that his hand no longer automatically reaches for the doorknob when he approaches doors. The combat veteran may instinctively duck when Fourth of July firecrackers go off in the street. Anthropologist Sherry Ortner describes *habitus* as "structures of agency," or "game instincts," in the serious game of living.[2]

The process by which Holy Communion creates *habitus* is largely unconscious, or "pre-conscious," as liturgical theologian Mary Collins

1. The French sociologist Pierre Bourdieu referred to *habitus* as, "the durably installed, generative principle of regulated improvisations," and also as, "systems of durable, transposable dispositions" (Bourdieu, *Outline,* 72 and 78).

2. Ortner says, "I find 'games' to be the most broadly useful image. But because the idea of the game in English connotes something relatively light and playful, I modify the term: 'serious games.' The idea of the 'game' is meant to capture simultaneously the following dimensions: that social life is precisely social, consisting of webs of relationship and interaction between multiple, shiftingly interrelated subject positions, none of which can be extracted as autonomous 'agents'; and yet at the same time there is 'agency,' that is, actors play with skill, intention, wit, knowledge, intelligence. The idea that the game is 'serious' is meant to add into the equation the idea that power and inequality pervade the games of life in multiple ways, and that, while there may be playfulness and pleasure in the process, the stakes of these games are often very high. It follows in turn that the games of life must be played with intensity and sometimes deadly earnestness. As a final note there is an assumption that there is never only one game" (Ortner, "Toward a Feminist," 12–13).

puts it.[3] It is embedded in the basic schemes of the sacrament: in synchronized acts that perform community or in acts of consecration or in who gets to serve the food and how. *Habitus* are absorbed through our involvement in, our repeated enactment of, the basic schemes as we participate. They resist conceptual articulation, being a type of formation lodged primarily in the body. They are less about our assent to a particular doctrine or agreement with an ideological stance, such as inclusion or reconciliation, and closer to the way we are able to avoid colliding with our own furniture in the dark. So, unless we get really uncomfortable with what's going on, or some jarring experience throws our negotiated appropriation of the meal out of joint, we don't generally notice the ways that the meal structures *habitus*. The result is that these schemes become inscribed on the body in the sense that they guide our perceptions and actions in ways that are more instinctive than deliberative.

In the previous chapter we encountered the idea of strategic misrecognition, the fact that we generally don't see ourselves shaping our own liturgical environment through our participation. Here we can begin to see another crucial aspect of this concept: *we do not see ourselves generating the very liturgical environment that structures our instincts beyond it.*[4] Even as we are reconstituting our worship in particular ways, it is shaping us. Even as we are reconstituting our worship through our actions, projecting basic organizing schemes onto the liturgical environment, those same schemes are instilled or reinforced in us. We create the environment that forms us every time.[5]

---

3. Collins (*Worship*, 259) writes, "People learn who they are and who they are becoming before God in their very physical positions and assigned roles in sacred assemblies, by what they themselves do and say, by what is said and done to them and for them, by transactions in which their participation is either prescribed or proscribed. This learning, because it is ritual learning, is pre-conscious, not consciously available to the liturgical participants. It is nevertheless taken into their identities and is formative of the world view from which their behaviors flow."

4. We do not see that the body of the participant "temporally structures a space-time environment through a series of physical movements (using schemes described earlier), thereby producing an arena which, by its molding of the actors, both validates and extends the schemes they are internalizing" (Bell, *Ritual*, 109–10).

5. It is worth noting here that in Bell's more secular perspective, there is a binary opposition at work here. She assumes that while participants believe that the liturgical environment is structured by a source beyond the community, in fact it is *only* the community, functioning within broader social systems and physical environments, that structures a particular ritual environment and thus the *habitus* of participants. From my own faith perspective, this seems to overcompensate for the misrecognition

The logic of beneficial violence that we enact in Holy Communion shapes us in this subtle way. For example, it's not that Holy Communion carries an explicit message that objectifying people is okay. Rather, without really noticing, we ourselves create opportunities for our instincts to be structured by objectifying practices that we do not see clearly. We get used to focusing our attention on Jesus as a subject (either present or remembered, depending on our theology) while acting in ways that treat the bread and cup as objectified body and blood (either real or symbolic) available for our use.

Similarly, it's not that the sacrament promotes violence as a moral or spiritual good. It's that we provide ourselves with regular occasions to engage in ritualized acts of collective violence (either real or symbolic) without looking directly at what we are doing. We repeatedly focus on the violence done to Jesus in the past instead: how it was tragic or inevitable or divinely necessary. If we have any misgivings about the enacted rite, we do it anyway. Both the ritualized violence and the deflected attention shape us.

The same is true for the logic of benefit. We don't set out to normalize surrogacy or to claim that our well-being is unavoidably predicated upon the inordinate suffering of others. We just get used to enacting that kind of relationship. We go along with the way the meal is done, adding our agency to it in a way that quietly schools our game instincts. Again and again we give thanks for Jesus' sacrifice and all that we gain, never questioning out loud or voicing outrage at that arrangement. We enact an economy of scarce, tightly controlled benefits. We defer to spiritual leaders through our roles and our postures in order to receive those benefits. All of this creates *habitus*, structuring our instincts for daily living. Over time, these ritual schemes begin to structure our perceptions and instincts in other contexts.

---

she is trying to bring to the surface. It assumes that the structuring of the liturgical environment cannot have any source whatsoever beyond human initiative. Given that we cannot ascertain with absolute certainty whether religious rites derive at least some of their structure from transcendent sources, it seems better to suggest a more open-ended alternative. Thus, we might say that even if the structuring of the liturgical environment comes in part from transcendent source, we misrecognize the nature of our liturgical activity if we do not acknowledge the ways in which participants' actions project basic schemes on the liturgical environment—even as they are simultaneously shaped by them. The Holy Spirit may, in fact, be involved in structuring our rites. Still, we who enact Holy Communion play more of a role than we generally acknowledge in determining what is done every time the table is set.

This formative impact of Holy Communion is strengthened by the "loose sense of totality and systematicity"[6] that such rites can generate. As we participate in the meal, our interaction with the environment creates a sense of fit between the different dimensions of our experience: that of our bodies, our communities, and the cosmos. Language, symbol, and action are also organized in ways that create a sense of a coherent whole.[7] Thus the ritual schemes are inscribed not merely as superior or expedient but as fitting with reality—as simply the way things are. Add to this the way that religious rites sacralize the schemes they use, and we can see how the logic of beneficial violence is inscribed not merely as the way things are, but as the way they are meant to be. Even if the violence at the center of the meal is understood as unfortunate or tragic or even wrong, it is engaged in a way that connects it to the divine. This adds to its sense of ontological givenness, or even of inevitability. "It couldn't be any other way," more than one person has said to me after hearing me lecture or preach on violence and Communion. Game instincts for living within systems of beneficial violence are inscribed as God-given reality rather than as something we help to construct.

Collusion or Resistance?

The impact of these violent structuring practices on our day-to-day behavior doesn't happen in a singular or direct way. As we noted above, *habitus* are more principle than pattern of behavior, more generative structure than habit. If we try to link the structuring environment of Holy Communion too directly to particular behaviors, we will oversimplify and miss the helpfulness of the conceptual tool of *habitus* altogether. As I said at the outset of this book, it's not like we finish sharing in Holy Communion and rush right out to rob the nearest convenience store.

More accurately, the *habitus* of Communion form or strengthen certain instincts as the basis for our own varying improvisations. The *habitus* of Communion shape these instincts by interacting with a multitude of other cultural practices that also form our dispositions for

6. Bell, *Ritual,* 104.

7. As Bell says, "The environment, constructed and reconstructed by the actions of the social agents within it, provides an experience of the objective reality of the embodied subjective schemes that have created it" (Bell, *Ritual,* 141).

action.[8] They must compete with all of the other practices forming our instincts, from media portrayals of violence to clothing options to bullying and intimate abuse. That's why, as we leave the table, our behaviors will vary from person to person, depending on the particular variety of structuring practices that we have experienced, and depending on our own choices.[9]

This perspective changes the question of how the logic of beneficial violence in Holy Communion shapes our behavior. Whereas before we might have asked simply, Does Holy Communion make us more violent? Or, does our participation in the sacrament cause us to accept violence more? Now we can proceed with a bit more nuance. To what extent do the *habitus* inscribed on participants by the eucharistic schemes of objectification, violence, and benefit collude with the *habitus* instilled by other violence-related practices in our culture? Where are the structures of agency mutually reinforcing, or where do the practices of Holy Communion provide some counterformation? In what ways are the *habitus* of Holy Communion insufficient to form us for nonviolent resistance in a world so soaked in blood?

A place where we can easily begin to see collusion at work is at the intersection of objectification and gender. The *habitus* of objectification structured by Holy Communion, for example, interacts with thousands of other practices that engage us in objectifying women.[10] Instincts for

8. The interplay being described here between the *habitus* of Holy Communion and the *habitus* of other practices should be of help to those students of performance theory inclined to object that the "frame" or "bracket" of the ritual allows participants to do things that they would never do elsewhere in daily life. It's true that in many cases the ritual frame permits and conditions participants to act in ways that would otherwise be objectionable, such as eating a pangolin (Douglas, *Purity,* 199) or Jesus' body. It is also true, however, that such bracketed behaviors can shape us nonetheless, creating *habitus* that then interact with other practices in our lives.

9. "The body is always conditioned by and responsive to a specific context. John Blacking underscores this point when he argues that 'it is from a specific historical and ethical context that the individual derives the expressive possibilities of his body.' Hence, ritualization, as the production of a ritualized agent via the interaction with a structured and structuring environment, always takes place within a larger and very immediate sociocultural situation" (Quoted in Bell, *Ritual,* 100).

10. It would be natural at this point for readers to wonder how liturgical practices that produce an objectified *male* body could structure *habitus* impacting women's bodies. My observation is that eucharistic *habitus* are easily generalized to both male and female (and nonbinary) bodies because of the preconscious, embodied character of those *habitus,* experienced in different bodies. Because practices that objectify women are more prevalent in general, we are likely to observe more collusion there,

objectification formed at the table collude with the *habitus* created by everything from lingerie catalogs to cosmetic surgery to news reports on the clothing and physical appearance of women politicians. They reinforce each other, helping to normalize the loss of the other (or the self) as *Thou* and even rendering objectification seemingly beautiful.[11]

This collusion can make women's resistance to objectification difficult. Depending on the other structuring practices in women's lives, the practice of regularly reducing Jesus to an object in worship can become one more contributing factor in their acceptance of objectification as a given, muting their instincts to assert their own subjectivity or to seek allies. For many women, the interplay of structuring practices also reinforces their own tendencies to objectify others. They may find it easier, almost natural, to treat other women (and some men) as objects, be they servants, celebrities, rivals, or saints. Remember that none of this is deterministic. It doesn't *make* people act a certain way. It simply contributes to our "game instincts," or the ways we tend to improvise our behaviors.

The liturgical *habitus* of objectification also colludes with various structuring practices in the lives of men. This is particularly true when the sacrament rehearses them in projecting a fantasized, willing subjectivity onto the one being objectified. A man's lewd comments to women in the street, his informal training in the male gaze through advertising and pornography, the importance he learns to place on his partner's physical beauty—all these are consonant with the kind of "you are for me" logic enacted in Holy Communion. Practices that objectify other men collude here as well, within the gay community for example, but also in targeting those men who are considered other because of their race, ethnicity, class, sexual orientation, faith, or what have you. Not the least, the eucharistic *habitus* of objectification interacts with the structuring effects of hero objectification. It reinforces and sacralizes a tendency to reduce Jesus and other hero figures to floating signifiers whose bodies become sites of projection more than discovery, impacting men's self-objectification and their acceptance of objectification by others as they aspire to such heroic models.[12] In all of this, the *habitus* of objectification

but the objectification of male bodies is related as well.

11. Procter-Smith (*In Her Own Rite,* 13) borrows language from poet Adrienne Rich, asking, "Does the liturgy 'translate violence' into beautiful forms, disguising its danger for women?"

12. For a helpful discussion of how men's violence functions in three modes—violence against women, violence against other men, and violence against self—see

in Holy Communion mutually reinforce other *habitus* created in the performance of particular masculinities.[13]

Moving from objectification to the eucharistic *habitus* structured by our enacted ritual violence, we can see how the *habitus* of violence formed by Holy Communion also collude with gender performance, and in similar ways. Instincts formed in Holy Communion for tolerating or participating in violence interact with the ways we are formed by all sorts of practices of male violence, from slasher movies to concrete acts of rape and abuse. The sacramental *habitus* collude with or at least fail to form resistance to the normalization of male violence against objectified others, be they women, children, or less powerful men. The *habitus* formed in Holy Communion reinforce our instincts to valorize or even sacralize certain kinds of suffering, whether in relation to women in abusive relationships or men in war. They collude with practices of passive bystander behavior, dulling our indignation and intervention when violence is inflicted on others. Instincts formed by the collective violence of Holy Communion also tend to shore up a perception of violence as a particularly male prerogative, since men commit the vast majority of violent acts, and since the vast majority of those who physically break the bread during the fraction are still men.

If you are starting to see the connections here, then it won't be surprising that the *habitus* related to benefitting from violence finds resonance in a variety of gender-based scapegoating and surrogacy practices as well. If a man mistreats a woman at home or at work, using her as a surrogate for the boss or other authority figure that he can't challenge openly, then the liturgical *habitus* created by our using Jesus for our own benefit can easily collude. Whether the woman finds some meaning in her suffering by identifying with Jesus or not, both female and male partners have a feel for how this game works. Similarly, if women are expected to

Kaufman, "Construction," 5.

13. It is worth noting here that structured dispositions such as these become deeply embedded in part because of the way an embodied performance of Holy Communion becomes "sedimented" in an embodied performance of gender. That is, a way of acting that is perceived to be in concert with God's way is also a way of acting that "succeeds" in performing a particular construction of gender identity and embodiment. It's not just the way the world appears to be; it's also the way we ourselves are. A helpful perspective in this regard is that of M. Elaine Combs-Schilling ("Etching," 104), who, in describing a Moroccan marriage ritual, suggests that "durable systems of domination are often ones in which the structures of power are so embedded within the body of self that the self cannot be easily abstracted from them."

stand in for men by doing the emotional work of grief and loss so that men can maintain a stoic performance of masculinity, then the *habitus* of surrogacy help both women and men to know the drill. Not the least, if a man's individual act of violence against a woman benefits other men by reinforcing and broadcasting the gender privilege that males generally enjoy, then the eucharistic *habitus* of our all benefiting from the violence done to Jesus may contribute to men's instincts about the tragic but typical character of such things. We feel bad about what happened, and may experience some slight guilt about being male, but what can we do? We accept the way things are.

Collusion with the *habitus* of benefit can be further clarified by adding the intersection of race and violence to the perspective of gender. In ethicist Traci West's book *Disruptive Christian Ethics: When Racism and Women's Lives Matter,* she wonders aloud whether Holy Communion in predominantly White cultural contexts colludes with other practices of White privilege, encouraging participants to take for granted the suffering and death of others for their benefit. She makes a point of describing broader societal practices outside of worship (hate crimes, police brutality, speeches by state officials) in which "persons of color are sacrificed to the mythological needs of White superiority."[14] She points out that people who have been formed by such practices will bring that formation with them to church. There, she observes, they rehearse thanksgiving for Jesus' suffering and death during Holy Communion in ways that merge with and inform White people's sense of entitlement. "Communion could function as a kind of liturgical reinscribing of the privileges of Whiteness," she suggests, "possibly fostering a lack of concern for the systemic ways they may benefit from the sacrifice of the health, safety, and well-being of 'alien others.'"[15] Her point is not that all Caucasian people display the exact same lack of concern about the cost of their privilege, but that the formative effects of broader cultural practices of White privilege may actually collude with what we have identified here as the *habitus* of surrogacy in Holy Communion.

Yet another perspective may clarify this third type of collusion even more: the use of torture—or "enhanced interrogation" as it is euphemistically called nowadays in U.S. military parlance.[16] In the era of Guanta-

---

14. West, *Disruptive,* 124.

15. West, *Disruptive,* 124.

16 'The following section may be a trigger for survivors of violence.

namo Bay detention camp, Abu Ghraib prison, extraordinary rendition, and the School of the Americas (now called the Western Hemisphere Institute for Security Cooperation), it is difficult for Christians living in the United States to claim that we have no moral or spiritual relationship with torture.[17] As a nation we not only torture people all over the world, but we also teach torture techniques to military forces in other countries. Add to this the growing number of torture treatment centers in cities across the U.S. serving hundreds of thousands of refugees who are living with the trauma of torture.[18] It is part of who we are.

Torture is a political technology of the body, to use the language of philosopher Michel Foucault.[19] When someone is tortured, his or her body becomes a site of negotiation, a means of producing particular relationships of power through the use of pain and minute physical control. Through often highly ritualized patterns of inflicting pain and fear, torturers break down the sense of agency and colonize the subjectivity of their victims. We might say the trauma of torture structures *habitus* of helplessness and compliance. It also produces a range of behaviors associated with trauma, such as hyperarousal or fear, lack of initiative, and dissociation. Beyond that, acts of torture often constrict the victim's capacities for relationship with anyone else who might offer hope or help, including God.[20]

As William Cavanaugh says in his book *Torture and Eucharist,* the primary goal of such practices is to create an "isolated monad," someone

17. "We must resist the urge to maintain the unfamiliarity of torture," writes William Cavanaugh, "to consign it to the past, or to a world of monsters. It is very much a part of our world, and we must make the mental effort, however uncomfortable, to put the ideas of 'governance' and 'torture' together" (Cavanaugh, *Torture,* 28).

18. At this time of this writing, the National Consortium of Torture Treatment Programs (NCTTP) listed thirty-three organizations around the United States, serving hundreds of thousands of survivors. "NCTTP Member Centers," http://www.ncttp.org/members.html.

19. Foucault writes of various means to produce productive and subjected bodies, including torture, describing "a 'knowledge' of the body that is not exactly the science of its functioning, and a mastery of its forces that is more than the ability to conquer them: this knowledge and its mastery constitute what might be called a political technology of the body" (Foucault, *Discipline,* 26).

20. "Traumatized people feel utterly abandoned, utterly alone, cast out of the human and divine systems of care and protection that sustain life. Thereafter, a sense of alienation, of disconnection, pervades every relationship, from the most intimate familial bonds to the most abstract affiliations of community and religion" (Herman, *Trauma and Recovery,* 52).

who is unable to resist or to build relationships that might lead to a community of resistance.[21] Survivors of torture released back into the general population become "walking signifiers" of the state's power, radiating fear-based practices that erode the relationships of others.[22] The "feel for the game" inscribed on the bodies of torture survivors is thus reproduced in society, fragmenting the social body. In these ways, torture is an extreme opposite of communion with God and others, a sort of anti-Communion ritual.[23]

At its best, Holy Communion should and can counter practices of torture and contribute to the re-formation of its devastating *habitus*. It may well do so to some extent already, but it could contribute more than it does. Holy Communion, after all, is also a political technology of the body: a way of inscribing certain instincts and particular relationships of power.[24] It should and can do more to help to re-member us and to nourish the resilience of the *habitus* of deep communion, re-inscribing those *habitus* on us through practices that embody our true connection with God and each other. It can potentially enact the deeper reality that regardless of the violent practices undertaken to dis-integrate us, we all belong, body and soul, to the Beloved Community of God.[25]

21. "With the demolition of the victim's affective ties and loyalties, past and future, the purpose of torture is to destroy the person as a political actor, and to leave her isolated and compliant with the regime's goals" (Cavanaugh, *Torture*, 45).

22. Cavanaugh, *Torture*, 45.

23. Cavanaugh comes close to this when he says, "Torture may be considered a kind of perverse liturgy, for in torture the body of the victim is the ritual site where the state's power is manifested in its most awesome form. Torture is liturgy—or, perhaps better said, 'anti-liturgy'—because it involves bodies and bodily movements in an enacted drama that makes real the power of the state and constitutes an act of worship of that mysterious power" (Cavanaugh, *Torture*, 30).

24. For Bell, as for Foucault, the body is the most basic level of power relations, the "'microphysics' of the micropolitics of power" (Bell, *Ritual*, 202.) Consequently, to the extent that liturgy is a technology aimed at affecting the body, it is also a "strategic arena for the embodiment of power relations" (Bell, *Ritual*, 170). Liturgical activities do not merely express or communicate power relations but in fact constitute an embodiment and exercise of power-in-relationship (Bell, *Ritual*, 196). Our communal worship enacts arrangements of power-in-relationship in a privileged way that inscribes them on the bodies of participants. It is in this sense that liturgy constitutes a *political* technology of the body as well (Bell, *Ritual*, 202).

25. This is an intentional play on the opening lines of the Heidelberg Catechism: "I, with body and soul, both in life and in death, am not my own, but belong to my faithful Savior Jesus Christ." It is also meant to avoid the pitfall of making the soul the church's only concern while the body remains controlled by the state. For discussion of this

More on that later. For now, it's important to say that the *habitus* of Holy Communion, as they are currently structured by the ritual logic of beneficial violence, also collude with practices of torture. At the same time that the sacrament provides comfort for some torture survivors, it may also collude with the *habitus* inscribed by torture. For example, the reenactment of violence may retraumatize survivors or reinforce the narrative of their torturer: that the violence done to them was necessary or even beneficial. For those who commit and sponsor torture, the meal can provide a "feel for the game" in which the suffering of an individual at the hands of the state serves a sacred end. For those of us who look on, eucharistic *habitus* can help make the "benefits" of those who suffer "for us" intuitively familiar to us. In this context it matters less whether we believe it's wrong and more that we get used to it. Even if we experience some disquiet because of the torture and execution of Jesus himself at the hands of the state, we still have the instincts for this game—it's horrible, what a shame, but it keeps us safe. Our public outrage is too easily stifled by the defense of waterboarding as a salvific necessity: it saves American lives and couldn't be accomplished any other way. Sound familiar? We know that tune by heart, even if we go to a church that sings different words. The *habitus* of Holy Communion collude when we are habituated to bow our heads and look away as others are made to endure unimaginable suffering in the name of our personal safety and national interests. We just get used to it.

In all of these ways and more, Holy Communion structures our dispositions for action in ways that contribute to, or fail to resist, broader cultural practices of violence. The point is not that Holy Communion is the ultimate cause of violence or even the most influential one. Especially for those of us who rarely participate, the Christian meal may have little influence on behavior. Rather, the point is that the sacrament in its current form has been historically and continues to be part of what Pamela Cooper-White calls a "mediating structure" that supports and maintains violent practices within societies more than it resists them.[26]

---

latter idea, see Cavanaugh, *Torture*, 9. Also, it my assumption here that the Beloved Community of God is not coterminous with the church.

26. "On one level, no woman is damaged by seeing a billboard of a woman in a stereotypically sexy pose as she would be by being gang-raped or murdered. But when we consider the deepest root causes of violence against women, it becomes clear that every specific form of violence supports and maintains the systemic perpetuation of them all" (Cooper-White, *Cry*, 65).

As we have noted before, the sacrament can also structure our instincts in more positive ways, and it does. In the ways named here, however, it reinforces a cultural matrix of violent practices more than it builds resistance to violence. Even if the sacrament is in some ways strategically liberating in a particular context, the collusion described here decreases the Christian meal's ability in its current form to subvert or resist violent practices in a reliably enduring way. That's key. The eucharistic *habitus* remain, waiting for the right collusion to allow the instincts to be expressed.

Is It Really a Problem?

You may still be thinking that Holy Communion doesn't really affect you negatively very much—maybe that it doesn't affect your behavior very much at all. You may be right. For example, it may be that Holy Communion just isn't that influential in your life. Many of us live our lives in ways that are only minimally influenced by our sacramental practices. Some of our faith communities celebrate Holy Communion in cursory and infrequent ways that don't really impact our daily practices and worldviews. Especially in Protestant traditions that have moved away from the sacrament and toward the preaching moment almost entirely, that wouldn't be surprising.

But what if it *were* an important part of your life? What if it were a frequent, focal practice in your church, and something that you experienced as being central to your life, and not just to your faith life? What if there were a theology and practice of Holy Communion that caused you to *want* to participate more deeply and more often? And what if the sacred meals shared in your faith community were the paradigm that shaped every other meal you participated in? That kind of influence, after all, is one of the goals of this book: a rich and engaging sacramental life that nourishes both body and spirit, and more clearly shapes how we live. Can you see how the choreography of beneficial violence might matter more, might form you more then?

It may also be that in spite of the structuring environment of our culture, you've been fortunate enough to be formed as a person who doesn't resort to violence or condone it when it is turned on others. Maybe you're a person who never really objectifies others, and who doesn't tolerate systems that objectify, exploit, and destroy other people.

If that's the case, then, like the impact of violent video games or advertising, the violent ritual logic of Holy Communion just isn't a problem for you. It's possible. Violent video games have been amply shown to influence behavior, increasing aggression and decreasing empathy, especially when combined with other factors, but maybe they wouldn't influence you even if you played all the time.[27] Advertising has been demonstrated to shape our views and our behavior, in spite of or even *because* of the fact that we dismiss them as trivial, tell ourselves we're smarter than that, and assume that we are not persuaded.[28] Still, maybe your perceptions of beauty, gender roles, happiness, or racial stereotypes remain unaffected despite the hundreds of ads we typically see and hear every day. Even if all that is true for you (I can't say it's true for me), might it still be a problem for others? Holy Communion engages us more holistically than video games or advertising—body, mind, and spirit—and presents itself not only as being true and real, but as *the way that God intends the world to function*. Might it be possible that in spite of what we tell ourselves we are doing, Holy Communion functions as a structuring environment that instills *habitus* beneficial violence in those who participate—other people at least, and maybe even you?

Habitus and Belief

In the previous chapter we looked briefly at some of the theological explanations that ease our anxieties about the violent character of the sacrament, but mostly we have steered clear of discussion about belief, theological language, or doctrine in relation to Holy Communion. I'm sure you've noticed. This somewhat artificial separation has been intentional in order to focus our attention on things that are very hard to see. Now seems like a good time to clarify that the game instincts we gain from enacting beneficial violence in worship most certainly interact with our beliefs as well as other practices in our lives. Our theological beliefs can sometimes play a role in reinforcing or suppressing the *habitus* that we have been trying to see. Theologians—and particularly feminist, womanist, postcolonial, and queer theologians—have by now created a large body of work critiquing the influence of traditional theologies

27. See, for example, Anderson et al., "Violent."

28. For discussion of the ways that advertising shapes our perceptions and behavior, see Boihem, "Ad." See also Kilborne, "Killing."

and language on the violent behavior of Christians.[29] Our journey here depends heavily on that work, and we would be examining an incomplete picture if we didn't acknowledge the ways that conceptual theology and the less discursive knowledges of ritualized practice can reinforce each other.

Nevertheless, it's also important to acknowledge the crucial difference between changing what we believe and say *about* Holy Communion, and changing its central practices as well. Historically, our beliefs about Holy Communion have been somewhat fluid, whereas the violent ritual logic of the meal has remained relatively stable and uniform, both geographically and over time.[30] Changing the ways that we are formed by the meal involves changing our habits. It's about altering the practices of the meal in a holistic way, and not just the theological explanations we give to it.

In some ways it's more like trying not to yell at your kids, if you have them (or your nieces and nephews, if that works). As a child, you think to yourself, "When I'm a grownup, I am *never* going to talk to my kids the way that my parents just talked to me." You're certain of it. Then, fast-forward fifteen or twenty years. You are looking at the Brazilian flag that your own child has carved into the coffee table in the living room. Or you are looking at the screen door that has been ripped open for the fourth time in a month. Or you are rushing a child to a doctor for stitches because his brother locked him out of the house and he pounded so hard on the door that one of the glass panes of the door shattered. (These are just hypothetical examples of course.) As you listen to yourself, you simply can't believe the words coming out of your mouth. They are words that sound so strange, so distant from the person you are, and yet so familiar. It's as if the words belonged to someone else. Then you realize, they *do* belong to someone else—your parents, to be exact. You feel like you've been possessed by them, that they have somehow taken over your body. How in the world did that happen! And how can you begin to change?

We don't stop saying regrettable things to our children simply because we suddenly realize that it's counterproductive, or read a parenting

29. For foundational work, a good place to begin would be Daly, *Beyond*; Reuther, *Sexism*; Williams, *Sisters*; Procter-Smith, *In Her Own Rite*; and Procter-Smith, *Praying*.

30. For a fairly concise discussion of the changing beliefs about Holy Communion in the history of the Western Church, see Macy, *Banquet's Wisdom*. For discussion of the ambiguity, instability, and inconsistency of belief relative to ritualized practices, see Bell, *Ritual*, 182–87.

self-help book. We stop gradually, by working on changing our habits: acknowledging the history that has formed us, recognizing the warning signs, and practicing alternate strategies. In the same way, we will never explain our way out of the violent ritual logic that has shaped our meal and influenced Christian societies for thousands of years. We're not going to curb the negative impact of these eucharistic practices simply by being smart enough to recognize their influence on us. The deeper change needed can happen only when we can begin to acknowledge the legacy of the Christian meal's logic of beneficial violence and then begin practicing alternatives that will resist that logic in an ongoing way.

Walking Away

As we come to grips with the daunting possibility of departing from the ritual logic of beneficial violence that we've used for so many centuries, it's tempting to try to walk away from the death of Jesus altogether. It's tempting to create sacramental meals that focus only on Jesus' resurrection or to act as if the crucifixion never happened at all. We may just want to focus only on Jesus' ministry and stick to celebrating the joy of positive themes like community, inclusion, and acceptance. After all, who wants to come to church and dwell on all of the nasty things that happened to Jesus anyway? It's depressing. It just drives people away.

But several problems arise with this approach. The first is a tendency, especially within more liberal communities of privilege, to mask the violence done to Jesus during Holy Communion while still retaining a vague sense that we benefit from what happened to him. The bread becomes the "Bread of Life," the cup becomes the "Cup of Blessing," but the prayers often still imply that Jesus did something for us, and often the words of institution are preserved as being indispensable.

The result is a kind of externalization of violence. It's there, but we don't have to look at it. All of that Good Friday unpleasantness is externalized from our consciousness—perhaps not entirely, but enough that we are able to continue participating in a relationship of surrogacy with little or no awareness of the cost beyond a bland sense of gratitude. This is the very definition of privilege: being able to benefit without having to see the cost. Parallels with other kinds of externalization are instructive here. The violence of poverty, for example, can be kept out of sight with property values, zoning laws, and police.[31] The violence of labor exploitation can be externalized using multinational corporations, immigration policies, maquiladoras, and the labor laws of foreign countries. Wars can be fought only in other lands, by poorer people who are disproportionately people of color. And all-White or even predominantly White neighborhoods and businesses can keep the violence of racism in the United States almost invisible, making racial unrest in urban centers seem unusual and surprising.[32] If our attempts to address the violence of Holy Communion only reinforce this kind of externalization, we are no better off.

The second problem is that meals with a narrow focus on the resurrection can lead to a kind of disengaged triumphalism. In our efforts to shift our practice away from the violence done to Jesus, we may inadvertently back ourselves into a kind of *Christus Victor* end-of-the-season banquet for the winning team. We may act as if the game is over—either because the cross has finished the conflict on some abstract level, or because we already know the eschatological outcome, or both. This kind of self-satisfied, "game over" stance can lead privileged Christians especially away from the struggle of God's continuing work and away from practices that rehearse resistance in a world where evil is pervasive and persistent. As theologian Darby Ray suggests:

31. William Kennedy speaks of a "middle-class cocoon" of ideology, saying, "To the non-poor the poor are all but invisible. The non-poor live in such isolation from the poor that they easily hide in their cocoon and blame the victims because they neither know their hurts nor understand the causes of such hardships as layoffs and unemployment. In non-poor churches there are no hungry people—or at least no visibly hungry people—so people lack any immediate feeling of hunger . . . Just as superhighways hide the realities of urban poverty from commuters driving by, so does the cocoon of ideology mask the realities of the world beyond the comfortable social location of the non-poor . . . What the cocoon does is cushion the problems and make the sufferings seem remote. It narrows the ideological horizons, circumscribes interpretations, and severely limits imaginations which could envision a better world" (Kennedy, "Ideological," 240).

32. During the writing of this chapter, protestors and police have been clashing in the streets for weeks just twelve miles away in Ferguson, Missouri, following the police shooting of an unarmed African American high school senior named Michael Brown. As I have left my writer's desk and my predominantly white suburb to join in peaceful protests, I've been reminded of the externalization in my own neighborhood, and the importance of a practical theological method that stays grounded in the concrete impact of theological work on people who are suffering.

> The challenge is not to vanquish it [evil] or imagine it already defeated but to learn to recognize its many faces and then to struggle to avoid it when possible, to confront it when it cannot be avoided, and to resist its dehumanizing effects when we find ourselves its victims. [Nel] Noddings expresses this thought: "It takes great conscious effort to subdue evil by living with it rather than stirring it up in misguided attempts to overcome it once and for all."[33]

Our challenge in the context of Holy Communion is to choose Christian meal practices that help us to "subdue evil by living with it," forming us for resistance to evil in nonviolent, ongoing ways, rather than simply celebrating its past or future defeat. This perspective points us toward practices of Holy Communion that don't even aim primarily toward the decisive vanquishing of evil, that don't imagine evil as defeated by the cross, and yet act as if the Beloved Community of God is always coming near. This is a significantly different mode of celebration.

One of the great dangers of engaging in practices that treat evil as pervasive and persistent is that this can work against our proper recognition of evil as radically contingent (depending upon some kind of corruption of an ontological state) rather than as ontologically constitutive (just the way reality is). Once we lose sight of the fact that shalom is the created state of things, it is easy for us to shift back toward liturgies in which Jesus' death was inevitable because evil is forever, and oppressors will always kill those who resist. From there it's not long before we are back to viewing Jesus' death as the outcome of his own principles and choices. This viewpoint places all of the responsibility for Jesus' death upon Jesus himself, rather than upon those who chose to kill him unjustly. The viewpoint thereby obscures the important truth that events didn't have to happen the way they did. Political and religious leaders could have chosen differently. Our challenge is to engage in practices that treat evil as persistent but still radically contingent in an ontological sense.

This leads us down a very narrow path. On the one hand, we don't want to fall back into claiming that Jesus' death was somehow necessary to the work God was and is doing. On the other hand, if it's not a necessary component of the story, we can easily find ourselves leaving it out. Herein lies the challenge: to remember Jesus' death as unnecessary, and to refuse to theologize as if it were, but to remember it as part of the story. It didn't have to happen that way, but it did happen.

33. Ray, *Deceiving*, 129.

A third weakness of trying to avoid the crucifixion altogether during Holy Communion is that then Communion can become an exercise
in denial: denial of Jesus' suffering and death, denial of our own suffering and mortality, and denial of the reality that we can never fully avoid
participating in objectification and violence. As we will see, it may well
be possible to celebrate Holy Communion without always including the
story of the crucifixion. Even so, we can't avoid it completely in our liturgical life together. We don't want our sacred meals to rehearse us in
a "No really! Everything's fine!" kind of denial of Jesus' death, especially
when this leads us toward a denial of suffering more generally. And it will
do us no good to pretend that we can completely disentangle ourselves
and simply walk away from all objectification and violence. Such meals
usually suffer from what liturgical theologian Lawrence Stookey calls a
"chirpy optimism," forming us in the ways of avoidance and offering only
brief, cathartic moments of happiness.[34] We will be better off engaging in
meals that gather up as much of the whole mystery[35] of Jesus' life, death,
and resurrection as possible, but in ways that interpret and respond to
violence and suffering differently.

34. Stookey (*Eucharist*, 98) writes: "Wanting to escape the morbidity and subjec-
tiveness of the 'perpetual Good Friday' mentality, eucharistic celebration has sometimes become as irrepressibly happy and exuberant as its antecedent was sorrowful
and introspective. At its best, this kind of eucharistic observance centers on the resurrection and reign of God to the exclusion of all else . . . At its worst, a triumphalistic
type of Eucharist centers simply on what is called rather vaguely, 'the celebration of
life.'"

35. I am increasingly dissatisfied with the term "paschal mystery," common among
liturgical scholars, for two main reasons. The first is that, while it purports to broaden
the focus of our attention from the death of Jesus to the whole of his incarnation,
ministry, death, and resurrection, the term "paschal" itself retains the suffering and
death of Jesus as the gravitational center of the concept. With its echoes of the sacrificial lamb of the Passover (Hebrew: *Pesach*) and its strong similarity to the Greek
paschō "to suffer" (a source of some etymological confusion in the early church), it's
clear where the emphasis lies. I somewhat prefer "incarnational mystery," or even "anastasial mystery," (from the Greek *anastasia,* meaning "resurrection"), although these
share the same flaw of narrowed focus. Second, the term fails to incorporate the larger,
social character of the mystery/revelation, including the web of social relations that
made Jesus' pre- and post-Easter ministry possible, as well as the emphasis on God's
kin-dom that was and is so central. Indeed, the use of the term seems symbolic of
the struggle within the scholarly community—sensing a problem, but believing that it
can be solved by a broadening of focus while still retaining the language of beneficial
suffering as the fulcrum upon which everything rests.

A Peculiar Grace

In chapter 2 we took some time to examine the grace of resilience, including the human ability to let go of habits formed by traumatic violence. I suggested that there is a trace of the divine in the possibility that our Holy Communion practices could actually recover, could change in spite of all the violence, oppression, and dominating power in which we live. That is a change, I believe, whose time has come.

It's time we stopped reenacting the violence inflicted on Jesus. The impulse to repeat that violence is something we can learn to let go. Our current practices of Holy Communion subtly shape our instincts toward beneficial violence and collude with broader practices of objectification and violence in our cultures. It is time for us to begin reaching beyond the costly benefits of violent surrogacy and focus our energy on acting in concert with God's resilient work in the world.

This is not a suggestion that we merely deemphasize practices that incorporate Jesus' body and blood, or that we return to those traditional practices only during Holy Week. It's not a proposal that we just add more layers of symbolism on top of the traditional, bedrock signs. It is a call for churches to stop breaking Jesus. At a minimum, we should stop for at least a couple of centuries and see what results.

At the same time, if our alternate meal practices are only going to avoid the cross altogether, rehearsing us in triumphalism or denial, we will be no better off. We need to find ways of walking away from the reenactment of violence done to Jesus but not from telling the whole story of Jesus, his community, and its ongoing ministry. We will need to recover and reimagine ways of meal sharing that carry on that ministry and that form us for ongoing discipleship in a world of suffering, resistance, and resilience.

The remainder of this book will lay out biblical, theological, and practical resources for that task. What does a truly alternate politics, a different arrangement of power, look like at the table? What does a truly alternate economics look like, something other than distribution of a scarce and valuable commodity by the few to the many? And what will still qualify as Holy Communion if we find alternatives to the ritual logic of beneficial violence?

Fortunately, within the Christian meal tradition are practices that are amazingly gracious and revolutionary. In spite of the effects of violence, in spite of centuries of being overshadowed and co-opted for other ends, these practices have persisted, albeit in attenuated form. We can still draw them out and begin to imagine what they might look like in our own communities today—if we dare.

PART II

5

The Trek toward Recovery

Facing the Legacy of Trauma

Diving Deep

In her poem "Diving into the Wreck," Adrienne Rich describes the experience of putting on scuba gear and descending to the ruin of a sunken ship. Her passage down to the ship has a mythic character, even as she aims to discover something down there beyond the "book of myths / in which / our names do not appear."[1] The weight of meaning and metaphor seems to increase as she descends, but her mask, as she says, pumps her blood with power. The meaning of the sunken ship itself is left somewhat open: it could be women's history, the personal history of an individual woman's life, the old mythology of patriarchy, or something more. Regardless of how readers connect, it is the way that Rich captures the mixed blessing of this exploration that has made it a touchstone image for several generations of feminist writers: "I came to see the damage that was done / and the treasures that prevail."

The next leg of our journey will focus on recovery in just these two senses of the word.[2] We will see both the damage that was done to the

1. Rich, "Diving into the Wreck," 23.

2. Here I am indebted to Flora Keshgegian, who speaks of Afrocentrism in a similar way: a recovery movement in two senses of the word. Keshgegian, *Redeeming,* 107.

meal practices of Jesus' ministry as well as some of the treasures that re-main. First, in this chapter, insights from trauma theory will help us to see how traumatic injury could come to be carried within some of the meal practices of the early church. We will ask whether some practices carry the performative memory of trauma more than others, and how this perspective can help us read the biblical meal stories. Then, in the next chapter, we will look more closely at biblical passages related to the Christian meal, sifting for the treasures that prevail.

Repetition Compulsion

Children who have been subjected to traumatic violence often reenact that violence in their play.[3] Lenore Terr compares the normal play of children with that of traumatized children, saying,

> The everyday play of childhood . . . is free and easy. It is bubbly and light-spirited, whereas the play that follows from trauma is grim and monotonous . . . Play does not stop easily when it is traumatically inspired. And it may not change much over time. As opposed to ordinary child's play, post-traumatic play is obsessively repeated . . . Post-traumatic play is so literal that if you spot it, you may be able to guess the trauma with few other clues.[4]

Fixation on the unresolved trauma, or we might say the domi-nance of that trauma in the landscape of a child's life, results in trauma-structured behavior that is played like an audio or video loop, over and over. It is generally easy to spot, as Terr indicates, because it so often includes a reenactment of the trauma itself. In *Trauma and Recovery*, Ju-dith Herman describes a five-year-old child who, though sexually abused in the first two years of life, denied any knowledge or memory of being abused. Nonetheless, says Herman, his play "enacted scenes that exactly replicated a pornographic movie made by the babysitter."[5] Through what Freud called repetition compulsion, the traumatic experience continued to intrude upon the life of the child, manifesting itself in "playful," repre-sentational acts that were clearly structured by the original abuse.

---

3. ¹The following passage may be a trigger for survivors of violence.

4. Terr, *Too Scared*, as quoted in Herman, *Trauma*, 39.

5. Herman, *Trauma*, 38.

Adults as well as children often feel compelled to reenact or echo an unresolved traumatic event that has shaped them, sometimes without conscious awareness. A survivor of rape may feel compelled to walk down the same alley where she was attacked. A survivor of childhood abuse may even harm others in order to re-create his or her early traumatic circumstances. Sometimes these reenactments are unconscious and disguised. Even so, says Herman, they tend to have a driven, tenacious quality about them. "Even when they are consciously chosen," she says, "they have a feeling of involuntariness."[6] It's also important to note that such behaviors often have a ritualized character as well. They are often repeated in prescribed, rule-bound ways and are experienced as carrying deep meaning and a weighty sense of efficacy.

Unfortunately, such behaviors may be a way of coping with the traumatic return, but they are rarely, if ever, a way toward recovery. They may provide temporary sense of being able to control or even master the trauma, but ultimately they do little to alleviate the survivor's chronic feelings of helplessness or being out of control in the face of the trauma's return. Therefore, they often induce shame as well. In this way, the behaviors usually reinforce the loop of trauma-structured behavior.

Mr. X sounds like a character in a movie, I know.[7] The doctors of STARTTS (New South Wales Service for the Treatment and Rehabilitation of Torture and Trauma Survivors) near Sydney, Australia, call him that in print to protect his privacy because he's a real person, like you and me. He is a survivor of both severe torture and its lingering legacy. Having survived the torture itself, he has also survived the ways that his own behaviors were shaped by traumatic violence.[8]

At the time of his arrest on political charges, Mr. X was around the age of forty, working as a junior public servant in his home country, married with children. Though he denied the allegations against him, he was imprisoned for two and a half years, during which time he was regularly tortured and raped by five prison guards. He was subjected to starvation, noise torture, mock execution, and much, much more. He was given forced enemas regularly. If he accidentally defecated during rapes, he was subjected to beating and electric shocks. His friends were murdered in front of him.

---

6. Herman, *Trauma*, 41.

7. The following passage may be a trigger for survivors of violent trauma.

8. Momartin and Coello, "Self-Harming."

After he was released, having signed a false confession, Mr. X strug-gled valiantly to continue his life. He suffered from flashbacks, night-mares, and dissociative episodes. He "woke up" on two occasions having broken a glass shower screen and then a glass wall in his house. He was afraid of the night, and of any group of males in the street.

He engaged in repetition compulsion as well, reproducing the particulars of his torture in his own behavior. He found himself follow-ing women in the streets, saying things to degrade and humiliate them. He began going to male prostitutes. Later, after moving to Australia, he frequented male baths, in an attempt to have more sexual encounters than he had experienced in prison. He kept track of the numbers on his calendar. These encounters sometimes included volunteering to receive beatings and engage in violent sexual acts. He would "wake up," bleeding, only after the sexual partner had left.

Fortunately, a sexual health clinic in Sydney referred him to STARTTS. He began visiting the center on a weekly basis. A year and a half later, when the case study about him was written, he had come to understand much more about his condition and had learned a number of new strategies for self-care. He had begun to examine and grieve his traumatic memories and to connect with his faith and ethnic communi-ties in Australia as well.

To be clear, he was not "all better." He still went to the baths, but he did not write numbers on his calendar. He used protection and had now gone to the hospital for treatment twice after "waking up" in the midst of violent sexual acts. He had begun to see the ways that torture had shaped him and how his compulsion to repeat his traumatic experiences didn't result in his mastery over them but perpetuated his suffering instead.[9] Slowly, painfully, he was working with others to re-form himself: his body, his habits, and his hope for what his doctors called "a future that is no longer merged with a traumatic past."[10] With a resilience that stretches the limits of our comprehension, he had begun to shift his focus. He was practicing how to refrain from enacting the traumatic return, how to live

---

9. "Compulsive repetition of the trauma usually is an unconscious process that, although it may provide a temporary sense of mastery or even pleasure, ultimately perpetuates chronic feelings of helplessness and a subjective sense of being 'bad' and out of control. The goal of the treatment is gaining control over one's current life, rath-er than repeating trauma in action, mood, or somatic states" (Momartin and Coello, "Self-Harming," 24).

10. Momartin and Coello, "Self-Harming," 25.

with the legacy of trauma in ways that reached instead for a life of healing and well-being.

Mr. X's lived experience bears witness to realities that will be important for our reading of biblical meal stories. To begin with, his life testifies to the ways that traumatic violence, particularly ritualized violence, can structure subsequent behavior. His story also shows how repetition compulsion may be an important way of coping but can actually short-circuit the difficult process of recovery. It reminds us that re-forming the *habitus* instilled by trauma requires so much more than changing our minds. Not the least, Mr. X's experience provides concrete support for a crucial possibility: although resilience may not be a final victory, and although it may not be the complete opposite of brokenness, it bears a trace of the divine nonetheless.[11]

Together, these realities suggest a way of reading the meal practices described in the New Testament through the lens of trauma. The characteristics of both repetition compulsion and recovery from trauma can help us to understand those meal practices in new ways. They can help us to see both the damage of trauma-structured behaviors and the treasures of resilience that are manifested as well.

Trauma and Performative Memory

Our reading of the biblical meal stories will be helped by the work of two scholars who have highlighted the relationship between trauma at the origins of Christianity and what Paul Connerton calls "performative memory."[12] Connerton uses this term to describe how societies pass certain *habitus* from one generation to the next.

To be clear up front, the point here is not that we who participate in Holy Communion all suffer from post-traumatic stress (although some of us do). Rather, we are trying to discern whether the use of Jesus' body and blood in Holy Communion is a trauma-structured practice that has

11. Lest we forget, Mr. X's experience also calls us to keep him in view, now that we are witnesses to his suffering and struggle. While his story has illustrative value, his life in all its particularity makes a claim upon our theological and liturgical work. It calls us to proceed with a sense of urgency and an eye to the practical outcomes of our deliberations for him and for survivors of violence like him.

12. Connerton (*How*, 21–25) defines performative memory (or "habit memory") most basically as the capacity to reproduce a certain performance.

been passed down to us as performative memory. The work of Flora Keshgegian and Stephen Patterson will help us to trace some connections.

Keshgegian suggests that it's possible to see the impact of unexamined trauma upon early Christian theology and practice. In her book *Redeeming Memories,* she asks us to look more closely at just how traumatic the crucifixion was for the community around Jesus.[13] His execution frightened his companions and sent them into hiding behind locked doors. It disrupted their sense of meaning and their expectation of the realm of God. It shattered their sense of trust—in both God and humanity—and left them feeling abandoned.[14]

Instead of being able to process and mourn that event as traumatic, Keshgegian suggests, those around Jesus needed ways to cope, to survive amid ongoing violence and loss. They found ways to justify what happened, to make it a good thing as well as a bad thing, to make it necessary, beneficial, even ordained by God. "A whole array of metaphors and descriptions were appropriated to narrate the death as accomplishing good," says Keshgegian. "Jesus' suffering was increasingly seen as something Jesus chose, indeed, the reason for his existence. Jesus gave up his life and died, for the sake of our salvation, for us . . . Over time a narrative thread was spun consisting of the cross, Jesus' undeserved suffering, and human sin."[15] Because this traumatic injury was never faced *as trauma,* she says, "the crucifixion remains an unexamined trauma at the core of Christian faith and theology."[16]

If a traumatic event is not witnessed to and validated as traumatic by a community of discourse, Keshgegian adds, the legacies of traumatic experiences can continue to be manifest in people's lives long after the originating event.[17] Survivors' needs for meaning and control may continue to be expressed in disguised and sometimes distorted ways, but

13. Keshgegian, *Redeeming,* 166.

14. Keshgegian, "Crucifixion," 8.

15. Keshgegian, *Redeeming,* 166.

16. Keshgegian, "Crucifixion," 3.

17. "Only when trauma is witnessed to as an event is it experienced and recognized as trauma and suffering. Without such witness and thus validation of the event as traumatic, the trauma manifests in ways that more often than not mask the experience of trauma and so, in a sense, put the trauma further out of reach. The lack of witness and the absence of an accompanying community of discourse that names the event for what it is leave no avenue for mourning and therefore facing the loss as loss. The trauma then is detached and suspended, unexperienced as trauma, unmourned and unaccounted for" (Keshgegian, "Crucifixion," 8–9).

they tend to persist. Significantly, she adds, "I have learned from those who study trauma that it can be passed on through generations, if it is not remembered and witnessed to fully, appropriately, and adequately."[18] If Christianity as a community of memory and practice retains this kind of unresolved trauma, then we might expect to find performative memories of it in practices such as Holy Communion. It's possible that we could even find some characteristics of repetition compulsion there—attempts to gain some control over traumatic suffering through repeated, ritualized acts.

Now, since the tasks of recovery from trauma include honoring what one has done to cope and to survive, it's important that we not simply condemn outright the meal practices that developed using Jesus' body and blood. During the process of recovery, Keshgegian says, "A survivor turns from blaming herself to being able to recognize and affirm what she did to enable her survival, as well as face the ways she may have injured herself."[19] Behaviors that might seem dysfunctional or even immoral in hindsight may ultimately be claimed as the assertion of a will to survive under terrible conditions. These behaviors can then be honored for the purpose they served, while at the same time freeing the survivor up to begin the work of rehabituating or reprogramming particular behaviors or responses. In light of our work in earlier chapters, we might call this inscribing new *habitus*. "Claiming these as survival techniques," says Keshgegian, "once useful but no longer effective, the survivor begins to see and know her own agency and power."[20]

This perspective opens up a way for us to honor the violent embodied logic that developed in some of the meal practices of the early church, while preserving the possibility that a particular practice or ritual logic was eventually counterproductive. We can honor, as a means of coping, those meal practices that seem to reflect or echo the radiating effects of torture, public execution, occupation, and war in the first centuries of our faith. We can honor the need to assign meaning to suffering, even if it means constructing a new narrative, in order to cope. At the same time, we can begin to undertake the difficult work of reprogramming that performative memory, replacing it with behaviors that are no longer structured by unresolved trauma.[21]

18. Keshgegian, *Redeeming,* 120.

19. Keshgegian, *Redeeming,* 42.

20. Keshgegian, *Redeeming,* 54.

21. One of the greatest challenges to the ideas presented in this book is the ongoing

The work of Stephen Patterson both amplifies and challenges Keshgegian's work in important ways. In *Beyond the Passion* he suggests that in some local communities early Christian memory and practice were structured not only by Jesus' death but perhaps even more by the traumatic violence Jesus' followers experienced themselves while the New Testament texts were being written.[22] The brutal violence of Roman occupation (crucifixion was common), the destruction of the temple in Jerusalem, and the periodic persecution of those early Jesus followers all influenced the ways that Jesus was remembered. As James Caroll writes in *Constantine's Sword*, "It cannot be overemphasized that the texts of the New Testament were being written at one of the most violent epochs in history."[23] Thus, some of the "readings" of the crucifixion that we find in the New Testament may signal the extent to which particular narrations of Jesus' execution became a means of coping for persecuted, dislocated, and traumatized local communities.[24] Similarly, meal practices that fo-

experience of trauma. Recovery from trauma depends, first and foremost, on a degree of safety. So, what about people who are not safe, who are still being hunted down by paramilitary patrols, who are still in abusive relationships? Who am I, from a position of safety and privilege, to say to the Nicaraguan artist who paints bloody images of Jesus and to the Filipino who participates in reenactments of the crucifixion each year, allowing nails to be driven through his hands because that is their lived experience, that their practices of Holy Communion are wrong? What about the powerful ongoing need to process and make sense of pain, suffering, and loss? What about the ability of the cross to make our own suffering seem purposeful, even redemptive? In the face of their suffering and need, we must tread carefully and listen. I can say only that traditional eucharistic practices appear to have harmful long-term effects for both those with privilege and those who are oppressed, even as they are strategically helpful in some ways. I would like to think that the alternatives presented here have the potential to be liberative for people experiencing continuing violence as well, but I do not presume to know whether such practices would be sufficient substitutes for current ecclesial Communion practices. See, for example, McKirdy, "Crux."

22. See Patterson, *Beyond*, ch. 2.

23. Carroll, *Constantine's*, 90.

24. Patterson (*Lost*, 247–48) says, "All of the books of the New Testament, save for the authentic letters of Paul, were written during the period bracketed by the Judean revolt (66 CE) and the Bar Kokhba rebellion (135 CE). This was one of the most violent and tragic periods in the history of the Jewish people in antiquity. The New Testament is a collection of books written by Jewish dissidents negotiating their tender existence in a very hostile environment. Its earliest texts show resistance; later texts, accommodation. Through all of them, though, the cross remains central. They tell the story of Jesus as the story of the cross because this was their story. Jesus died by the hand of the empire. Thousands of Jews did. And many Christians, most of them Jews, did as well."

cused upon giving meaning to violence or gaining some sense of mastery over it may be the result of traumatic violence that was currently being experienced by Jesus' followers, as much or even more than the crucifixion itself.

More recently, in *The Lost Way*, Patterson elaborates on the relationship between trauma and text, suggesting the flip side: that less traumatized early communities actually existed and produced noticeably different texts (and practices) within the early church. He points out that the early Christian community in Edessa, in what is now Turkey, was not under Roman rule. They didn't live with oppression and the looming threat of martyrdom at the hands of the Romans. Because of that, he says, the memories of Jesus they preserved in the noncanonical Gospel of Thomas have a different focus. The Jesus remembered in Thomas is less a martyr and more a sage.[25] Salvation in Thomas (and perhaps in the source known as Q) comes not from Jesus' death but from his teaching. In terms of practices, baptism was less an act of dying and rising with Christ and more a return to Eden, to the prefallen state of Adam and Eve. It was a shedding of the old self and of shame.[26] We would expect the earliest meal practices of the community in Edessa to differ as well.[27] If Patterson's hypothesis is correct, then we have good reason to look for early meal practices that were *less* structured by violence, as well as those

25. "Edessa was not a Roman city. Its leaders cared little if an odd band of Jews settled there to meditate on the wise sayings of their slain leader, Jesus. The followers of Jesus likely settled in Edessa among the many other Jews who lived there and gradually came to blend into the multifaceted culture of this lively caravan town. They were not persecuted. They did not fear death—at least violent death. Martyrdom was not to be their fate. Consequently, their Jesus was not the model martyr. He was the model sage" (Patterson, *Lost*, 153–54).

26. Patterson, *Lost*, 225–29.

27. While Patterson doesn't include it in *The Lost Way*, there is a text related to this claim: the Anaphora of Addai and Mari. This somewhat early (third-century?) Communion prayer is generally acknowledged to have come from Edessa. In earlier manuscripts this Communion service has no words of institution, and the epiclesis doesn't ask for the elements to become body and blood. Admittedly, a prayer said privately by the priest does mention commemoration of the body and blood of Jesus, and a section of the prayer heard by the congregation includes reference to redemption though Jesus' blood. The notable absences might also simply be a remnant of a historical period before the words of institution entered Communion prayers more generally. Even so, the prayer remains useful as an example of an early eucharistic tradition that was later harmonized with the broader tradition emphasizing body, blood, and sacrifice more and more, as later manuscripts show. See Jasper and Cuming, trans. and eds., *Prayers*, 39–44.

that were shaped by it more. Practices might vary by region, or we might even find very different kinds of practices within a single community, with an earlier stratus being eclipsed during a later period of persecution.

A Gracious Letting Be

Together, these insights provide us with a new way of reading the New Testament meal texts that acknowledges the legacy of trauma. If unresolved trauma can become embedded in behaviors and passed down as performative memory, then the reenactment of violence in early Christian meal practices may well have been a ritualized form of processing trauma, even a kind of repetition compulsion.[28] If it's possible that such repetition was a means of coping or even resisting[29] under extremely difficult circumstances, then we may be able to read those practices in a way that honors them while acknowledging how they were maladaptive or damaging in the long run.[30] And if the violent persecution of some

28. It is not my contention here that trauma was the only, or even the "real" reason (in some reductive sense) for the particular structuring of the meal practices that came to predominate. There were other influences. Nor am I contending that the lingering effects of trauma were the only reasons that this particular type of meal practice gradually subjugated all other meal practices. I *am* contending, however, that it was a significant factor, and that trauma theory can help us to undertake the difficult task of incorporating the death of Jesus into contemporary Communion practices without inscribing participants within schemes of surrogacy and beneficial violence.

29. Hal Taussig argues convincingly that the body-and-blood tradition was itself a means of resistance to the Roman Empire, replacing a libation for the emperor with one for the crucified Jesus, and invoking a covenant in Jesus' blood that signified a sociopolitical bond of resistance. It is certainly true that ways of coping with trauma can also be forms of resistance. The process of recovery from trauma often includes honoring such resistance. It is my position, however, that this kind of resistance usually takes place in a mythologized space in which the subjects of violence have been cast as willing victims who chose their fate, since this is a less terrifying alternative to helplessness and loss of control. Recovery from trauma often includes coming to terms with forms of resistance that were needed but not necessarily based in reality. It is also my position that this particular means of empire subversion was particularly vulnerable to cooptation by the empire. Thus, a means of coping, itself a form of resistance, was eventually subverted by a ritual logic of beneficial violence that ontologized the empire's violence more than performing an alternative. See Taussig, *In the Beginning*, 130–35.

30. Flora Keshgegian ("Crucifixion," 13) notes the incidence of coping and survival strategies "that are effective in allowing one to resist and live through the suffering," but that "become, at best ineffective and even more so, dangerous when one no longer needs them, so to speak."

communities of Jesus' followers but not others created multiple trajectories for the meal, then we may be able to find evidence of a variety of meal practices in Scripture.

The goal of this recovery work cannot be to leave the lingering effects of violence behind. Recovery from trauma is rarely linear, and never fully complete. For people like Mr. X the work of recovery is a long and difficult process, filled with setbacks and sudden turns in the road. The struggle is far more complex than the discussion here has conveyed.

Even so, that doesn't mean that the legacy of trauma must inevitably be handed on. Survivors of abuse can sometimes manage to avoid passing on the destructive aspects of *habitus* inscribed on them by traumatic violence. There is a peculiar grace, instructive for our eucharistic practices, in the possibility of mourning Jesus' death as trauma, but also in a kind of "letting be," an "unrehearsing" of the habit memory of trauma, moving toward a future that does not forget, but is no longer merged with the traumatic past. God is resilient, and while God remains with us in the midst of the traumatic return, willing and able to bear that pain again and again, God is not confined there. In resurrection, in the gathering of frightened disciples to continue the meal, in the emergence of new leaders, God continues to call us onward.

With that in mind, let us turn to the biblical texts. As we shift our attention, this would be a good moment to breathe a little. You may remember, at the beginning of this book, I mentioned that there would be a point, after we had come through some particularly difficult work, when it might help to go outside and look at something beautiful. This is that moment. You might take a walk, have a cup of tea, go to an art gallery or a garden, or just spend time with a pet. When you're ready, we'll go and see what kind of biblical resources we can find to help recover and reimagine Holy Communion.

6

To Arrive Where We Started and Know the Place for the First Time

Reading the Meal Stories Again

The Resilience of Subjugated Knowledges

"We shall not cease from exploration," writes T. S. Eliot in the last of his *Four Quartets*, "and the end of all our exploring / will be to arrive where we started / and know the place for the first time."[1] In this chapter we will continue our recovery mission, but in a different mode. Rather than focusing on recovery from trauma, we'll be searching the familiar meal stories of the New Testament in order to discover them anew: to shine a light upon eclipsed practices and foreground visible but overshadowed ones.[2] We will use what liturgical theologian David Power calls a hermeneutic of liberative retrieval, not just assuming that oldest is best but reclaiming with a critical eye.[3] We will ask what treasures from the storehouse of

---

1. Eliot, "Little Gidding."

2. For the concept of foregrounding, which Garcia-Rivera describes as "lifting up a piece of the background and giving it meaning," see Garcia-Rivera, *Community*, 35–37.

3. Power (*Sacrament*, 9) says this of liberative retrieval: "No retrieval of tradition, however, is possible unless it is noted that the renewal of sacramental liturgy belongs in a context in which many alienations have to be overcome. There is the alienation of the inner self, between rationality and feeling. There is the alienation or estrangement between humans and the earth which they inhabit. There is the alienation of

tradition will be most helpful in addressing the problems we have already raised here. As liturgical theologian Marjorie Procter-Smith says, it will be a process of "reclamation and reconstruction," one that combines the mining of texts for fragments of memory with more imaginative work.[4]

We will also rely upon philosopher Michel Foucault's concept of subjugated knowledges. Foucault speaks of two kinds of such knowledges. One type consists of blocks of historical knowledge that have been masked or filtered by systematizing thought but which "allow us to rediscover the ruptural effects of conflict and struggle."[5] In other words, we will be searching for signs of struggle over practices of Holy Communion, particularly in the biblical texts that speak about the meals of the early Jesus movement. We'll ask: with what practices is the text in dialogue? What is the text arguing against or trying to suppress? How were these texts actually received by the communities in which they were read?[6]

The other type of subjugated knowledge Foucault describes is local, specific, and often popular knowledge (*savoir des gens,* or "knowledge of the people") that is disqualified as primitive, naïve, or inadequately rigorous for systematizing thought. Thus we will also be looking for local meal practices that have been disqualified as primitive (e.g., "proto-eucharist," "*agape* meal," or "Jewish-Christian meal") by later efforts at systematization, including contemporary scholarship.

Where Foucault uses the term "insurrection" to describe the reemergence of these subjugated knowledges, we will focus on persistence and resilience. We will be looking for meal practices (which are in some ways less discursive knowledges but knowledges nonetheless) that are

---

women, subjugated to patriarchal order in social action and often in the very act of liturgy. There is the alienation between races, with the subordination of other races to the white throughout the history of Christianity and the history of liturgy itself. The retrieval of the mystery of God given to believers in sacramental tradition and action must therefore be assessed through its capacity to emancipate and reconcile into fuller participation."

4. Procter-Smith, *In Her Own Rite,* 57.

5. Foucault, "Two Lectures," 81–82.

6. Andrew McGowan ("Is There," 76) writes, "Stanley Fish, for instance, suggests that while a text may obtain a life of its own independent of authorial intent, it does so neither invariably nor arbitrarily, but in meaningful ways, in terms of relation to some interpretive community. . . . What is proposed here is, in effect, giving further consideration to the questions of ancient reception or 'reading' and not merely to those of origins of texts, and to privilege certain pieces of evidence that illustrate the continued interplay of text and ritual in community."

less stuck in the repetition of traumatic violence and more intent upon carrying forward the radical meal practices of Jesus' ministry. We will try to discern and foreground practices that have been resilient in spite of the crucifixion and the persecution of the early church and persistent through centuries of distortion and suppression. This approach is based on the conviction that our practices of Holy Communion carry within them a great resilience and not just damage. Indeed, it is that resilience, that persistence of *and for* the sake of the Kin-dom of God, in spite of suffering and death, that holds great promise.

Just to be clear, we are not searching for the Original Meal, the One True Meal, as if it could be excavated and placed on a velvet pillow in a glass case. It's just not that simple. As we will see, it's becoming clearer to scholars that there is no singular point of origin, no lone, paradigmatic event. The historical picture of early Christian meal practices is actually a much richer, more complex tapestry. Besides, as Dwight Vogel, my professor of liturgical theology, used to say, the study of Christian origins is like a game of connect-the-dots in which half of the dots are missing. Any picture that we end up with will always be at least partly conjecture. So few early documents are left, and so much is lost in the translation from lived practice to text. Add layers of textual editing along with the fact that a text may be expressing an ideal or a critique rather than what was actually being practiced, and it gets even more difficult to nail down a single origin. Our recovery work will necessarily include some reconstruction and reimagining. This makes a humble and prayerful approach to our work all the more important.

It's not as if all the sacramental meals of today's church are just knockoffs, bereft of value. As I have been saying all along, much that has survived in our current Communion practices is worthwhile, even crucial to the project of nurturing meal practices less dependent upon beneficial violence. Many of us find connection with God and each other at Communion. Sometimes we manage to gather in ways that give us a glimpse of the Beloved Community of God. Our approach, then, will be to search for a variety of subjugated ancient practices, reimagining their use today alongside some practices from today's sacramental meals.

Clearing Some Room to Move

As we begin looking at specific biblical sources, a quick review of some relatively recent developments in the study of eucharistic origins will give us a bit more interpretive elbow room. We'll start with the words of institution, since they are often considered to be the essential component that divides Holy Communion from all other meals.

Probably the most important recent shift in scholarship about eucharistic origins, for our purposes at least, is the increasing consensus that the words of institution were not actually spoken as a liturgical formula during the Communion prayer until the middle of the third or even the fourth century.[7] Think about that for a moment. Drawing significantly upon the work of Andrew McGowan, liturgical theologian Paul Bradshaw points out that even when the institution narratives do begin to be inserted into early liturgical texts, "they appear to be innovations in eucharistic prayers rather than the continuation of an ancient tradition."[8] The institution narratives appear to show up in prayer only gradually over time, and at first are inserted parenthetically, apparently for instructional or explanatory purposes.[9] Bradshaw and McGowan conclude that earlier on, the supper narratives were neither liturgical texts nor liturgical instructions. For centuries they were used only as teaching stories, geared more toward explanation of the origin of particular beliefs than toward prescribing liturgical practices.[10]

The possibility that the words of institution were not recited during the meal for centuries doesn't erase the fact that the upper room narratives were being told very early on in at least *some* Christian communities. The shift does, however, require that we rethink the position of these stories during the era of the earliest meals of the emerging church. Rather than representing a single core liturgical pattern of the entire eucharistic tradition, the institution narratives were originally a secondary means of explanation. They were origin stories used outside of the meal itself to connect existing meal practices with new interpretations and beliefs. These stories probably had little impact on the actual meal practices at first. Only gradually, over a period of centuries, did the stories find their way into the liturgy itself, eventually becoming performative language and thereby changing the practices of Christian meals dramatically—hundreds of years down the road.[11]

7. McGowan, "Is There," 15.

8. Bradshaw, *Eucharistic,* 11.

9. Bradshaw, *Eucharistic,* 15.

10. Bradshaw, *Eucharistic,* 14.

11. Enrico Mazza describes what he calls a process of the "paschalization" of early Communion prayers, in which the instituting words of the *Birkat-ha-Mazon* (Deut

A more profound challenge to the words of institution, if a less unanimous one, is the questioning of their historicity. Describing the impact of the field of biblical studies during the twentieth century, liturgical theologian Nathan Mitchell concludes, "It is no longer possible to affirm, without qualification, that during his historical life Jesus consciously and explicitly 'instituted' sacraments like baptism or Eucharist."[12] Even if Jesus did actually say the words of institution, which some scholars doubt, there are multiple versions of the story, with sometimes-conflicting memories of the event, and layers of retelling. As we'll see shortly, the New Testament includes three different upper room traditions. This makes it difficult to claim that we know exactly what Jesus was trying to initiate in terms of sacramental practice, if he was trying to do so at all.[13] What are called the command formularies ("Do this in remembrance of me," "Do this, as often as you drink of it . . .") become more of a question than a clarification. Jesus may not have actually said, "Do this," to his disciples, but even if he did (or even if he didn't actually say it but *was* trying to teach particular meal practices), what exactly did he want people to *do* at sacred meal gatherings? What is the "this" in "Do this"? The variety of meal practices in early Christian communities suggests that the answer to this question was anything but clear.[14]

A variety of early meal practices? Yes. Beyond the late insertion of the institution narratives, scholars have pieced together an emerging picture of localized meal practices that were more diverse from the start, and for a longer period of time, than was previously believed. Communion prayers, for example, may have varied from one community to the next and were not necessarily patterned after the model of upper room

8:10) and the earliest Communion prayers, or "paleoanaphora" (Mal. 1:11) were replaced with "paschal themes," particularly the upper room narrative. See Mazza, *The Celebration of the Eucharist*, 61.

12. Mitchell, "The Impact of Twentieth-Century Approaches to Scripture," 16. Also, Bradshaw, *Eucharistic Origins*, 16.

13. "This appeal to what are called 'institution narratives' is not without ambiguity. Both the story of the baptism of Jesus in the Jordan and the story of the Last Supper are told differently in the New Testament sources. This becomes more complicated when it is recognized that later tradition, homiletic and liturgical, diversifies the interpretation even further" (Power, *Sacrament*, 153).

14. "Even those who thought that Jesus had said 'Do this in my remembrance' did not necessarily interpret this to mean, 'Do this *in exactly the same order*, in my remembrance.' It is more likely that they understood the command to mean that whenever they ate a ritual meal together, whatever form it took, they were to eat and drink in remembrance of him" (Bradshaw, *Eucharistic*, 13).

narratives.[15] This early diversity also included a variety of food and drink, such as bread and water instead of wine, or the complete absence of a cup, or the inclusion of other foods such as milk and honey, cheese, oil, salt, fruits and vegetables, and possibly fish.[16] "In some places there was still concern about what kinds of food were appropriate for Holy Communion in the late fourth century," says McGowan, "as evidenced by regulations at the councils of Carthage and Hippo."[17] People had to be reminded to stop bringing other kinds of food (besides bread and wine), because there were still services of Holy Communion that included other food and drink as late as the year 393.

Particularly interesting for us in Bradshaw's discussion of local variety is his reference to the marginalization of some of these early practices. In defending McGowan's view that bread and water Eucharists were widespread into the second and third century, he says:

> This wide dispersion of instances of 'bread-and-water' Eucharists across both 'orthodox' and heretical groups is a strong indicator that it was not the preserve of any particular segment of early Christianity, but rather the survival of a primitive tradition that had once rivaled the use of wine, and only became pushed to the fringes later.[18]

His description of early, developing traditions, of rivalry and later marginalization, is just the sort of struggle we will be looking for as we begin to tease out the evidence of meal practices that were being eclipsed during the New Testament era.

To be fair, limited evidence exists as to just how prevalent this early variety was. The hints of variety found in written records could represent a few communities or many—though the evidence from early councils and across communities would argue for the latter. McGowan challenges the opposite tendency. He argues that we have for too long assumed uniformity among early meal practices based on very little evidence. Also, as Bradshaw, Taussig, and others have pointed out, texts often refer to

15. "Just as there is nothing to suggest that the narrative of institution found a place in eucharistic prayers before the fourth century, so too there is no indication that eucharistic thanksgivings were patterned in any distinctive way after the model of Jesus but rather assumed diverse forms" (Bradshaw, *Eucharistic*, 93).

16. For discussion, see McGowan, *Ascetic*, ch. 3; and also Taussig, *In the Beginning*, 7.

17. McGowan, *Ascetic*, 89.

18. Bradshaw, *Eucharistic*, 55.

practices in only one locale without saying so, leading us to assume uniformity across locations.[19]

Another important shift has been the increasing recognition that *all* the meals of Jesus' ministry are the source of Holy Communion, not just the upper room. This approach has replaced earlier attempts to draw the entire eucharistic tradition from a single, founding meal. As Phillipe Rouillard said in 1979, "The sources of the Christian Eucharist are not to be found exclusively in the Last Supper but also in a certain number of meals in which Christ the Savior took part during his earthly life and in the course of his appearances after the resurrection."[20] Nathan Mitchell would later challenge the upper room paradigm more forcefully, and with greater implications for the content of the meal, when he wrote about the miraculous feeding stories in 1997, saying, "The stories challenge Christians to remember that eucharistic origins lie not in Jesus' *last* meal, but in *all* those events wherein Jesus (as guest or host) satisfied hunger, announced the unbridled joy of God's arrival in the present moment (= 'God's reign'), and offered healing and hope to the poor and needy."[21] This shift in perspective has begun to decenter the upper room as the sole, defining origin, allowing the emergence of a more complex picture of the contexts out of which the sacramental meal emerged.

A final trend in scholarship worth noting is one that traces a historical shift away from full meals that emphasized sharing and the realm of God toward more sign-oriented meals that focused on eucharistic elements—and on Jesus himself. Half a century ago liturgical scholars would speak of full meals as *agapes* or proto-eucharists,[22] with the implication that Christian meal practices only really became Holy Communion once the full meal had been reduced to bread and cup as signs. More recently, many scholars have been more tentative, sometimes speaking of "change"

---

19. See, for example, Taussig, *In the Beginning*, 36.

20. Rouillard, "From Human," 45.

21. Mitchell, "Impact" 73.

22 Where Dix defined an *agape* as "what was left of the *chabûrah* meal when the eucharist had been removed," the whole concept of an *agape* meal as a category distinct from Holy Communion has now become a dubious one (Dix, *Shape*, 95). Bradshaw (*Eucharistic*, 29) writes: "It [the concept] served as a useful, vague category in which to dump any evidence for meals that scholars did not want to treat as eucharistic, regardless of whether the text itself described the meal as an *agape* or by some other title." The breakdown of this category pushes us to acknowledge evidence once easier to dismiss—to label the evidence either simply heretical, or, if not an *agape*, then a "proto-eucharist." Forms of the meal once ignored are now, so to speak, on the table.

rather than "development." Nathan Mitchell, for example, describes the shift without dismissing earlier practice as proto-eucharistic, saying, "As virtually all scholars agree, one can already discern in the New Testament itself, a movement *away* from concern about community meals to concern with 'cultic moments' and 'cultic elements' (most specifically, with the elements of bread and wine identified with Jesus' body and blood, and interpreted in terms of his saving death for all)."[23] Here we see not only acknowledgement of a change that appears to be occurring as late as the New Testament era or later, but also a hint of criticism about the loss of concern for the sharing of full, community meals.[24] Among scholars attempting to reach back past the initial diversity of community practices to the historical Jesus, this criticism is much more pronounced. Scholars such as John Dominic Crossan tend to view the decrease in open commensality and egalitarian sharing of a full meal as a major loss.[25]

Plurality at the Origins

Taken together, these shifts point toward a new, emerging picture of eucharistic origins and development. "Whereas earlier generations of scholars were concerned to find the common core behind the variety," says Bradshaw, "scholars today tend to be more interested in what the variety says about the particular theologies of the Eucharist that were espoused by the individual writers and their communities."[26] Dom Gregory Dix represents the earlier view when he said, in 1945, "The intricate pattern of local variety overlaid on the unchanging apostolic core of the rite is

23. Mitchell, "Impact," 72.

24. See also Marxsen, *Lord's Supper*. Following him, see Riggs, "From Gracious."

25. Crossan (*Birth*, 438), for example, says, "The Common Meal Tradition involved originally a full meal ritualized precisely as such. The specific bread/wine or body/blood ritualizations were not intended to remove that reality and should not have done so . . . The point in all of this is not whether ritualizations are done before, during, or after the meal but whether the meal itself is an intrinsic part of the eucharistic symbolism. Bread and wine should summarize, not substitute for, the Eucharist; otherwise, it is no longer the Lord's Supper."

26. Bradshaw, *Eucharistic*, 2. Also, Jonathan Schwiebert (*Knowledge*, 2) says, "historians are dealing with more than differences of *opinion* about who Jesus was and what he taught. We are also dealing with practical differences regarding what is or is not done by members of a concrete movement. Sooner or later, to be intelligible historically, such concrete differences require the existence of *separate groups*" (italics original).

the product of history."[27] McGowan, Bradshaw, and others have set aside the biases of this earlier scholarship to consider all the available evidence, along with the possibility of a nascent Christianity that is "an essentially pluriform movement with diverse theologies and diverse practices."[28] This doesn't mean that we have to give up entirely on the particular practices of Jesus himself and his first community. It simply means that we can't claim to know those founding practices with as much certainty, and it makes less sense for us to focus only on a single, founding event. This includes the traditional words of institution.[29] Consequently, we will look for traces of the meal practices of Jesus' ministry more generally, together with the creative, contextual work of early Christian communities.

The picture that has emerged, then, is of a New Testament era in which a variety of parallel forms of Christian meal gatherings exist in different locations. They include different foods and unstandardized, even improvised prayers. None of these prayers includes an institution narrative as a liturgical recitation (or a liturgical framework), and not all communities are even aware of the upper room narratives.[30] Meal practices based on Jesus' ministry are still in use and, as we will see, are at times in competition with one another, as are a variety of catechetical meal stories.[31] Full meals (that are not merely *agapes*) are only beginning to give way to a focus on the importance of symbolic or cultic elements. With this picture in mind, let's look at some particular traditions within the New Testament.

27. Dix, *Shape*, xiii.

28. Bradshaw, *Eucharistic*, viii.

29. "The conclusion to be drawn, therefore, is that our data does not witness to a single origin or single meaning for early Christian meals. Rather, the meal apparently came to exist as a center of communal self-identity based on its own inherent meaning in the culture. It needed no further justification. Various communities then applied differing interpretations to their meals utilizing various models and traditions, including the tradition of the Last Supper of Jesus. But in doing so they were not referring to an authoritative command or model; that simply does not exist in our data. The early Christian communities exhibit a great deal of creativity in their adaptations of meal tradition to fit their own special social situations" (Smith and Taussig, *Many*, 43).

30. "The Last Supper tradition does not witness to all the meal traditions in the early church . . . There are other meal traditions in the early church that refer neither to the Last Supper tradition nor the idea that the meal is a commemoration of the death of Jesus" (Smith and Taussig, *Many*, 43).

31. "The biblical canon, that is, should not be understood as the product of a peaceful consensus, but as the result of protracted struggles for authority between competing communities" (Schwartz, *Curse*, 146).

1 Corinthians

Paul's discussion of the Lord's Supper in chapters 10 and 11 of 1 Corinthians is usually considered to be the earliest mention of Holy Communion in the New Testament. Scholars disagree whether it is actually the earliest source, but it was written down years before the Gospels. Paul's assertion that he is handing on what he "received from the Lord" is frequently used to argue for a very early origin of the upper room narrative and, by extension, of liturgical practices using Jesus' body and blood.[32] This passage is also the one used most often in Communion prayers: "The Lord Jesus, on the night when he was betrayed, took a loaf . . ." Together, these factors make 1 Corinthians a good place for us to begin.

Where did Paul learn this story? He says that he received it from Jesus (1 Cor 11:23), but he never met Jesus in the flesh. So either he received it from other followers of Jesus during his formation in this new way of faith, or he received it in a vision. The latter option raises the possibility that the body-and-blood version of the upper room story (there are several versions) actually originates with Paul.[33] If this is true, then Paul himself, who never knew Jesus in person, and whose writings show little interest in Jesus' ministry during his life, was combining his own (more objectifying) received vision of the meal's origins with early Christian meal practices he already knew.[34] If Paul learned from others what he told the Corinthians, this raises the question of location. Which community or communities taught Paul this story? He spread that story in his journeys, but it started out somewhere in his travels. Perhaps he learned it in Antioch. Perhaps it came from the church in Jerusalem.[35] Either way,

---

32. See, for example, LaVerdiere, *Eucharist*, 31.

33. "What Paul plainly says is easy to overlook: '*I received from the Lord what I handed on to you.*' His language is clear and unequivocal. He is not saying, 'I received it from one of the apostles, and thus indirectly it came from the Lord,' or, 'I learned it in Antioch, but they had gotten it by tradition from the Lord.' Paul uses precisely the same language to defend the revelation of his gospel and how it came to him. He says he did not receive it from any man, nor was he taught it, but swears with an oath, 'I received it through a revelation of Jesus Christ' (Galatians 1:11–12). This means that what Paul passes on here regarding the Lord's Supper, including the words said over the bread and the wine, comes to us from Paul and Paul alone!" (Tabor, *Paul*, 146; italics original). This is also Lietzmann's position. See Lietzmann, *Mass*, 208–9n2.

34. If the body-and-blood tradition begins with Paul, who had never met Jesus, we can see how it might be easier for him to objectify Jesus, seeing him as more of a floating signifier than a subject.

35. For example, Crossan and Reed, *In Search*, 341.

it would likely have been a region where Roman occupation had a strong impact on both daily living and on how Jesus was remembered. This fits with the possibility that meal practices involving body and blood arose in communities that were continuing to suffer from traumatic violence.

Now, it may be that Paul's upper room story reflects the basic outline of the Christian meal practices that he has learned—a structure that fits with the pattern of Hellenistic meal gatherings of the era. A blessing is offered for the bread; a meal is shared (the *deipnon*); a blessing is offered for a ceremonial cup; and then some kind of discussion, singing, or entertainment follows (the *symposion*). This doesn't mean that the violence done to Jesus is being reenacted during the meal in Paul's congregations at this stage, but it's possible that the body-and-blood story is being recited as a teaching tale after meals in at least some locations.

What's often missed is that Paul appears to have learned more than one story for explaining the meal, and possibly more than one format for the meal itself. Just a bit earlier, in the tenth chapter of 1 Corinthians, Paul uses a christological retelling of the exodus story to make a point about morality and meals at the church in Corinth. It's a catechetical story about the meal, just as the upper room story is later, in chapter 11. "Our ancestors," he says, "were baptized into Moses in the cloud and in the sea, and all ate the same spiritual food, and they drank the same spiritual drink. For they drank from the spiritual rock that followed them, and the rock was Christ" (10:1–4). This is clearly a reference to baptism and the sacred meal. In this framework, however, the bread is understood as manna. The cup holds not wine but *water*, and it is understood to be water from the rock.[36] "If Paul and his readers had been familiar with Christians who used water instead of wine in their Eucharist," says Bradshaw, "even though their own practice was different, such an image would have been perfectly intelligible, and indeed might even have been current in those circles."[37] This imagery taps into a whole tradition that associates the messiah with a return of manna. More will be said on that when we get to the feeding of the five thousand.

We might easily dismiss these verses about manna and water as just conversation in a letter, not reflective of any bread-and-water practice or

36. It is true that in the following verse we see Paul working to connect the water image to Jesus ("and the rock was Christ"), but it is a bit of a stretch to argue that Paul is trying to turn the water into blood. More likely, he is just trying to link the First Testament story to Jesus more generally.

37. Bradshaw, *Eucharistic*, 53.

tradition, except for a couple of striking coincidences. The language of spiritual food and spiritual drink appears nowhere else in the Bible, but it does appear in one of the earliest Communion prayers we have, found in an early church document called the Didache. The Communion prayers of the Didache have no reference to Jesus' body and blood, but one of them does refer to spiritual food and drink. "You gave food and drink to human beings for enjoyment, so they might thank you," it says, "but you graced us with spiritual food and drink and eternal life through [Jesus,] your servant."[38]

Here in chapter 10 of 1 Corinthians, Paul also seems to be aware of a different order of events at the meal: "The cup of blessing that we bless, is it not a sharing [*koinonia*—"companionship," or "community," or perhaps even "communing"] in the blood of Christ? The bread that we break, is it not a sharing [*koinonia*] in the body of Christ?" (10:16). This cup-bread order is the reverse of what is found in the upper room story but the same order that appears in the ninth chapter of the Didache. These commonalities and others are enough to convince scholars like Enrico Mazza that Paul not only knew the prayers of the Didache but had used them himself.[39] This would make the eucharistic prayers in the Didache very early (at least in oral tradition) and would strengthen the possibility that Paul himself is working here to combine practices closer to the Didache's stream of tradition ("The cup of blessing . . . The bread we break . . ." [1 Cor 10:16a]) with the story and theology of the bread and cup as Jesus' body and blood ("Is it not . . . ?" [1 Cor 10:16b]).

McGowan and Bradshaw move in this direction, suggesting that Paul's reference to "the cup of blessing which we bless" and the "bread which we break" in chapter 10 gives us a clearer picture of actual meal practices at Corinth than the supper narrative in chapter 11. They see in chapter 10 more of a concrete description of what "we" do: a *berekah* or blessing (rather than words about body and blood) said over "the cup of blessing" (a common Jewish expression[40]) and the breaking of bread, possibly with a blessing (along the lines of the blessing for the bread in

---

38. Niederwimmer, *Didache*, 155.

39. Following the work of Feuillet, Mazza (*Origins*, 96) concludes, "If this analysis of Feuillet and our own analysis of the food-drink order are correct, we can conclude that Paul was acquainted with and used both of the eucharistic texts of the *Didache*, not only *Didache* 9, but also *Didache* 10. Therefore, the entire eucharistic liturgy used by the *Didache* would be earlier than the First Letter to the Corinthians."

40. Bradshaw, *Eucharistic*, 47.

Didache 9 or the traditional Jewish *birkat ha mazon* or bread blessing). In other words, Paul is describing something closer to meal prayers such as those in the Didache when he actually talks about what they do at the meal. McGowan concludes that, overall, "Paul envisages a eucharistic meal that is formally quite unlike the Last Supper he narrates."[41] Even if the order of elements in chapter 10 isn't strong enough evidence of actual practice in Corinth, the discussion in chapter 10 does seem to indicate Paul's awareness of multiple stories and practices.

What, then, do we make of the upper room narrative in chapter 11? Bradshaw suggests that while the cup of blessing and the "bread that we break" were familiar practices to the Corinthians, the body-and-blood interpretation that Paul *thought* he had previously communicated to them was not explicit in their prayers and had faded in their minds since his visit.[42] That's why he needed to retell them the whole story of the upper room in his letter. He writes out the whole thing in order to remind them of the meaning that he attaches to the meal: the proclamation of Jesus' death until he comes (11:26). This would be in keeping with Paul's ongoing promotion (against opposition?) of Jesus' death as particularly significant.[43]

But what about the repetition of the command formulary, "Do this in remembrance of me" after both the bread and cup? Isn't this the memory of Jesus' command to repeat these particular ritual acts with the bread and cup—identifying them with Jesus' body and blood? Not necessarily. As McGowan points out, it is more likely at this stage that the call to "do this" refers more generally to offering a blessing or prayer of thanksgiving over the bread and the cup.[44] Only much later would the act

---

41. McGowan, "Is There," 79.

42. "The fact that Paul feels compelled to give his readers catechesis about the true meaning of the rite itself implies that its import is not fully manifest in the words that were actually used" (Bradshaw, *Eucharistic*, 47).

43. "Perhaps most importantly, throughout 1 Corinthians Paul seems so intent upon reminding the church over and over again of the particular significance of Jesus' death (1:13, 17, 18–25; 6:14, 20; 11:26). One might well guess that Paul's opponents here would have assigned little importance to any of the content of the early Christian creedal formula Paul cites in 15:3–4: 'that Christ died for our sins in accordance with the scriptures, that he was buried, that he was raised on the third day according to the scriptures.' The opponents were not interested in Jesus' death as a saving event" (Patterson, "Paul," 38).

44. "Even if read prescriptively or performatively for liturgical purposes, the narrative and the call to 'do this in memory of me' would seem to lead to 'thanksgiving' (or 'blessing,' which was often the equivalent) over the bread and cup, which is what

of reciting the words about body and blood make its way into the meal itself, so early communities of Jesus' followers would have understood the command to be more general.

Several traces of struggle have begun to emerge here. The first is between Paul's reassertion of an interpretation of the meal in terms of Jesus' body and blood on the one hand and what the Corinthians are actually doing at their meals on the other. Paul's reference to cup-bread blessings, including language from the Didache, may represent one side of the struggle, while the "Don't you remember?" implications of his extensive teaching about Jesus' body and blood may indicate the other. Looking back at the situation as we do, from long after the time when the ritual logic of body and blood eclipsed all other Christian meal practices, it's easy for us to think that Paul is simply teaching established orthodoxy and widely accepted practice. This particular tension, however, raises the possibility that Paul is writing because his preferred interpretation of the meal is more unstable, even contested, than secure.

A second area of tension can be detected between the catechetical story of the upper room and the catechetical story of the manna and water in the desert. That may not even seem like tension to us, since we are conditioned to view the upper room story as a foundational, even historical narrative and this brief reference to the exodus narrative as a minor illustration. If neither of these stories was actually being used liturgically during the meal, however—if they're both stories that were being told outside the meal proper to give it meaning—then we begin to get a different picture. If, as Bradshaw suggests, we are seeing here the remnant of a bread-and-water meal, then this may be a catechetical story that was part of that practice. Paul may be giving us a glimpse of a distinct stream of tradition, familiar to the Corinthians, that used water instead of wine and understood the bread and cup very differently. It's not surprising that Paul mentions the manna framework but asserts the upper room more strongly. This is in keeping with the epistle's overall intent to emphasize the saving significance of Jesus' death in opposition to others in Corinth who do not.

This brings us to the most obvious traces of struggle in 1 Cor 10–11. In chapter 11 Paul warns the Corinthians that any among them who eat and drink "unworthily" will be liable for Jesus' body and blood. He says

---

Jesus is said to have done, more easily than the recitation of the words 'this is my body that is for you' and 'this cup is the new covenant in my blood' or similar" (McGowan, "Is There," 80).

that those who eat and drink "without discerning the body" (changed in some ancient manuscripts to "the body of the Lord") eat and drink condemnation against themselves. He even goes so far as to blame this unworthy eating for sickness and even death in the Corinthian church. Clearly, Paul is pretty upset with somebody, and something is seriously wrong with the sacred meals in Corinth.

For centuries, these verses have been used to argue that any of us who participate in Holy Communion without discerning the body *on the table* do so to our own detriment. It certainly seems that Paul is promoting an understanding of the bread and cup as body and blood of Jesus here, and it's possible that he is unhappy with some in Corinth who oppose this interpretation and its accompanying narrative. At a minimum, he's unhappy that they have forgotten the interpretive framework he favored and had promoted. But let's be clear: the central problem here is not that the Corinthians are skipping the words of institution. Most likely, no one is using them during the meal itself yet. Paul has not gotten himself this worked up because the Corinthians aren't reenacting the upper room story that he has taught them. He's not even primarily concerned about the bread and cup in particular. He says he's upset because of what he has heard: church members with more privilege are eating separately from members who are in need. In so doing they have failed to discern the single body, the emerging church, that is *around* the table, thereby missing the point of the meal, which is to enact an alternate social, political, and spiritual reality.[45]

"When you come together," Paul says to the Corinthians forcefully, "it is not really to eat the Lord's supper"(1 Cor 11:20). In other words, what you're doing isn't even really Holy Communion because the wealthier church folk in Corinth, the people who work fewer hours, have already eaten (and gotten drunk!) by the time the people who work late at Wal-Mart and Waste Management have taken the bus to get there, so to speak (11:21, 11:33). Worse yet, those who have more may actually be finishing their meals in front of those who have little (11:21)! As a result, those who are poor come to the eucharistic meal and are not only

45. Richard Hays (*First*, 193–94, 200), for example, says, "The problem that Paul is addressing at Corinth is not (overtly) a problem of sacramental theology; rather it is a problem of social relations within the community." Elsewhere he says, "'Discerning the body' here cannot mean 'perceiving the real presence of Christ in the sacramental bread'; this would be a complete non sequitur in the argument. For Paul, 'discerning the body' means recognizing the community of believers for what it really is: the body of Christ."

humiliated (11:22), but are actually going hungry (11:21). This is what has Paul so furious. He can't believe that in a community that supposedly practices meal sharing in the way of Jesus, the wealthier people are now segregating themselves and their food while people who are hungry, perhaps even starving, stay that way.

This kind of segregated, hoarding excuse for Communion, says Paul, actually makes things worse (11:17). It merely mimics the class distinctions of the larger society. It perpetuates the typical disparities of resources, health, and respect rather than breaking them down. It divides and thus weakens the church as a body, showing contempt for the church (11:22) by denying the deeper communion that we share across boundaries.[46] The Corinthians' sacred meals are worse than doing nothing because the meals allow the Corinthians who live in comfort to *feel* like they are spiritually and practically in sync with God and others when they really aren't.

From Paul's conflict with the wealthier Christians in Corinth we gain a couple of important insights into the kind of meal practices he championed. Most importantly, nobody goes hungry and nobody enacts divisions. Especially when it comes to those in need, a meal that qualifies as the Lord's Supper must actually feed people. It has to be enough of a meal that people don't go away with their stomachs growling, and it has to involve a kind of sharing that redistributes resources without reinforcing class distinctions. So, an actual meal where everybody shares the same food and where resources get spread around. Might we go as far as saying that it's not really the Lord's Supper without people who are poor? Paul is very clear, after all. When the privileged try to celebrate Holy Communion among themselves without actually feeding those in need, it's not Communion.

Paul may mostly avoid Jesus' life and teachings in his writings. He may want to emphasize Jesus' death instead, and the bread and cup as his

---

46. It is difficult for us to overestimate the importance Paul placed upon the church's unity and the deeper communion shared across boundaries by all who were in Christ. He is willing to go up against Peter and James when their meal practices exclude Gentiles (Gal 2:11–12), and here he is willing to discount any eucharistic meal that excludes the poor by not providing the same sustenance for all. Further, for Paul, being baptized into Christ means there is neither Jew nor Gentile, neither slave nor free, and neither male nor female (Gal 3:27–28). Sharing in the one loaf means not just that we all eat the same food, but that we who are many are one body (1 Cor 10:17). Paul calls that kind of community *koinonia* in the body of Christ (1 Cor 10:16). Jesus called it the kin-dom of God.

body and blood. Here, though, it is clear that he is combining these emphases with an insistence on the socially radical meal practices through which he has been formed.[47] For Paul, that social radicalism is fundamentally tied to Jesus' death and our participation in it. Nonetheless, it is quite possible that here we are seeing traces of the resilience of socially radical practices that have continued despite a new layer of emphasis upon Jesus' death.

Our overall reading of 1 Corinthians 10 and 11 has valuable gifts for us. We can see that Paul is most likely working with multiple sources when he writes about the eucharistic meal. The passage gives us an entrée into the Didache tradition from the New Testament, opening the possibility that both Paul and the Corinthians drew upon that source. We gain a connection to the practice of using bread and water with Paul's reference to the bread as manna and the cup as water from the rock (10:3–4). (Imagine if that imagery had found its way into liturgical practice and developed into a theology of transubstantiation!) We gain some perspective on Paul's assertion of the upper room narrative—both the ambiguity of his having received it "from the Lord" (1 Cor 11:23) and his need to reassert it for the Corinthians. This last issue is particularly important because it raises the strong possibility that the eucharistic meals in Corinth bore little resemblance to the practices described in Paul's upper room narrative. Most likely, no explicit explanation was yet recited during Corinthian eucharistic meals, and no interpretive scheme had yet come to predominate.

The Upper Room Narratives of the Synoptic Gospels

The upper room stories in Mark, Luke, and Matthew include the body-and-blood material found in 1 Corinthians 11. As we noted earlier, this would fit with the persecution of Christians and the ongoing violence of Roman occupation during the period when the Gospels were being written. Along with the body-and-blood tradition, though, the Synoptic

---

47. "Paul may have come to eschew the sayings tradition because in the form in which he encountered it (for example, in Corinth); it did not emphasize the very thing that Paul considered to be crucial to entering into the socially radical position of this new movement: the death of Jesus. Paul shared with the Jesus movement its social radicalism; he simply could not arrive there by the same route. For them, the reign of God was present in the spoken word; for Paul it became real only when one could accept the cross as one's own death to the world" (Patterson, "Paul," 39–40).

Gospels also introduce us to a second supper tradition from another source. We might call it the eschatological vow tradition. The authors of the Synoptic Gospels have woven this second narrative so tightly into the body-and-blood narrative that this second tradition can be difficult to see, but it's there.

Over the last century, biblical and liturgical scholarship has been hampered by the desire to make these two narratives cohere with a single historical episode, labeling one of them an eschatological memory and the other a cultic memory of the same event. More recently, Xavier Léon-Dufour has distinguished by genre two originally separate traditions: a narrative tradition that recounts both a Passover meal and a farewell discourse incorporating eschatological sayings, and then a shorter "cultic" or "liturgical" set of interpretive sayings linked more specifically to actions over bread and cup. More importantly, he has suggested that the combination of these two genres was the work of the Gospel writers themselves, not earlier tradition.[48] This would mean that some twenty years after Paul was working to combine meal traditions, the Gospel writers are still trying to negotiate between a variety of stories and practices, much later than scholars had previously thought.

Paul Bradshaw pushes Léon-Dufour's argument even farther, challenging the assertion that one tradition is more cultic in character. Bradshaw emphasizes that at this stage both traditions are etiological stories, "intended to furnish an explanation of the basis for beliefs rather than of the origin of certain liturgical patterns."[49] They are the same genre, both carrying mnemonic patterns that have the potential to shape later ritual practice. The classification of the body-and-blood tradition as more cultic may stem from our perspective in history, long after that particular story found its way into ritual practices.

We can still see traces of the Gospel writers' attempts to harmonize these two traditions. Bradshaw points out the awkward repetition of the phrase "as they were eating" in Mark 14:18 and again in 14:22. The story

---

48. Bradshaw, *Eucharistic*, 6.

49. Bradshaw, *Eucharistic*, 14. Admittedly, these stories may have already begun to influence actual meal practices—increasing the attention given to the elements of wine and bread, for example. But this is quite different from saying that the stories were intended to provide liturgical guidelines, that they functioned primarily in that way, or that they reflect meal practices already developed. If there were an increasing emphasis on symbolic elements, in fact, that would only strengthen part of the perspective I am proposing: that meal practices preoccupied with beneficial violence gradually grew up around and eventually eclipsed all others.

seems to start over, indicating a second source. Bradshaw also points to a contradictory situation in Luke where Jesus vows not to drink of the fruit of the vine in 22:18 and then does just that two verses later in 22:20.[50] "If the evangelists were still making somewhat clumsy attempts to conflate the two sets of sayings as they composed the Gospels," he says, "it would seem very unlikely that they had already been integrated in earlier Christian history."[51] Thus, we get a glimpse here in the Gospels of the ongoing tension between two different accounts of the meal.

This second tradition, the one that focuses on Jesus' vows, includes more details about a full, shared meal. Mark's version of it includes no mention of bread breaking specifically but incorporates the widespread practice of dipping bread into a common bowl (14:20), just as it appears in John (13:26). More importantly, Mark's Gospel includes a vow, an eschatological promise, made in connection with the cup: "Truly I tell you, I will never again drink of the fruit of the vine until that day when I drink it new in the kingdom of God" (14:25). This connects the meal with the concept of the Kin-dom in a way that is absent in Paul.[52]

Luke either elaborates upon Mark (arranging the two traditions differently) or draws more fully from his awareness of a subjugated tradition or both. He adds an eschatological promise in conjunction with the meal (not the bread specifically) as well as a connection with the Passover meal. "'I have eagerly desired to eat this Passover with you before I suffer; for I tell you, I will not eat it until it is fulfilled in the kingdom of God.' Then he took a cup, and after giving thanks he said, 'Take this and divide it among yourselves; for I tell you that from now on I will not drink of the fruit of the vine until the kingdom of God comes'" (22:15–18). The dominant theme here is that of eating and drinking with Jesus in the Beloved Community of God.

The Synoptic Gospels' second version of the upper room story not only gives us another alternative to the body-and-blood tradition, but it also reconnects the meal to the Kin-dom of God that was so central to Jesus' teaching. Mark casts the expectation farther into the future ("until that day" [14:25]) whereas Luke leaves the time frame more open-ended

50. Bradshaw, *Eucharistic*, 7.

51. Bradshaw, *Eucharistic*, 10.

52. While I agree that Paul has his own eschatological promise ("You proclaim the Lord's death until he comes"), it also seems clear that he carefully avoids the language of the *basileia* of God. Attempts to equate the eschatological character of these two streams of the tradition gloss over the tension between them here.

("until it is fulfilled" [22:16] and "until the kingdom of God comes" [22:18]). Either way, an association is made between the meal itself and the Beloved Community of God that Jesus said had drawn near.

We know from Paul's writing that some communities early on knew the body-and-blood story but not the story of Jesus' eschatological promises in conjunction with the meal. With this second upper room tradition, it becomes just as likely that the opposite was also true: some Christian communities during the New Testament era knew the story of Jesus' promises to eat and drink with them again in the Kin-dom of God but had never encountered the sayings about Jesus' body and blood.[53] It's also possible that some communities *had* encountered that story but simply disagreed with it. That possibility is not so far-fetched as we might think, as we'll see when we turn to John.

What would it have been like to participate in Holy Communion in such a community? What was the meal like when the stories told to explain it emphasized only the promise that Jesus would eat with them in the Kin-dom of God? For those of us who have always seen the upper room through the dominant lens, it can be difficult to fathom. It may have resembled the format of the Didache tradition. It may have followed the conventions of Hellenistic meals more generally. What we do know is that the stories told in conjunction with it connected it explicitly to the *basileia,* the Beloved Community of God. We can also see that those who gathered did so with a heightened expectation that Jesus would be with them, either in the near future or even at the meal, but *only as a subject,* not as a ritual object.

John

John's Gospel provides us with the third supper narrative, one dramatically different from either of the other two. John also describes a final meal that Jesus shares with his disciples before his arrest. John, however, doesn't even mention the food, beyond a mention of Jesus dipping a piece of bread in a dish and offering it to Judas. Instead, John's focus is

---

53. "It is equally probable that there were other Christian communities that knew nothing of that particular tradition but may have been aware only of stories that Jesus celebrated the Passover with his disciples and engaged in discourse with them, including making eschatological statements, all of which had no direct effect in shaping the pattern of their regular ritual meals together beyond a heightened expectation of his imminent return" (Bradshaw, *Eucharistic,* 10).

on a meal that emphasizes a practice of serving others that disrupts the typical social hierarchy. Though the language of the *basileia* of God is less prevalent in John, we can still discern a connection between the practices of serving one another at the meal and the Beloved Community of God.

Imagine a period of time in John's community, perhaps before they had ever heard the body-and-blood narrative, when *this* was the catechetical institution narrative told in conjunction with the meal: Before his arrest, Jesus takes off his outer robe and ties a towel around himself, like a servant. He pours water into a basin. He washes each of the disciples' feet, drying them with the towel wrapped around him. In words that carry baptismal overtones, Jesus says to Peter, "Unless I wash you, you have no share with me" (13:8).[54] Afterward, he returns to the table and gives his disciples a very explicit command, instituting a practice. He says that they should do for each other what he has done for them—not right then, but in the future.

We have no way of knowing the extent to which this story was reflected in the practices of John's community. As a subjugated practice, there is limited evidence of footwashing as a foregrounded or ritualized part of meal gatherings elsewhere in the New Testament. Even so, the command formulary in John 13:14–15 and the warning to Peter in 13:8 suggest either that this was a practice somewhat formalized in John's community, or that the story was a push toward encouraging regular practice.

This was not a meal in which participants merely prayed about crossing boundaries of power and privilege once they moved out into the world, or in which they gave thanks that the Spirit had somehow accomplished a breakdown of distinctions that was never actually enacted. It was also not, as often occurred in the church's later footwashing rituals, a "ritual of reversal" in which the hierarchy is exactly inverted (with only those in power washing the feet of the poor, for example), which simultaneously maintains, even reinscribes, the social order.[55] The command is for disciples of all varieties to wash one another's feet at or before the meal. This disrupted the common practices of the time, in which only

54. For discussion of the possibility that footwashing may have been an initiatory practice in John's community, see Johnson, *Rites*, 20–22.

55. There are numerous examples of this in history. For example, "In 694 the Seventeenth Synod of Toledo commanded all bishops and priests in a position of superiority under pain of excommunication to wash the feet of those subject to them" (Thurston, "Washing").

servants or slaves (mostly female[56]) washed the dirty feet of guests, who wore sandals or no shoes at all. The central focus of this meal was that it engaged in a counterpolitics, an alternate way of enacting power in relationship during the meal. It was a meal that didn't simply gesture symbolically at an alternative or critique the dominant arrangement. It helped participants begin to live out an alternative social order.

Historically, the sixth chapter of John's Gospel has been used to bring John's supper narrative into harmony with the focus on Jesus' body and blood found in 1 Corinthians and the Synoptic Gospels. Within chapter 6, however, is clear evidence of struggle. Jesus' bread of life speech shifts suddenly—from a discourse in which he claims to be bread from heaven only in the sense of feeding students as a teacher (the food being his teaching) to a "clarification" at the end of verse 51 that the bread is his flesh, and then a threat that focuses on practice: "Unless you eat the flesh of the Son of [Humanity] and drink his blood, you have no life in you. Those who chew [Greek *trogon,* "gnaw," "or "munch"] my flesh and drink my blood have eternal life" (John 6:53–54). The presence of this kind of strident, threatening rhetoric should alert us to some kind of conflict. Against what is this graphic passage arguing? And what accounts for the sudden shift in language?

A good place to begin is the all-but-unanimous view of biblical scholars that verses 51c–58 are a later insertion into the passage.[57] This helps us to see that the conflict about eating Jesus' flesh and drinking his blood came later than the composition of the original text but probably still happened within the Johannine community.[58] The surrounding passage is an earlier sapiential (wisdom) tradition in which Jesus' teachings ("the food that endures for eternal life, which the Son of [Humanity] will give you" [John 6:27].) are what make him the bread that comes down from heaven, and belief in him is the key to eternal life.[59] Without the later insertion, it's clear that the imagery of this passage does not point to

---

56. It's hard not to notice that the only people washing feet in the New Testament, other than Jesus, are women (Luke 7:38; 1 Tim 5:10). More generally, Jesus' teaching about serving others rather than being served would have engaged more men in work that seems to have fallen mostly to women (and still does, in many contexts).

57. Brown, *Gospel,* 287.

58. Brown, *Gospel,* 286.

59. "The form of the discourse in 35–50, although it has amalgamated to itself some extraneous material, represents a far more primitive, sapiential form of the discourse." Brown, *Gospel,* 287.

body and blood, but to manna (6:31, 33) and perhaps water (6:35) in the wilderness. The images sound somewhat similar to Paul's manna-and-water reference in 1 Cor 10:3–4. John 6:51b–58 are thus inserted as a correction, intended to overwrite the sapiential manna-and-water tradition with the threat that one must, in fact, eat and drink the body and blood of Jesus in order to obtain eternal life.[60]

So, who is arguing here? Some scholars have described a conflict between the main body of the Johannine community and so-called Jewish Christians who resisted a higher Christology, or even those in the Jewish community who argued against following Jesus.[61] The strong language of the editorial insertion, according to this interpretation, is a function of the separation of the Johannine community from its Jewish roots in the synagogues. Other scholars see the work of an editor who is writing at time when "docetic spiritualism has raised its head within Christian ranks," suggesting that Jesus never really had a body at all.[62] Both of these suggestions have some foundation and may be contributing factors, but they share the same bias. They use labels like "Jewish Christian" and "docetic Christian" to dismiss the earlier version of the passage as "not really Christian" in order to side with the more orthodox theology of the insertion. It is just as likely, however, that the practice of eating Jesus' flesh and drinking Jesus' blood was itself a later introduction to the Johannine community, perhaps from the communities we associate with Paul.[63] Before the time of the argument, then, the Johannine community already possessed the high Christology expressed in John's Gospel, but without an institution narrative that focused on beneficial violence.

The leaders of the Johannine community, including the Gospel's later editor, came to agree with this new way of understanding Holy Communion, but clearly some members of the community did not. The dissenting group's Christology was not necessarily low, given the overall theology of John's Gospel. Their theology wasn't necessarily primitive

---

60. Admittedly, the earlier version of this discourse does not describe a meal as directly as the other passages we have examined so far. Even so, the language, themes, and structure of verses 22–51a have led more than one scholar to wonder about its connection to community practices: Perry, "Evolution," 26–28. See also Brown, *Gospel*, 236–37, especially n55.

61. "The objection and answer in vss. 52–53 may reflect a dispute of the evangelist's own time, for the Jewish apologists against Christianity attacked the Eucharist" Brown, (*Gospel*, 292).

62. Sloyan, *John*, 73.

63. This is the position of John Perry. See Perry, "Evolution," 29.

either, although it had been present in the Johannine community longer. What we can say with some certainty is that some of the Johannine
Christians disagreed with the meal interpretation (and possibly with meal
practices) that were being introduced. If verse 66 is part of that same later
editorial work, then it appears the issue was important enough to split
the community: "Because of this many of his disciples turned back and
no longer went about with him." The possibility that the community's
original eucharistic practices were actually continuing, either within the
community or outside it within a splinter group, would account for the
dire warning in verses 53 and 54.

We don't know why the community's leadership chose to add the
body-and-blood focus for Holy Communion to their meal. John Perry
speculates that the experience of persecution and expulsion from the
synagogues caused the leaders of the Johannine community to adopt
this more passion-oriented eucharistic practice.[64] That would fit with the
connections we have been making between the performative memory of
trauma and ongoing experiences of trauma at the time the text was written, but the evidence in this case is only indirect.

In all, we gain several additional resources from our rereading of
John's supper narrative in chapter 13 and the controversy in chapter 6.
We gain a third upper room tradition, finding here a story of a "final"
meal that describes (and commands) a completely different practice.
Here footwashing, and perhaps more generally service to each other during the meal, provides the ritual framework with the potential to form
participants in alternative class and gender relationships. In the same way
that for Paul sharing the same food across social boundaries was indispensable for any meal that could be called the Lord's supper, so footwashing here is what distinguishes a sacred meal in the way of Jesus. This can
be tied to teachings in the Gospels about the centrality of serving others
(Mark 10:42–44; Luke 22:25–27).

---

64. "I suggest it was probably the shock that occurred when Jewish officials began
forcibly expelling Jewish Christians from the synagogue (9:22; 16:2) that disposed the
leader(s) of the Johannine community to adopt a passion-oriented Eucharistic practice
. . . A passion-oriented Eucharistic practice would suddenly have seemed appropriate
to the leadership of a church experiencing persecution, for it reinforced the Fourth
Evangelist's teaching that Johannine Christians must be prepared to endure the same
suffering as Jesus in God's service (15:18–21; 5:15). The new practice was probably
introduced, therefore, to help galvanize the community's willingness to continue their
mission at a time when they were confronted with an alarming escalation of hostility
and discouragement" (Perry, "Evolution," 29).

After 1 Cor 10:3–4, John 6 seems to give us a second instance of manna-and-water imagery. Although verses 22–51 are not explicitly tied to the meal, the later insertion indicates such a connection, at least in the mind of the editor. The imagery of Jesus as manna, bread from heaven, who feeds his followers with the Word and gives them drink that quenches forever, would certainly fit with Paul's bread-and-water eucharistic imagery in the tenth chapter of 1 Corinthians. We should be cautious about assuming that the Johannine community practiced bread-and-water Eucharists at an earlier stage, but we can say at least that the manna-and-water symbolism seems to be an earlier interpretation here, and that generally speaking, bread-and-water Eucharists were probably an earlier tradition in the communities where they were practiced.[65] It is possible that we can see here an earlier manna-and-water tradition being eclipsed. This will be even clearer when we consider the story of the feeding of the multitude, which begins this passage in chapter 6.

Lastly, the traces of struggle in chapter 6 give us the clearest evidence yet of resistance to the body-and-blood tradition. Some opposed it strongly, perhaps even to the point of schism. Some were deeply invested in other meal stories, and perhaps other practices, that they considered to be faithful to Jesus' way. Thus, it appears that the path by which the body-and-blood interpretation came to eclipse all others was not as smooth and natural as we might have thought.

The Feeding of the Multitudes

The story of feeding the multitude is the only catechetical narrative for Holy Communion that appears in all four Gospels. We might say it's the only institution narrative for Holy Communion in all four Gospels, though there are no explicitly instituting words attributed to Jesus in it. Consider that for a moment. Try to step outside the tendency to view this story through the lens of the upper room. At a time when the meal stories of various local Christian communities were in competition with each other, this story was an independent narrative and was more widely known than any other. It is also the only miracle story, apart from the

---

65. "The geographical clustering of these witnesses . . . along with the theological diversity of the groups discussed, also suggests that the pattern may not actually be an ascetic emendation of a normative ritual pattern at all, but rather was the primitive tradition in these areas or communities" (McGowan, *Ascetic*, 173).

resurrection, that appears in all four Gospels.[66] In Mark and Matthew the story even appears twice, in slightly different versions! For a while in the history of the early church, then, this narrative was widely known, and may even have been the primary narrative associated with the meal, not only for one local community, but quite possibly for many.

Several important discoveries emerge when we can bring ourselves to stop reading this story as a secondary narrative and an echo of the upper room. First, the abundance of food in the midst of scarcity evokes the story of manna in the wilderness as a central theme. Hungry people get fed—actually, not symbolically. An economy of scarcity is replaced with a manna economy, reminiscent of the economy in Exodus where reliance upon God, sharing the same food, and prohibiting hoarding result in enough for everyone. This connects easily with Paul's reference to manna in 1 Cor 10, as well as with the original language of bread from heaven in the sixth chapter of John. It becomes even clearer here that both Paul and John's community knew of this tradition in relation to the meal, even if they were in the process of subjugating it to the one they preferred.

This narrative also evokes the messianic banquet. A reference to manna would have been understood by many Jews of the time to be the new manna that would signal the coming of the Messiah.[67] Combined with the abundance of food, the presence of new manna connects the feeding narrative strongly to the messianic banquet as a framework for the meal. Fish were also a sign: "There can be no doubt," argue Richard Hiers and Charles Kennedy, "that some Jews, particularly those in apocalyptic circles, expected that fish would be the main dish at the Messianic banquet."[68]

It would be tempting at this point to suggest that the feeding narratives represent an early practice of fish-and-bread meals, either from Jesus' pre-Easter ministry or from the earliest stages of the church. Unfortunately, there is essentially no documentary evidence of such a

---

66. Mitchell, "Impact," 71.

67. "Israel remembered that God had fed [God's] people with manna in the wilderness at the time of the exodus . . . and there is ample evidence that the Jews expected a renewal of the gift in the coming time of salvation. . . . The importance of the Jewish expectation of a coming messianic distribution of manna for the Christian eucharist is seen in the feeding miracles of Jesus and in the discourse on the heavenly bread of life in John 6 . . . and in I Cor. 10 (where the manna of the Exodus is presented as a type of the eucharistic bread)" (Wainwright, *Eucharist*, 22).

68. Hiers and Kennedy, "Bread," 37.

practice outside of these stories.[69] If there ever was an early Christian meal practice that emphasized bread and fish somewhere, it must have ended very early. More to the point, as Andrew McGowan says, it would be odd to suggest that bread and fish had been assigned a particularly central meaning at this early stage.[70] Christian meal gatherings were still full meals, with little emphasis on any particular sacral food or drink apart from a regular Jewish blessing over cup and bread that would have been a normal part of such gatherings. We have no reason to assume that fish would have been eaten as a sign-act any more than that bread would have been broken as sacral food or wine poured as sacred drink.

Although the slight possibility remains that the feeding stories originally arose in a community that used fish more centrally, then, the use of fish in the feeding narrative was more likely catechetical—evoking a strong sense of the messianic banquet for participants who understood the symbolism. For Hiers and Kennedy, the meal of bread and fish would have been understood by early Jewish Christians as an "anticipation if not epiphanic participation in the blessed life of table-fellowship in the Kingdom of God."[71] The story would have helped them to sense that as they ate together, the Beloved Community of God had come near.

Strangely, the number of times that fish are mentioned in the feeding stories decreases as one moves from Mark to John. "The fish, at least in the later synoptic accounts and in John 6," note Hiers and Kennedy, "seem to have been something of an embarrassment, and so were de-emphasized if not eliminated entirely."[72] The later Gospel writers found the symbol of fish to be objectionable, so they talked less about the fish in a way that placed greater emphasis on the bread. Overall, Hiers and Kennedy see the eclipse of the feeding narratives to be part of a broader shift in early Christian meal practices from the messianic banquet and

69. McGowan, Ascetic, 129. Also Hiers and Kennedy ("Bread," 24), who are sometimes misrepresented, say, "There is no definite evidence that early Christians ate fish as eucharistic food."

70. "While the use of various foods in eucharistic meals in the broader sense adopted in this study, i.e., of communal meals with a ritual character, seems not only possible but quite likely in the earliest period, it is odd to suggest that fish may have had a peculiarly sacral meaning at a stage (i.e., prior to the composition of the canonical Gospel texts) when even bread and wine had not, or at least not everywhere, taken on the fully sacramental character familiar from later tradition" (McGowan, Ascetic, 130).

71. Hiers and Kennedy, "Bread," 46.

72. Hiers and Kennedy, "Bread," 36.

the Kin-dom of God toward a focus on immortality achieved through the eating of sacral food.[73]

Lastly, it's worth noting that while the feeding narratives in the Synoptic Gospels all use the same four verbs as the upper room narratives (take, bless or give thanks, break, give), John's feeding of the multitudes has one striking difference. In John's version, Jesus takes the loaves, gives thanks, and then distributes the bread to those who were seated. That's right: he doesn't break it. That can't be accidental—it's too important. Either this difference was simply part of the earlier form of the tradition, or else John, whose supper narrative had no such verbs, left out the breaking intentionally. Either way, it's a clear trace of difference between streams of the tradition.

Overall, the feeding narratives offer some startling insights. They include a strong affirmation of manna-and-water imagery, widely understood in relation to meal gatherings. They connect the Christian meal as a manna economy with the tradition of the messianic banquet. We can detect what look like traces of the subjugation of a tradition that used fish imagery as a sign of the messianic banquet, and we even find a biblical precedent for a threefold eucharistic action: Jesus took, blessed, and gave.

The Breakfast on the Beach

The last two meal stories we're going to look at are the resurrection meals in John and Luke. No meal narratives have suffered more from being read through the lens of the body-and-blood tradition than these. The emphasis upon the upper room narrative as Jesus' so-called Last Supper, when it is manifestly not Jesus' last meal with his disciples in Luke and John, is an interpretive label that prevents us from seeing these later meals in their own light.[74] It encourages us to read them looking back toward the upper room rather than looking forward to what is unfolding in the resurrection. Thus, the resurrection meals are traditionally read as mere echoes of the upper room rather than as ongoing meals that might clarify or even update the so-called Last Supper narratives. We categorize them as later catechetical additions with no particular bearing on eucharistic practice

73. Hiers and Kennedy, "Bread," 47.

74. Other brief passages in Luke-Acts not covered here that do mention resurrection meals only strengthen this position. See, for example, Luke 24:41–42 (more fish!) and Acts 10:40–41.

and so miss the possibility that they are examples of what early followers of Jesus believed he actually meant by "Do this."[75] When we begin to
read the resurrection meals as independent narratives, though, we catch
a glimpse of the faith of communities that interpreted—even practiced—
the meal quite differently. We can also find traces of the Gospel authors'
work to integrate competing meal narratives in order to resolve the tension between traditions.

The story of Jesus' breakfast with his disciples on the beach after
his resurrection is generally understood to be a late addition to John's
Gospel, probably added by a redactor. What's intriguing, though, is the
scholarly opinion that the meal story itself is quite early in its origins.[76]
This would mean that while this story wasn't included in the original version of John's Gospel, it *didn't go away.* It survived during the intervening
years, either within John's community or more broadly in other church
circles. It was considered to be important enough by some later editor
that it was added (or added back) into the story. What we have, then, is a
long-standing tradition with no indicated awareness of the upper room
narrative that is being deliberately preserved at a late point in the production of the Gospel text, despite efforts within John's community (in
chapter 6) to promote a focus on Jesus' body and blood.[77]

The breakfast on the beach, in its current form, is clearly meant to
echo John's feeding-of-the-multitudes narrative in chapter 6. If it was
originally an independent meal narrative with no reference to the feeding
of the multitude, it has been harmonized here to evoke that earlier event.
It is the only other story in John's Gospel besides the feeding narrative
specifically located on the Sea of Tiberias.[78] It is also a meal that includes
both bread and fish. And whether they are the result of harmonizing
work by the editor, or they were part of an earlier form of the tradition,
even the verbs used to describe Jesus' actions at the meal are largely the
same. "Jesus came and took the bread and gave it to them, and did the

75. See, for example, Brown, *Gospel*, 1080–81.

76. "Although added to the gospel at its last stage, John xxi apparently draws
upon very old material from the Galilean tradition of post resurrection appearances"
(Brown, *Gospel*, 1094).

77. Brown (*Gospel*, 1081) says, "We believe that the redactor has incorporated here
some ancient material that was not included in the first edition of the Gospel, including the story of Jesus' first post-resurrectional appearance to Peter." He also says, "An
important, motive, then, for adding ch. xxi was the redactor's desire not to lose such
important material."

78. Brown, *Gospel*, 1099.

same with the fish" (21:13). Just as in the feeding narrative, he takes the bread and gives it but does not break it. This strengthens the likelihood that the absence of the breaking in chapter 6 is not accidental.[79]

If, as seems likely, this meal story was originally told separately from the fishing story in verses 1–8, then an even more astonishing meal narrative comes into view. By itself (I've taken the liberty of including only verses 4, 9, 12, and 13), the story would look something like this:

> Just after daybreak, Jesus stood on the beach; but the disciples did not know that it was Jesus. When they had gone ashore, they saw a charcoal fire there, with fish on it, and bread. Jesus said to them, "Come and have breakfast." *Now* none of the disciples dared to ask him, "Who are you?" because they knew it was the Lord. Jesus came and took the bread and gave it to them, and did the same with the fish.

Without John's recognition of Jesus from the boat in verse 7, the disciples' recognition of Jesus in verse 12 ("they knew it was the Lord") makes much more sense.[80] Jesus is made known to them in an invitation to share the same food as before: a meal of bread and fish! It is a stunning alternative to the broken-body tradition. "Finally," as Raymond Brown says, "they knew it was the Lord when he gave them bread and fish in the same manner as he had distributed bread and fish after the multiplication in this same region."[81] It was the messianic banquet all over again—or still.

The continuity of language and imagery here opens up a breathtaking theological vista, like a broad valley hidden just beneath the surface of the ocean. From this perspective, an essential theme of the breakfast on the beach is the persistence of the meals of Jesus' ministry. It's about how the messianic banquet is resilient—the feast of manna-like abundance that feels like paradise, like the Beloved Community of God has come near. *That* meal. It persists in spite of all the damage that has been done. The disciples, in spite of their disillusionment and fear, dare to accept hospitality from a stranger again, to eat what is given them, just as they did when Jesus sent them out. And what happens? In so doing they

---

79. This story is also missing the verb "bless." Jesus does not bless the bread, either.

80. "Originally, in one of the stories that lies behind xxi vss. 1–14, the meal of bread and fish that Jesus offered his disciples led them to recognize him as the risen Jesus. An element of this is still found in vs. 12, but attenuated by the fact that a recognition of Jesus by the Beloved Disciple and Peter is recorded in 7." Brown, *Gospel*, 1098.

81. Brown, *Gospel*, 1094.

find that *God* has been resilient. God has already been at work, has been working all along. When they join in the practice of continuing the fragile, risky, messianic feast, the Beloved Community of God comes near once again, and they can even sense Jesus in the midst of it. His ministry persists, and in some way so does he—not as an object to be used, and not as a way of validating the beneficial character of the violence done to him, but as the Crucified One, who wants the disciples to continue his ministry. "Do you love me?" he asks Peter in the following verses, "Feed my sheep" (John 21:15–17).

From this passage we gain one of the clearest examples of a meal tradition in which resilience is a key theological theme. The continuing meals of Jesus' ministry give the disciples hope and begin to transform them. We also gain a new perspective on the reoccurring trope that Jesus often appears as a stranger at first. Perhaps there is something critical in the way that the disciples accept food from a stranger. If we add in some of the verses that follow, we may even gain a new set of instituting words: "Do you love me? Feed my sheep."

The Meal at Emmaus

In what scholars call stage 1 of the Emmaus tradition, before the Lukan insertions about suffering and fulfillment of prophecy, the story probably looked more similar to the breakfast on the beach.[82] Jesus' disciples encounter him as a stranger on the road. In spite of all that has happened, in spite of their fear, they follow both local custom and the hospitality of Jesus' ministry and invite the stranger to stay with them. Significantly, this echoes the kind of itinerant meal sharing that was central to Jesus' ministry and is found earlier, in Luke 10:8–9: "Whenever you enter a town and its people welcome you, eat what is set before you; cure the sick

---

82. Fitzmyer, *Gospel*, 1560. An earlier version of the story might have looked something like this: "Now on that same day two of [the disciples] were going to a village called Emmaus, about seven miles from Jerusalem, talking with each other about all these things that had happened. While they were talking and discussing, Jesus himself came near and went with them, but their eyes were kept from recognizing him[. . .] As they came near the village to which they were going, he walked ahead as if he were going on. But they urged him strongly, saying, 'Stay with us, because it is almost evening and the day is now nearly over.' So he went in to stay with them. When he was at the table with them, he took bread, blessed it, and gave it to them. Then their eyes were opened, and they recognized him; and he vanished from their sight" (Luke 24:13–16, 28–30).

who are there, and say to them, 'The kingdom of God has come near to you.'" When the disciples share a meal with this stranger, they experience this same pattern of hospitality and the Beloved Community of God again. They experience the continuation, the resilience of Jesus' ministry. Their eyes are opened and they recognize, in the stranger they have welcomed, something of the divine, something they understand to be the persistence of Jesus himself.

A couple of details in this story are striking. First, Jesus is at a table, and he's with disciples, not long after Luke has shared his upper room narrative with its "Do this in remembrance of me," but Jesus never says anything here about his body or blood. Why not? Here is a unique opportunity for Jesus to demonstrate what he meant by his earlier command. He offers a blessing, which he does in almost all of the stories we've discussed, then simply breaks the bread and gives it to the disciples. It seems unlikely that Luke glossed over any reference to Jesus' body because he assumed its inclusion to be understood. The absence in this story of any reference to Jesus' body or his blood supports the possibility that the story was once an independent tradition, unrelated to the upper room narrative. The fact that Jesus doesn't mention his body and blood also supports the scholarly position that the words of institution were not recited during the meal itself until a later era. Even more importantly, the absence of reference to body and blood here means that in this narrative, Jesus is present *only* as a subject. In this first demonstration, there is no indication of Jesus as a ritual object beyond the use of the verb "break" (which the breakfast narrative avoids), and even that's pushing it.[83] Luke's efforts to harmonize this story with the upper room may evoke the body and blood indirectly, but it's actually a stretch. You have to read it into the text. What's actually there is hospitality to a stranger, prayer, and a meal that is an epiphany, a citation or performative reiteration of a meal that helps the Beloved Community of God to come near, recognized by the disciples.[84]

83. Some might object here that Jesus' question, "Was it not necessary that the Messiah should suffer these things?" back on the road points readers toward a more sacrificial interpretation of the Emmaus meal. Since Luke inserts the theme of the necessity of Jesus' suffering at other points during his gospel, it is safe to assume that he has done so here as well. See Fitzmyer, *Gospel*, 1565 n26.

84. By "citation" here I am intending a kind of performative reiteration that perpetuates a convention or mode of behavior, perhaps even sedimenting that behavior. This usage is similar to Judith Butler's use of "citation" as the re-performance of a gender norm that sediments gender performance. For discussion, see Butler, *Bodies*, 12–16.

Second, there is no mention of a cup at all. It's hard to imagine that this is simply an abbreviation, when Jesus' actions are clearly important to the story. What is more likely is that this story comes originally from a context in which the cup did not play as central a role or was missing altogether. Andrew McGowan has demonstrated that there is solid evidence for bread-only forms of Holy Communion in the early church— yet another variety of practice.[85] It's doubtful that the Lukan community participated in bread-only Communion, though, given the upper room narrative, especially in its longer form. Probably Luke is using earlier materials that witness indirectly an earlier, bread-only tradition.[86] We are again seeing traces of struggle between two different traditions of interpretation, and perhaps two different meal practices as well.

From this passage we gain another example of a meal tradition that focuses on the resilience and continuation of the meals of Jesus' ministry. We get a glimpse of a bread-only eucharistic tradition unaware of Jesus' body and blood as ritual objects. We can see a connection with the itinerant meal sharing of Jesus' ministry, and we can see Luke's efforts to conflate this tradition with his overall narrative of the upper room.

A Wealth of Resources

We've only begun to uncover the variety of meal traditions in the New Testament. In this chapter we've looked only at the longest and most developed meal stories related to Holy Communion, those that most clearly indicate streams of meal practice within local communities. We haven't looked at any of the minor stories, and we've hardly touched upon the many teachings about meals attributed to Jesus. All of those other passages most likely influenced the practices of particular communities as well. Then there's the vast array of Communion practices that the church has tried across the centuries, as well as continuing arguments about whether the elements are Jesus' body and blood, that we haven't even touched.[87]

85. McGowan, *Ascetic*, 181–82.

86. "This evidence is not, however, without value as a possible trace of eucharists of this kind [bread only] at a very early point" (McGowan, *Ascetic*, 234–35).

87. A good example of the ongoing struggle is found in Ignatius's letter to the Smyrneans, in which he describes a group of Christians who have stopped participating in the community's Holy Communion rites because they refuse to accept that the bread is Jesus' body. Like Paul and the editor of John, Ignatius predicts the demise of those who disagree. See Bradshaw, *Eucharistic*, 88.

Even with this limited sample, we have already found a wealth of resources for the work of recovering and reimagining Holy Communion. There wasn't just one meal tradition that gave rise to Holy Communion. There were a number of them, in small, local faith communities trying to figure out how best to carry on Jesus' ministry. In this brief survey we've seen six distinct streams of tradition, not including the one that focused on Jesus' body and blood:

1. *A manna-and-water tradition,* drawing from the Exodus and Numbers wilderness stories, tied to a theme of abundance and to Jewish belief that new manna would be a sign of the Messiah.

2. *The feeding of the multitude,* with bread, fish, and abundance all functioning as signs of the Messiah but also bearing the marks of Jesus' ministry: a manna economy in which all share the same food and all get enough to eat.

3. *An eschatological promise tradition,* a pre-arrest meal, including Jesus' vow not to eat or drink again until his goal is accomplished, bound up with the eschatological promise of eating together in the Beloved Community of God.

4. *A footwashing tradition,* also a pre-arrest meal, but one that focuses on serving others in ways that can disrupt social hierarchy, especially through footwashing.

5. *The breakfast on the beach,* a postresurrection meal tradition that emphasizes the resilience and continuation of the messianic feast. It focuses on the kind of sharing and abundance that characterized Jesus' ministry and, through it, the resilience of Jesus himself, encountered in/as a stranger.

6. *Emmaus,* a bread-only, postresurrection meal that also emphasizes the resilience of the meals of Jesus' ministry, this time including the practice of hospitality, especially to strangers or itinerant guests.

Before Holy Communion began to be standardized across different locations, local communities of early Christians shared a variety of meals, informed by a variety of stories like these, as their particular ways of continuing Jesus' ministry. Many of them were shaped by the Hellenistic *symposion* format, and many of them carried forward the blessings and prayers of Jewish meal practices. When we begin to imagine the way these stories functioned before they were systematized and some were subjugated, we discover a storehouse of treasures. Some of those stories corresponded with a community's particular meal practices: blessings offered over bread and water, or bread only, or maybe the mutual washing of feet. Communities experimented; they tried different things. Some of the things they tried proved too difficult to sustain. Some communities told of a meal where Jesus said that the bread and cup were his body and blood, but many others did not. Some of their stories and practices spread from one community to others. Some, undoubtedly, did not and have been lost to us altogether. As we have seen, Paul and the writers of the Gospels gathered many of these stories, mostly favoring the body-and-blood narrative and subjugating other meal narratives in the process. This did not happen without some struggle, but it happened nonetheless.

In the centuries following the New Testament era, and perhaps even during it, the variety of interpretations and practices began to diminish. Written prayers and rubrics were eventually shared between communities—even imposed at times after we get to Constantine—competing, in a sense, with oral tradition and local improvisation. Other changes occurred as well. The full meals of Jesus' ministry were gradually displaced by a symbolic amount of food that focused narrowly on bread and wine as sacral elements. The sharing of abundance, of food brought by participants, was progressively replaced by much scarcer, sacral food that became the closely guarded possession of a growing class of clergy. The body-and-blood narrative moved in and eclipsed all other meal traditions across geographic locations. Particularly with Constantine's endorsement of the church, the need for the liturgy to explain itself to the uninitiated resulted in the insertion of the words of institution into Communion prayers, such that a ritual logic of beneficial violence became even more explicit. Meals that had been ritualized practices of *actual* sharing, *actual* feeding, even *actual* eating with tax collectors and sinners came to be members-only practices that gestured ritually at these things, claiming in prayer to do them while practicing something increasingly different.[88]

88. Maxwell Johnson (*Rites,* 5–6) speaks of the shift toward more closed meals when he writes, "It is important to underscore the fact that nowhere do the Gospels record anything specific about rites of entrance or preparation for this meal sharing with Jesus. Rather, to use our own now traditional sacramental language, the meal itself was not the *culmination* of initiation but appears, rather, as the *inception,* that is, the very *beginnings* of initiation, the 'sacrament' of initiation, or the rite of incorporation into Christ . . . Conversion itself, it seems, was a *consequence* of, not a precondition for, such meal sharing." Soon after Easter, the church reversed the process, requiring the catechumenate and baptism before Holy Communion.

Also, over time, the convivial table of sharing and *koinonia* that had been a hallmark of Jesus' ministry was gradually conflated with an altar of sacrifice.[89] All these changes helped to overwrite the variety of meals practiced by early followers of Jesus—with some dire consequences in history, particularly as the church came to political power.[90]

At this point it would be easy to conclude that the historical development of early Communion practices was a straightforward fall from an idyllic, Eden-like purity into violent and vain attempts to consolidate power and control death, but that is not the case. The various practices that preceded these changes were not perfect by any means, and much of what is truly amazing and transformative about Holy Communion has remained in spite of the changes of the first several centuries. The point, rather, is that *some* things went wrong with Holy Communion. Our task, our calling in this era, is to continue what is best in our current Communion practices, to recover from the trove of history what we discern as most faithful to Jesus' ministry and God's desires, and to summon our

89. Some readers may disagree with the idea that Holy Communion was not originally associated with sacrifice or altar, but the various strata of New Testament teachings and stories about the meal lean in that direction. The table of the eucharistic meal as a sacrificial altar is scarcely even a biblical concept, apart from the obvious connection between table and altar created by meat that had been sacrificed. While many indications point to an understanding of Jesus' martyrdom as a sacrificial offering developing during the New Testament era, it is anachronistic to suggest that the upper room narratives bear signs that the meal itself (as opposed to Jesus) is a sacrifice in practice (and not just in written metaphor), or that the table is an altar. Heb 13:10 is the passage most often used to justify this trajectory of theology and practice. It's true that this verse states that Christians have an altar, and associates an altar with eating. The book of Hebrews also articulates the clearest example of a developing theology of sacrificial atonement. Even so, at this stage the reference is most likely metaphorical only (as in, We have an "altar," in quotes, Heb 13:10). It is more accurate to say that a theology of sacrifice grew up around the meal practices of Jesus' ministry and eventually became the dominant ritual and theological framework. The table becomes an altar. The idea of the meal as a "sacrifice" may well have originated with the need for early communities to justify their meals as being a substitute for temple sacrifice or sacrifice to the emperor. Just as Jewish communities were moving away from literal animal sacrifice and toward a "sacrifice of praise" after the destruction of the Jerusalem temple, so early communities of Jesus' followers used Mal 1:11 to justify substituting a meal for a temple sacrifice: "For from the rising of the sun to its setting, my name is great among the nations, and *in every place* incense is offered to my name, and a pure offering."

90. As an example of this shift to power, James Carroll (*Constantine's*, chs. 8–21) traces the parallel development of anti-Semitism in Christian theology as Christianity went from being a persecuted sect of Judaism to a religion of the empire.

own passion and creativity in assembling Christian meal practices that collaborate with God's Beloved Community, always coming near.

One of the most difficult questions remains, however: If we do this, if we gather up various, brightly colored scraps of fabric from Communion practices past and present, and if we use them to help create new Christian meals that don't rely upon beneficial violence, will it still really be Holy Communion? This is the question to which my students return again and again each time I teach a course on Holy Communion and violence. If we do something different, will it still be a sacrament? Will it still count, will it still be valid? Will it be what Jesus wanted, or what God wants? In the next chapter we will turn to this question, looking at examples of new, creative approaches to Christian meals, and recovering a different theology of sacramentality in the process.

7

Resistance, Resilience, and Risk

Practical Possibilities
for Recovering Communion

Signs of Resilience

On Sunday afternoons by a fountain in the Boston Commons, an unlikely group of people gathers. They are the worshipers of Common Cathedral, an outdoor congregation of people who are experiencing homelessness, and their friends.[1] They are businesspeople and students, people who are just scraping by, and some who are not. They all gather there together. They have been meeting there by the fountain every week—rain, snow, or shine—for the last *twenty years*. Perhaps because this congregation grew out of the Episcopal Church, they serve Holy Communion every week. They also share food, clothing, healing prayer, and conversation. In 2001 they even started Ecclesia Ministries Mission, helping to establish similar street ministries in more than eighty cities in the United States, Brazil, and the United Kingdom. One of the communities they helped to start, the Street Church program of the Church of the Epiphany in Washington, DC, gathers in Franklin Square, just four blocks from the White House. These faith communities don't participate in Holy Communion

---

1. Please see www.commoncathedral.org.

so that they can be inspired or formed to go out and help people who are poor. They *are* people who are very poor, as well as people who are not, communing together. Their spiritual union is also a practical union. They are practicing Holy Communion with a mixed guest list.

On Sunday and Monday evenings each week, people trickle into a small storefront in Brooklyn, put on aprons, and begin to cook dinner together. They are the members and friends of St. Lydia's, a dinner church. When the food is hot and the table has been set, they sit down together and share a meal—an actual, full meal—that includes Holy Communion. Amid candlelight and conversation, people who are sometimes strangers and often different from one another in a variety of ways eat and drink together—and then clean up together afterward. Theirs is not just a furtive gesture at a meal, a small taste that only points to the full meals of Jesus' ministry. It's not a symbolic substitution for the difficult work of sitting down and sharing one's table with a person who is "other." Rather, Holy Communion at St Lydia's asks people to both share and receive meal hospitality with people who are not just their family or friends. They are practicing Holy Communion with a full meal.[2]

There's more. On April 1, 2014, a group of Roman Catholic bishops held Mass on the border between Nogales, Arizona, and its partner city, Heroic Nogales, Sonora, Mexico. The bishops served Holy Communion across the international border. Communion elements were passed between the heavy vertical beams that make up the border wall there. Border guards looked on, and volunteers made sure that nothing illegal was passed across the boundary. The sacrament was celebrated as an act of solidarity with Mexican immigrants on both sides of the border. It was also an act protesting dehumanizing U.S. immigration policies and procedures. Most of all, this sacramental meal both enacted and signified the deeper reality of communion that the border denies.[3] With much less news coverage, local faith communities have actually been celebrating Communion services like this one along the U.S.-Mexico border for decades. Sometimes the participants coordinate with the border patrol, and sometimes there are tense face-offs. Sometimes the Communion elements cross the border, sometimes participants must celebrate within shouting distance. These practices of Holy Communion do not simply insist that the meal somehow unifies us with alienated and oppressed

2. Please see www.stlydias.org.

3. Zapor, "At Border Mass."

people who remain absent from our eucharistic meal. They do more than point toward our metaphysical solidarity in Christ. They also enact that unity in a practical way, through their resistance to laws, physical barriers, and agents of the state that would define the participants as separate from one another. Each of these celebrations of Holy Communion on the border is a gathering of alienated bodies.

Many other examples exist. The Banquet, a soup kitchen in Sioux Falls, South Dakota, asks all the volunteers from area churches who serve meals to also take turns sitting and eating with the guests.[4] The food pantry at St. Gregory of Nyssa Episcopal Church in San Francisco takes place every week in the sanctuary, with the food arranged around the Communion table.[5] In each of these cases, people of faith are working to recover more radical (from the Latin word *radix,* meaning "root") meal practices that were part of Jesus' ministry: enacting solidarity, sharing resources with those in need, mixing the guest list, and so on. In different ways, they are reintegrating characteristics of the Christian meal that they have come to associate with Jesus and his ministry.

The original community around Jesus shared actual meals with a variety of people, many of whom were poor and alienated. Those who gathered not only heard proclaimed but also experienced the Beloved Community of God coming near. In the contemporary movements outlined here, people who have been formed both by the sacramental meal and by their reading of Scripture are instinctively working to weave back together aspects of the meal they perceive as having become dis-integrated over time. More than doing something novel and creative, they are working to pull ancient, more radical meal practices back into use. If these movements show a certain amount of innovation or social experimentation, then that is in keeping with both the early and later history of changing eucharistic practices.[6] And although these contemporary communities might not see it this way, I suggest that these recovered meal practices were largely subjugated and overwritten by an overwhelming emphasis on practices aimed at signifying God's (and our) participation in a system of violent surrogacy.

This brings us to one other contemporary practice. It's one that doesn't necessarily show up in the previous examples but is also

4. Please see www.thebanquetsf.org.

5. Please see www.saintgregorys.org/the-food-pantry.html.

6. For discussion of social experimentation in the meals of early Christianity, see Taussig, *In the Beginning,* 145–71.

happening, and has much to learn from the radical ways of eating together already mentioned. On Sunday mornings here and there across the United States, local churches are already moving away from the ritual logic of beneficial violence in Holy Communion. The congregations I know of are part of the United Church of Christ, the Disciples of Christ, and the Mennonite Church USA. A few Baptist congregations (American Baptist and Alliance of Baptists) also participate, and there may well be others. In these Communion services people have begun to seek alternatives to a narrow focus on the elements as Jesus' body and blood. Their prayers still give thanks for God's activity in history, and in Jesus' life in particular, but they tell a different version of the upper room story, or a different meal story altogether. These congregations too are searching for something. It's true that at times their eucharistic prayers merely shy away from the difficult parts of Jesus' suffering and death. At other times their prayers sound as if they are still groping for alternative narratives and theologies. Even so, these congregations are beginning to let go of a focus on the reenactment of violence. They are allowing the crucifixion to shrink to size, leaving room for other meal practices to resurface.[7] Many of them have not yet integrated their liturgical changes with the kind of radical meal practices described above. In their search, however, they are creating a space where such practices could easily reemerge.

In this chapter we will consider how these various movements might be integrated in the life of a congregation. We will begin to map out the particulars of an approach to Holy Communion that focuses more on radical meal practices than on reenacting Jesus' execution. Rather than drawing us into a ritual logic that tries to cope with traumatic violence and ends up trapped in a loop of reenactment, the practices outlined here work to resist and heal the ways that violence forms us. They aim to counter the ways we are formed to accept violent surrogacy as a given in the world. They are meant to help us mourn suffering and nurture resilience. They are chosen to help us risk sharing, and to risk encountering otherness, in order to experience the deep communion we all share.

---

7. In *Redeeming Memories* Flora Keshgegian writes: "After the survivor has moved through the process of dealing with the abuse and it begins to 'shrink to size,' so to speak, so that it no longer dominates her life, her energy shifts toward integrating this past into the rest of life" (54). Later, she writes, "In a very real way, Christianity needs to do the same: to decenter crucifixion and resurrection toward a redeeming memory more inclusive of Jesus' life and the history of God's people . . . What would it mean to begin to tell the story of Jesus' life so that the crucifixion became one, albeit critically important, moment in that narrative?" (184).

We will seek an experience of God in practices as practical as they are symbolic—practices intentionally shaping in us *habitus* of the Beloved Community of God.

By engaging in these practices, we will be working to reintegrate aspects of the meal that have become separated from one another. Imagine yourself walking into a local church. (I am thinking of a church near where I live, but you can probably think of one that's similar.) It's not a huge church. It's a midsize congregation with an old, sturdy building and a historic sanctuary. If you walk in at the basement level, you find that the congregation has a thriving ministry among people who are homeless or are experiencing food insecurity. The congregation I'm thinking of serves hundreds of meals every week and provides a variety of other services. So as you walk into the basement, you find there sojourners from the streets eating. If you go up the stairs to the fellowship hall, on a Sunday but occasionally at other times of the week as well, you find a potluck: members of the congregation share tables, conversation, and their own food with one another. Everyone shares with everyone else. If you go through a doorway and down the hall, you come to the beautiful sanctuary, where there is a third kind of eating during worship. It's a more ritualized meal, more minimalist, and it includes more prayer. The prayer and ritual are meant to help open people to the reality of our deeper communion with God and one another.

Three ways of eating, one congregation. Rachel Held Evans critiques this kind of division, saying, "We have one place for the uncool people—our ministries—and another for the cool people—our worship services. When we actually bump into one another it can get awkward, so we try to avoid it."[8] Her version lacks the crucial addition of the potluck, but it helps us to get at the ironic division of different meal types in our churches. One of the major ideas of this book is that these different types of meals were at one time *all the same meal*. To differing extents in different early communities, there were meals that included guests (especially hungry guests), that involved potluck-style (or at least rotating) sharing, and that were steeped in prayer and ritual action. These meals, with their initial diversity and experimentation, devolved into three separate kinds of meal practices over time. One of the goals here, then, is to strategize about how these practices might be woven back together in the lives of local congregations.

8. Evans, "Is Your Church too Cool?"

Last but not the least, we will be looking for eucharistic practices that don't divide the practical from the spiritual but seek the sacramental in the practical. Like the ministry of Jesus, these approaches to Holy Communion go beyond symbolic efficacy, beyond the insistence that it is primarily our words and sign acts that accomplish the rite's spiritual ends. These practices enact concrete alternatives to the politics of subordination and atomization. They weave the fabric of community and solidarity. They ritualize an alternative to the economy of scarcity and distribution by the few, focusing on actual feeding and sharing. Not the least, they go looking for God in acts of kindness and generosity as much as in material things. They seek the surprise of the divine *Thou,* found in the act of sharing and in the face of the other. They strive for a glimpse of the deeper communion of our existence. They do not seek the Holy in a person who has been made into a thing.

In the process of exploring the possibilities, we will begin to see the outlines of what I will call *practical sacramentality*. By this I mean a way of engaging sacramentality in which efficacy is found in the practical effects of rites at least as much if not more than in their symbol and story. We are not looking for a Communion rite that (a) has real spiritual effects (reconciliation with God, experience of real presence, and so forth) and then (b) also has some positive, practical effects that flow from it. Rather, we will be seeking ways that sacramentality and sacramental efficacy can be found primarily in the practical results themselves: in the actual meeting of strangers across boundaries, in the actual sharing of one's food, and in the actual feeding of hungry bodies. By working against the historical drift toward sacramental practices that are primarily acts of signification, we will work to recover a practical sacramentality that has been lost along the way. This approach, I believe, can relieve us of the burden of producing strained, sometimes convoluted theories about how Christian meal rites achieve their ends. It can also help us to more fully recognize the practices suggested here as sacramental—at least as sacramental as the practices we currently call Holy Communion, if not more so. At the root of what Holy Communion has become are difficult, uncomfortable, exhilarating practices around food that can form us as people who are better at collaborating with a resilient God intent upon *shalom*. These are not just admirable ethical practices. They're ways of collaborating with the Kin-dom of God coming near.

So, you might ask, when the glowing possibilities described here are worked out in local faith communities, will it actually be Holy

Communion? Will it be the real deal, something that qualifies as a sacrament? A lot will depend on what you choose to do in your context. I expect that faith communities will need to take these suggestions and see what works: experimenting, learning from their own successes and mistakes, adapting from other communities, and striving for something that sustains the depth and sacramentality of the meal.

The suggestions here will likely be only a starting point for new discovery and creativity. For your faith community, it's probably better to just start somewhere, using the guidelines and examples here in your search for a meal of deep and holy communion with God and others. As we noted at the outset of this journey, quoting Millard Fuller, we more often act our way into thinking differently than the other way around.

Nevertheless, I do think that the results, while perhaps awkward at first in their difference from what we expect Holy Communion to be, can still be Holy Communion. They can still be sacramental meals, grounded in Scripture and in the founding practices of Jesus and the community that surrounded him. They can still be meals in which the Holy Spirit is able to move graciously alongside us in a peculiar and particular way. My hope is that as we move toward meal rites more focused on the *habitus* of the Beloved Community of God and less centered on symbolic acts of beneficial violence, our meals will come to be recognized as the recovery and reimagination of Holy Communion. Here, then, are some ways to begin.

We Open the Meal
(The *Habitus* of Hospitality)

We can begin by sharing Holy Communion with as many different people in our local communities as possible, engaging in what people in the United Church of Christ like to call extravagant hospitality.[9] Nonmembers as well as members; unbaptized as well as baptized; people of other faiths and people of no faith; youth, children, and adults; people of various races and ethnicities; people with differing abilities and capacities; people who are lesbian, gay, bisexual, transsexual, intersex, and straight; people in prison, in rehab, in locked wards, in homeless shelters;

---

9. "As many as possible" is meant to acknowledge a limit here. There are people who we may not be able to welcome if they are a danger to other people or are committed to the destruction of the community, for example.

people who have a basic understanding of the meal, and people who don't; people who have the appearances of righteousness, and those who are more clearly in trouble—the list goes on. This will mean working to make the meal more accessible for people of differing abilities and for people in our communities who speak different languages. It means using food and decorations and songs, and even leaders, that come from more than one local culture, ethnicity, or race—not as a gesture, but as a necessity. It means rethinking all of the "club for saints" language during the meal, which has placed a stumbling block in front of so many through the centuries.[10] It means making sure than survivors of violence can still participate, even if that means supervising or finding a new church home for a perpetrator. It means expanding our idea of the Christian meal as centered in the sanctuary as we move out into the community to be with others. It means letting go of the comfort of a meal that is primarily "just for us," in favor of something more important. As theologian Tom Driver once said, "If there are no hungry people in the vicinity of the church, the church should be moved."[11]

As with many of the suggestions in this chapter, it's possible that you already sense, on some level, the need for this kind of change. You may already sense that Holy Communion is always reaching beyond the in-group meal in the sanctuary toward a more expansive gathering. That has been an undercurrent in Communion services across the centuries. In his book on the history of baptism, Maxwell Johnson points out that before the crucifixion and maybe for a short time afterward, meal sharing appears to have been the beginning of the process of initiation into Christian community, rather than the end of it.[12] People were invited to these amazing meals where Jesus brought together all sorts of different people to eat and pray. If those people were intrigued by what they experienced, they were invited to learn more, to enter more deeply into the movement, and eventually to move toward baptism. Not only was this meal open, but

---

10. The following sentences may be a trigger for survivors of traumatic violence.

11. Driver, *Liberating*, 222.

12. "It is important to underscore the fact that nowhere do the Gospels record anything specific about rites of entrance or preparation for this meal sharing with Jesus. Rather, to use our own now traditional sacramental language, the meal itself was not the *culmination* of initiation but appears, rather, as the *inception*, that is, the very *beginnings* of initiation, the "sacrament" of initiation, or the rite of incorporation into Christ . . . Conversion itself, it seems, was a *consequence* of, not a precondition for, such meal sharing" (Johnson, *Rites*, 5).

it opened outward: it was a meal that needed, and perhaps even required, guests (Luke 14:15–24).

"Open commensality" is the term John Dominic Crossan has popularized to describe this openness.[13] Given that social stratification within societies is usually defined in part by who is welcome at one's table, Jesus' ministry of welcoming people who didn't ordinarily eat together was not just a prophetic sign act but also a counterpolitics, an alternate way of ordering power and community.

Of course, it's pretty clear that to whatever extent the meal was open to begin with, at least some of the early communities shut that down fairly quickly. Within decades after Easter, in contexts like that of the Didache, Holy Communion had already become a private meal only for the baptized: "Let no one eat or drink of your thanksgiving [meal] save those who have been baptized in the name of the Lord, since the Lord has said concerning this, 'Do not give what is holy to the dogs.'"[14] People who were considering baptism but had not yet taken the plunge were often allowed to stay for the first part of worship, but they were actually asked to leave before the meal. Notably, the preservation of this saying attributed to Jesus—about not throwing the children's food to dogs—is probably evidence of an early argument about the openness of the meals in particular and of the movement more generally. If this saying in the Didache (see also Matt 7:6) represents one side, then the story of Jesus' conversion to a broader view by a Syrophoenician woman (Mark 7:26) or a Canaanite woman (Matt 15:22) represents the other side. On one side, the meal is open only to the house of Israel (Matt 15; Mark 7) or to the baptized (Didache). On the other side, even Jesus himself is understood to benefit from sharing with people considered to be other.

In spite of this later struggle, it seems likely that open meals (rather than meals only for Jesus' inner circle) were a crucial and controversial part of Jesus' early ministry. The unflattering stories about Jesus being labeled a friend of tax collectors and sinners (Mark 2:15–17 and parallels) are a good indication of this. Add to this the teachings attributed to Jesus about welcoming strangers and guests (e.g., Matt 22:2–10; Luke 14:12–14), and it's clear that this ideal remained an important theme in some communities of the early church, even if early communities found the practice difficult to sustain.

13. For an introduction to open commensality, see Crossan, *Jesus*, 66–70.

14. Niederwimmer, *Didache*, 144 (brackets original).

Rather than creating a place where we eat primarily with our own family and friends, then, we can orient the meal outward, toward hospitality with those outside first, and then among those already part of the community as well. We practice hospitality as rehearsal for daily life, but also as a way of enacting a generous, open faith here and now. We structure the invitation, the location, and the meal itself so that not only the presiders but all of us can engage in this hospitality. We'll see this idea developed in more detail in the next section, but for now it's enough to say that we can begin by removing as many barriers as possible to the meal.

This opening of the table is not the anxious hospitality of shrinking churches. (If we're honest, our hospitality to some may drive others away.) It's not focused on getting more members or souls for Christ. It doesn't presume a mandate to convert, or that we possess the truth and are showing misguided people the true path, either. It is less a missional model and more what my colleague Damayanthi Niles would call a pilgrimage model: going out to find the sacred. In this mode, we turn outward in search of spiritual knowledge and experience. We seek God in the journey, the changing terrain, and the stranger. All these and more offer us new insight, as well as a reaching sense of mystery.

Importantly, Niles adds that this opening outward often includes pushing toward the "next other" rather than being satisfied with "our others." So we keep going on pilgrimage, avoiding the tendency to turn inward. The Christian meal is always going to be in danger of sliding back into a means of creating intimacy and belonging among people who already know and like one another. It's always going to be on the verge of losing its subversive impact, its effectiveness as a counterpolitics. What we have failed to realize historically is that when we lose these radical functions, when the meal becomes too comfortable, too manageable, and too socially acceptable, we also lose a crucial aspect of its sacramentality.

Each time I've taught a course on Holy Communion and violence, the final assignment has asked groups of students to experiment with designing and leading a meal rite that approaches violence differently and still tries to be Holy Communion. Each time, I've stressed the importance of hospitality to others, and each time the final assignment has included a suggestion that people outside the class be invited to participate. When the time comes, though, there haven't been any guests. I suspect this is because the class has formed a bond. Many of the students are survivors of violence themselves or are close to someone who has survived violence. During the month of intensive classes (the course is taught during our January term at Eden Seminary), they sometimes share their stories, and a solidarity develops within the group. Our meeting begins to feel like safe space. So, it's understandable that students would want to end the class with a "just us" kind of meal. Who could blame them? This points to the great difficulty of ongoing hospitality. How do we keep going on pilgrimage to find the sacred once we have found a sense of community? Perhaps the upper room story does us a disservice when it holds up a more private, disciples-only meal as paradigmatic of Jesus' meals—and our own.

If it is not a meal preoccupied with proselytizing, then this approach is not merely a community potluck stripped of its particular Christian character either. Hospitality may require some attention to language that is accessible, but if we lose the distinctive gifts of (humble) Christian prayers and ritual acts, we are missing the point. I would be saddened if my Jewish friends felt that they had to water down their Seder meal because they had invited me. I would not expect my Muslim friends to forgo traditional greetings in Arabic if they invited me to an Eid al-Fitr meal. So also we will lose something crucial if we "leave out the Jesus stuff," or "go easy on the churchy parts" on the chance that we might make others uncomfortable. Of course to truly welcome others we will need to negotiate our terms with those who gather, so we can't afford to be rigid. That's simply part and parcel of hospitality.

We Insist on a Mixed Guest List
(The *Habitus* of Solidarity and
the *Habitus* of Seeking God in the Other)

This may seem like the same thing as hospitality, and the two are intimately related. When we insist on a mixed guest list, though, we are adding a requirement: that we share the meal with people who are not only guests in some sense but also different from us. What if we actually *need* to encounter people who are genuinely different from us, who are "other" to us, or from whom we are alienated, in Holy Communion? We're not talking about, "Oh, wouldn't it be nice if we had more diversity in our congregation." We're talking about, "What are we going to do? We can't have Holy Communion without them"—where "they" are the people in our communities who live across boundaries of ethnicity, wealth, sexual orientation, differing ability, or social status. In the way that a *minyan* of ten people is required for traditional Jewish worship, it would not really be Holy Communion unless we were bringing together different kinds of people.

That may be a tall order, but Jesus seems to have done this with some regularity. As we just saw above, Jesus and his disciples were remembered as eating with tax collectors and sinners (Matt 11:19; Mark 2:15; Luke 5:29–30). Luke's Gospel also remembers Jesus eating with Pharisees (Luke 7:36, 14:1). If we combine these stories with teachings in the Gospels about going out and inviting people who are poor or differently abled to share a meal (Luke 14:21), or about inviting people who cannot repay us to our banquets (Luke 14:13–14), we begin to get a sense that the practice of mixing people together at meals was a common part of the collective memory of Jesus' ministry. Again, there was disagreement early on, and the degree to which this ideal was actually practiced in the emerging communities of the Jesus movement is unclear.[15] Even so, the practice of bringing together different types of people for meals remained a live issue in the decades after Jesus' execution. If nowhere else, we see this in Paul's disagreements with other leaders about eating with Gentiles (Gal 2:11–12) and in his disagreements with the wealthier Corinthians about eating with people who were in need (1 Cor 11:21–22).

Partly this practice of insisting on a mixed guest list is about enacting solidarity. It's about actually seeking out meals that allow participants to stand with people who have been dis-integrated or segregated from them; it's about re-membering community that has been fragmented. Then our sacramental meals both signify and enact the deeper reality we noted in chapter 4: that regardless of the (often violent) practices undertaken to dis-integrate us, we all belong, body and soul, to the Beloved Community of God.[16] We see this happening when the disciples gather to eat together in spite of the terrorizing influence of the crucifixion (e.g., Mark 16:14; Luke 24:33–43). Our meal sharing acts out the deeper communion we all share, even if appearances argue otherwise. Holy Communion becomes a liturgical counterpractice that actively resists the isolation caused by all sorts of violence: war, border policing, policies of segregation, dehumanizing prejudice, abuse, and more. Of course this will mean actually seeking out opportunities to eat together in caring,

15. See Hal Taussig's discussion of written ideals versus actual meal sharing across boundaries in the early communities of the Jesus movement. Taussig, *In the Beginning*, 153.

16. See note **25** in chapter 4, above.

empowering ways with those of us who have been particularly isolated, including veterans (our own and those from other countries), rape survivors, immigrants, or sexual minorities. This solidarity is not undertaken as charity, initiated only by the powerful, but as the fulfilling of a mutual need: a need for healing, and a need for solidarity across boundaries that helps the Beloved Community of God to come near.

So, for example, Mark Lewis Taylor writes in the book *Cross Examinations*, "The disciplines of torture should meet, in the practice of the Eucharist, a counterpower, one that unleashes worlds of life amid the deathly unmaking of worlds that war and torture spew forth."[17] What would it mean to ask point-blank: Okay, what do we have to do to create a Holy Communion event that works to re-member torture survivors into community? Or traumatized veterans? Or survivors of abuse? How would that open new possibilities for local church practice?

This solidarity will likely look quite different from community to community. A predominantly African American congregation may decide that their mixed guest list this season should include solidarity with ex-offenders, but not the large, Euro-American congregation down the street that might easily colonize the meal. Not yet, anyway. Or a predominantly working-class congregation may decide that the time is right to go and dine with Mexican immigrants, but without inviting certain prominent members of the community who might show up only for the photo op. That might come later, after the congregation has more practice and better strategies for this new way of doing things.

In addition to solidarity, the mixed guest list is also importantly about experiencing someone who is other to us as a *Thou*. It's about the revelatory surprise of discovering someone as both a three-dimensional subject and a window to the divine. Whether we see in them the *imago Dei* (the image of God that they were created to be) or the face of Jesus (as in Matt 25:34–40), Holy Communion with a mixed guest list can help us to encounter the holy in the face of the other. Here I am thinking not only of Buber's *I-Thou* relationship, but also of the trace of the divine in Emmanuel Levinas's face-to-face relationship that calls forth obligation: "The face opens the primordial discourse whose first word is obligation, which no 'interiority' permits avoiding," he says in *Totality and Infinity*.[18] Elsewhere he adds, "The trace is not just one more word: it is the proximity

17. Taylor, "American," 276.

18. Levinas, *Totality*, 201.

of God in the countenance of my fellowman."[19] Of course this assumes that we have not fixed our gaze so intently upon the eucharistic elements that we miss the sacramentality of the assembly.[20]

This kind of encounter with the sacred in the other will not just happen automatically. If we merely throw together people who are different from one another, they are just as likely to go away having experienced nothing but awkwardness. (There is likely to be some of that in any case.) So we will need to coach people: help them to feel comfortable, attend to the language of sacred encounter in our litanies and prayers, and yes, catechize. By this I do not mean that we should try to convince participants that something sacred and mysterious happens whenever they encounter another person at this holy meal. It doesn't always. I mean that we should introduce them to the possibility, using the stories of Jesus and a robust theology of *koinoia* (here meaning "enacting community/communion with God and others"), while offering no guarantees.[21]

Undertaken in this way, Holy Communion can help to form in us *habitus* that work against the tendency toward objectification, be it of Jesus or other people. Rather than seeking an experience of the holy in an in-group dynamic, simultaneously reinforcing our experience of those not present as "other," the meal can send us again and again on pilgrimage, toward neighbors who are other to us, in order to discover them and God at the same time. It can help train us in overcoming our fear and our objectifying tendencies. And it can put our own self-righteousness

19. Levinas, *Entre*, 57. It should be noted here that I am using "other" in a slightly different sense than either Buber or Levinas, choosing to foreground our experience of people who are less known to us, or who live on the other side of some kind of boundary (physical, political, social), while not wholly excluding those who are better known to us.

20. Beyond the individual other, such sacred encounters can help to make manifest the deeper reality in which we live as well: the truth that the poor (or the wealthy) are us, the whole city is us, even the ecosystem is us. An experience of *koinonia*, in which we experience communion with God and others at the same time, can extend beyond the human community, opening onto another crucial aspect of the Beloved Community of God: the sacramentality of creation.

21. Helpful to our discussion is the fact that the *koinōn-* root from which *koinonia* comes includes the meanings "sharing" or "participation," implying an act of giving or joining in. It's not always easy to capture the active sense of *koinonia* in English. The term is rich and complex in the New Testament, and especially in Paul, including companionship, mutual support (spiritual and financial), spiritual union, and more. It seems likely that Paul is using this term in many of the same ways that Jesus used the language of the *basileia* of God. See discussion of the term *koinonia* in Kittel, *Theological*, 3:798–809.

in check. As Brian McLaren once said in a lecture, the experience of the realm of God in the other undermines the mentality that says, "You should be like me because I'm (fill in the blank)."[22] As it shapes us, this kind of meal holds out the possibility that the Beloved Community of God, which seems to need a good variety of folk, will come near.

In Luke 24, Cleopas and another disciple meet a complete stranger on the road. In chapter 6, above, we noted that, in spite of the crucifixion, an instrument used to strike terror among the disciples, they choose to invite this stranger in. As people formed by their participation in Jesus' ministry, as well as by local custom, they take a chance and welcome him anyway. Yes, the disguised divine stranger is a common trope, both in biblical literature (e.g., see Gen 18) and beyond it. And yes, we tend to think of the breaking of the bread as the act that breaks the spell of mis-recognition, somehow dissolving the disguise to reveal that the person wasn't really a stranger at all. But what if we tell the story this way? The disciples welcome a stranger who never ceases to be a stranger. When they take the risk of continuing the meal practices of Jesus' ministry (as well as the Greek tradition of *xenia* or welcoming the stranger), something about the act of breaking bread together triggers their sense of the holy. The disciples sense, with tears and sighs of relief, that the Beloved Community of God is still coming near. They sense that Jesus is with them precisely because they experience the Beloved Community of God, and because they are once again surprised by the sacred in the face of one who is other to them. The stranger remains a stranger (even while becoming a friend?), but the disciples can discern the deeper truth: "Where two or three are gathered in my name, I am there among them" (Matt 18:20). And, "Just as you did it for one of the least of these . . . you did it for me" (Matt 25:40). The Kin-dom comes near not in the guise of the stranger, but because of him. The story is a lesson for all who gather to share the meal: a lesson about resilience and resistance to terror, and the surpassing value of taking a risk for the sake of one's neighbor and Jesus' ongoing ministry.

We can read the twenty-first chapter of John the same way. A stranger on the beach offers a breakfast of bread and fish to Peter, Thomas, Nathanael, and two other disciples. It's a risk. Should they accept? The disciples are demoralized and frightened after the events in Jerusalem.

22. I attended McLaren's lecture, called "Light Fires, Issue Permission Slips, Invite Others into the Interpretive Community," given at the Festival of Homiletics in Minneapolis on May 21, 2014.

Yet they have been formed over time by their participation in Jesus' ministry, so they are already in the habit of encountering the divine in the face of the other. *That's* why they are able to see Jesus in this stranger, who does not cease to be that unknown person on the shore. The instilled *habitus* of the Beloved Community of God reproduces behavior (accepting hospitality in this case, as in Luke 10:8–9) that is a crucial sort of citation or performative reiteration of the feeding of the five thousand, performed by the disciples and a stranger.[23] The Kin-dom comes near once again, and the disciples recognize Jesus in their midst, even if the person they have met is still a stranger on the beach.

We Share Leadership of the Meal
(The *Habitus* of Sharing Power)

We can consistently ask a variety of people to lead us in the meal. The role of presider at Holy Communion has been staunchly defended, with few exceptions (such as the Christian Church, Disciples of Christ) throughout the church's history. Arguments about who is qualified, or who can most appropriately embody Jesus as host, have served to shore up (gendered) clerical authority and transform the meal from one of sharing into one of distribution: acts of deference to clergy in exchange for food (see chapter 3, above). The shared leadership of two, three, or four presiders, including a variety of laypeople as well as ordained ministers, can disrupt the ritual scheme of enacted deference to clergy and model the kind of counterpolitics we have been discussing.

Specifically, both women and men should help lead. Women have for centuries prepared the eucharistic food, cleaned up after the sacramental meal, and sometimes even helped to serve it, while men have claimed the central role of presiding. We should err on the side of changing the social hierarchy, but not so much so that we end up creating a ritual of reversal, merely reinscribing the social hierarchy by presenting a temporary exact mirror image of it. We will need to mix it up. Children, youth, and elders should help lead—not as cuteness on display or the patronizing inclusion of an older generation, but as leaders who are properly trained and can lead us in word and action. The races, sexual orientations, socioeconomic

---

23. Butler points out that citation can also be used to resist or invert a norm, and there is room for the breakfast on the beach to be a citation of a Sabbath economy that inverts the dominant economy, but that is not my primary intent here. For discussion, see Butler, *Bodies*, 12–16.

locations, and differing abilities of a particular congregation are crucial considerations and will help to enrich the leadership of the meal. This can be flexible, changing with the seasons of a congregation's life, and we should be careful not to let this pattern of sharing stagnate into set quotas.

By shared leadership I do not mean that a variety of laypeople assist the (usually male) pastor. If the pastor remains in charge during the meal, serving as lead presider and directing other presiders in their roles, then we will have done nothing more than ritualize more visibly the dominant hierarchy. Real shared leadership will require preparation of the leaders, careful attention to who gets to do which parts of the prayers (so that clergy don't get all the important parts), and more.

At the same time, shared leadership doesn't mean that clergy should step away and let anything happen. This is not a veiled call for the end of ordained clergy. As an ordained person myself, I have understood my vows of ordination to mean that I have a responsibility to ensure that the sacramental meal retains its grounding in Scripture and tradition, even when I only play a small role or no visible role at all. The training of lay presiders, not just in what to say but also in hospitality, power sharing, and the generosity of spirit of a good presider, is part of the ordained person's responsibility. The pastor or priest may also help the congregation with a continuing cycle of evaluation and adaptation of the meal, as different seasons of the congregation's life bring new leadership and new guests.

To some extent, sharing leadership may mean being willing to negotiate even the format and language of the meal with those who participate. It can be frustrating to explain the congregation's approach over and over, negotiating with new participants who bring the same patriarchal baggage time and again. Without such humility and willingness to converse, however, our hospitality can easily become a colonizing practice, even if we are leaving the church building to be hospitable. When those of us with more privilege, credentials, or wealth control the meal and merely allow the powerless to be guests, hospitality can begin to look like that of missionaries who presumed to invite native peoples to "come over here," and who often arrived with armies a few months or years behind them. At its best, our hospitality flows from an understanding of mutual benefit and shared power: both others and we ourselves need to be received and stretched. This means the meal may change, depending on our negotiations.

In chapel at Eden Seminary we often call on more than one presider for each Communion service. Recently in the last chapel service each semester we've enlisted four, two of whom are nonordained students. Our Communion table is round so that the community can more easily encircle it. The presiders surround the table as well, leading the congregation in prayers that we speak and sing (and sometimes dance!) together.

I can imagine a congregation in which a variety of leaders is actually required to celebrate Holy Communion. We may have to recruit, to go looking for congregants to help, as part of our preparation. We may have to schedule the meal in a week, or on a weekday, when a broad variety of leadership can be present. All the issues of representational politics apply. What if the two Korean members get tired of representing all people of color at Communion? What if there are only straight people in church on a given Sunday? And how do we share power with our guests? We will need to allow ourselves a degree of fluidity and a measure of grace as we persevere in making shared leadership an ongoing reality.

We Bring Our Own Food
(The *Habitus* of Generosity)

In their book *Saving Paradise*, Rebecca Parker and Rita Nakashima Brock describe a fresco in Rome, in the catacomb of Priscilla. The fresco includes the depiction of a group of women, most likely at or coming to worship, with the inscription, "Bring it warm!"[24] I love the idea of early Christians baking at home, bringing their own bread to share for the sacramental meal, and putting up their equivalents of posters to encourage others to do the same. It's possible that the practice of bringing one's own food to share, especially with those who were hungry, occurred regularly in at least some early Christian communities, and it may have continued into the fourth century.[25]

Think about that for moment: how would it change our spiritual formation over time if we could only celebrate Holy Communion by bringing our own food to share with each other, food that has come from our own kitchens, our own tables, or even our own gardens? What if

24. Parker and Nakashima Brock, *Saving Paradise*, 30.

25. See earlier discussion of the variety of food that continued to be part of the meal in chapter six. The assumption here is that, if people had to be discouraged from bringing "unofficial" food to the sacramental meal, then people (not just clergy or sacristans) were most likely bringing food.

the holy food was not the church's food but our food, and the virtue of generosity was learned by doing? What if the sacramental meal included a variety of foods, as it did early on, and what if the giving of it was central to its meaning? What if it were not only women, but men and children as well who prepared such food? What if we celebrated our ability to give by including it in prayer, giving thanks for the chain of farmers and grocery clerks, and even the earth for "these gifts of the earth and our labor," as the United Church of Christ *Book of Worship* says?[26] And what if we encouraged those of us with no food to bring water, or the gift of their company?

To some of us this may sound hopelessly inconvenient: Crock-Pots, tinfoil, cleanup, and lost baking dishes. Some churches have run afoul of local health codes with their potlucks, and more than a few of us have experienced six pots of baked beans and no main course. (Perhaps this is why some wealthier congregations now choose to have their all-church gatherings catered.) Nonetheless, potluck-style Communion moves intentionally in the opposite direction. After all, the church potluck is a long-standing way that the early church practice of sharing one's own resources has been carried forward. That's something worth celebrating. If we bring our own food to the eucharistic table, an element of sharing our own resources will be restored.

All Serve Food to One Another
(The *Habitus* of Sharing)

Along with bringing our own food from home, we can work on changing the way everybody gets something to eat. This could mean a buffet table, or joint dish preparation (one group of students in my class asked each of us bring ingredients so we could chop, mix, and eat pico de gallo together), or even a moment where we all serve a few particular elements to each other around the Communion table as part of a larger meal. We have occasionally tried this kind of "holy chaos" Communion at Eden Seminary, using just the traditional loaf and cup. The only rules are (1) we're all serving one another, (2) everybody gets fed, and (3) no one can serve her- or himself. All are encouraged to serve a few people and then hand off the elements to someone else. It takes a while and usually

---

26. United Church of Christ, *Book of Worship*, 48.

includes some nervous laughter and standing around, but the result is far different from the usual distribution.

And that is the point. The goal is to change the economy of Holy Communion from one in which the sacred food is a scarce commodity controlled and doled out by a religious elite (clergy, elders, or both) to one in which all participate in sharing so that we all might experience abundance. It's an economy that moves us away from the roles of either official *in persona Christi* benefactors or deferential recipients and toward being friends who collaborate with one another and with God in order to help the Beloved Community of God come near. This alternative economy shifts our meals away from a Christology of consumption, in which our primary role is to be grateful consumers, toward a Christology of emulation, in which our principal task is a kind of holy sharing that reflects Jesus and the way of his ministry. We all share prayerfully, following the lead of the Risen One instead of eating him. In the sharing itself we seek the deeper communion we have with God, Jesus, the Holy Spirit, and other people.

We Eat a Full Meal Together
(The *Habitus* of Commensality)

You've probably guessed this from previous suggestions. We can share an actual meal rather than just a taste of bread and juice or wine. We can sit down together at tables and eat enough to satisfy our hunger, passing the salt and pepper (or soy sauce and mango chutney) and actually spend time interacting. Now, for those of us who are not avid conversationalists, polite discussion with acquaintances over dinner can seem like something closer to punishment than to heaven on earth. I can identify with this. So, maybe we will need discussion prompts. Or maybe we just keep it short. In any case, we will need to attend to this aspect as well. The point is to eat together like we do at home—or wish we did—with family or invited friends.

Although a variety of nutritious foods can be encouraged, the menu need not be elaborate every time. Those of us with more wealth, in developed nations, may assume that a full meal entails a variety of foods and significant abundance. Among the first generations of Christians, however, for plenty of people bread and wine, or bread and water, were a full meal. That was all the food some of them had. So a simple meal may be just fine, and may be easier to sustain over time. We just need enough so that those of us who are hungry can be fed.

The seating arrangement is likely to be a bit more complex than the menu. We will need to seat people very intentionally so that typical cliques and snubs don't get played out as God's way of doing things. We also want to create opportunities for participants to encounter God, Jesus, or Beloved Community in someone who is other to them, explaining that possibility regularly. My sense from experience is that this sort of thing can't be legislated, but it can be regularly encouraged, even including an invitational process each time all are seated. We will want to think carefully about how we arrange the room, about the size of tables, about where leaders will sit (no head table!), and so forth. We may even need some people to volunteer to sit with anyone who is being left out.

In keeping with "the cup of blessing that we bless" (1 Cor 10:16) and other ritual moments that were a part of Jewish and early Christian meals, we may want to include particular foods as part of our prayers and ritual acts. We will need to be careful though that such moments do not shift our focus from the whole meal or reduce the meal to only the traditional eucharistic elements over time. The whole meal should be blessed, and foods from a variety of cultures should count as sacred food.[27] If we are going to give particular meanings to such foods, I would suggest multiple coding as a way to keep the metaphors active. We might say something like, "May this bread be for us bread of life, manna from heaven, and the bread of your presence, and may this cup be the cup of salvation, water from the rock, and the wine that Jesus promised to share with us anew in your Kin-dom."

We Redistribute Resources
(The *Habitus* of Sabbath Economics)

This is the idea that our sacramental meals will actually feed hungry people—not just through a collection to be shared with them later, but at the actual meal. As we bring our own food and share it with others at the meal, or come with nothing but our hungry bodies, we all participate in the redistribution of wealth. This, again, is the practice of

27. Here I am thinking of preposterous situations described by international students who come to Eden Theological Seminary from Africa. They spoke of circumstances in which wine was imported at great expense by very poor Anglican congregations in central Africa, since grapes aren't grown anywhere in the region.

an alternate economy. The meal rehearses us in focusing more on the Beloved Community than on amassing capital. We shift our focus away from the scarce, protected commodity of sanctified bread and cup toward the assembly and its sanctified activity as a source of sacramentality. We enact an economy of abundance, what Ched Myers calls a Sabbath economy, giving thanks for the gift of God's abundance (recognizing our resources as a gift) and seeking to correct the imbalance created by human greed.[28] We gather and weave community rather than engaging in what Nancy Eiesland calls "segregationist charity,"[29] knowing that when we feed everyone, including "the least of these who are members of my family" (Matt 25:40), the Beloved Community of God and even Jesus himself are served as well.

This practice may prove to be the most difficult to sustain. We can't simply say to one another that all are welcome, hoping that hungry people will come to our worship. If we *need* people who experience food insecurity in order to help the Beloved Community of God come near, then we will have to advertise, going out to the highways and byways (Luke 14:23). We will have to adapt the meal, to move the church if necessary (borrowing Tom Driver's image), in order to create a context that draws hungry people. If people who are homeless or very poor are among our guests, we will need to adapt to their needs and the issues they face. A large percentage of people who are homeless have mental illness. Also, if you ask any congregation that has welcomed people who are homeless into their building, they will tell you that security can be an issue. How do we strive for the safety and dignity of all? How do we cope with theft or vandalism? How do we create a meal format that is safe for the children of our congregation and our guests? How do we continually work against the unintentional distinction between haves and have-nots? There are no simple answers, and I will not pretend to provide them here. My hope is that congregations can learn from past successes, experiment, and then

---

28. According to Myers (*Biblical*, 5), Sabbath economics can be summarized by three axioms: "1) the world as created by God is abundant, with enough for everyone—provided that human communities restrain their appetites and live within limits; 2) disparities of wealth and power are not 'natural' but the result of human sin, and must be mitigated within the community of faith through the regular practice of redistribution; 3) the prophetic message calls people to the practice of such redistribution, and is thus characterized as 'good news' to the poor." As Myers points out, this has ecological implications as well.

29. Eiesland, *Disabled*, 74. My thanks go to Rebecca Spurrier for sharing this concept.

share with one another what work has worked in their contexts. What I can say here is that this more difficult way of engaging in Communion brings with it the chance to do something truly remarkable, and the possibility that people will leave with both a feeling of accomplishment and a sense that God has accomplished something in our midst.

We Refuse to Use Jesus' Body and Blood, or Reenact the Violence Done to Him (The *Habitus* of Resisting the Objectification of Victims)

As I suggested in chapter 4, we can refrain from using Jesus' body and blood, real or symbolic, in our sacramental meals. For a couple centuries at least, we can refuse to reenact Jesus' execution and see how it goes. We can insist that in whatever sense Jesus is understood or experienced as being present (in Spirit, in memory, in real presence), our words and actions should treat him only as a subject, a person, a *Thou*. Jesus was brutally objectified by Roman authorities. In spite of this, when those who had worked with him dared to gather, they remembered, even experienced him as a subject, still. Only gradually did practices that reobjectified him come to eclipse all others. We owe it to him not to continue. He is not ours to use. His body is not ours to be. It's difficult to avoid objectification altogether, especially when a person is no longer around to resist our characterizations or projections. Even so, we can acknowledge this and try to be responsible to Jesus as a person with subjectivity and sociohistorical particularity.

This shift will still require a certain amount of vigilance to prevent the meal from being mapped over by violent surrogacy over time. As Chauvet, Girard, and others have acknowledged, the meal is always in danger of sliding back toward the sacrificial.[30] Similarly, the Communion table is always in danger of being conflated with a sacrificial altar. These two pieces of furniture, and the practices associated with them, were not originally the same. The early church made them so. Tables used for sacred meals in homes gradually came to be understood as altars of sacrifice, a rhetorical move meant to subvert literal practices of animal sacrifice, but that eventually overshadowed and subsumed the original table for eating. Thus, the table *became* an altar. Protestant Reformers attempted to reverse this conflation in the sixteenth century, swapping

---

30. For example, see Chauvet, *Symbol*, 308.

out altars for something that looked more table-like, and insisting that it be called a table. Today, however, it's quite common to hear Protestants casually refer to the table as an altar. So we will need to pay attention and continue to work out creative ways to resist the fascinating draw of violence.

We Broaden Our Focus from Objects to Practices
(The *Habitus* of Broad Sacramental Sensibility)

We can widen our attention from the food and the table as the sole locus of the holy to include all of us and what we're doing. Humans have a natural tendency to invest objects with sacred significance. That's not necessarily a problem (though at times it leads us to superstition), and I certainly don't want to skip over the sacramentality of creation. If God shines in and through all things, these things include our food and table. Yet we tend to get distracted by those objects and lose sight of the broader sacramentality that includes the assembly and what we're up to. So, we will want to invite one another to notice, to be open to the many ways that the Beloved Community of God can come near when we celebrate the sacrament. We may want to shift our language away from the table and the food toward our activities. My translation of Rom 14:17 would read something like this: "For the Beloved Community of God is not food and drink, but righteousness, peace, and joy in the Holy Spirit." It's primarily how we act, how we do what we do together, that can help the Beloved Community of God to come near.

We Shift the Meal's Focus from the Crucified Jesus Back toward the Beloved Community of God Drawing Near
(The *Habitus* of Kin-dom Seeking)

This may seem odd given that our current meal practices all point to Jesus—his presence, his saving activity, his institution of the meal, and more. And I would hardly suggest leaving Jesus out, but if we allow the crucifixion to shrink to size and look more broadly at Jesus' life and teaching, he seems to be pointing beyond himself.[31] In fact, he seems far more interested in focusing our attention on the Beloved Community of God and how to participate in it, and he seems less interested

31. Keshgegian, *Redeeming Memories*, 184.

in getting the spotlight himself. The goal here is to direct our energies toward collaborating with God's resilient, ongoing work, as Jesus himself did, rather than continuing to focus only on Jesus and the violence done to him—and thus remaining caught in repetition compulsion. We can fill our prayers and songs with language about the Beloved Community of God, giving thanks that it still comes near in spite of everything. We can sing and pray about the joy of collaborating with the activity of the Holy Spirit in our midst. We can still talk about Jesus, including his crucifixion, but in ways that allow the central focus of his work and message to shine through (more on that in a moment). We can give careful attention to how we do what we do, seeking to thoughtfully and graciously continue the way of Jesus. A biblical touchstone for this is Luke 10:8–9. Jesus says to his disciples, "Whenever you enter a town and its people welcome you, eat what is set before you; cure the sick who are there, and say to them, 'The [Kin-dom] of God has come near to you.'" Luke 10:8–9 outlines programmatically a ministry in which eating and drinking are directly connected to the Beloved Community of God.

We Work to Help The Beloved Community
to Come Near without Trying to Force It
(The *Habitus* of Collaborating with God)

One way that we have gotten ourselves into trouble historically is by praying in ways that assume that we can *make* our meals sacramentally efficacious with the proper formula of word and action, every time we gather for Communion. We generally attribute this consistency to the Holy Spirit rather than ourselves, but the result is the same: the presumption that the desired result will follow from the rite when performed. This is especially true at the end of the meal, when we use language like, "We give you thanks that you have made us one with Christ and each other at this table." What if we have not been made one? How do we know if we are one with Christ? The prayers assume that the meal has accomplished its ends, regardless of what has actually occurred.

The desire to generate a reliably reproducible spiritual outcome is understandable, but it has led us to a kind of liturgical overreach that interferes with the honest work of attending to what is actually happening. This work includes being open to the Spirit, being sensitive to others, creating the conditions for the Beloved Community to come near as best we know how, and refusing to fake it when what Ronald Grimes calls "ritual infelicities" occur.[32] Creating the right conditions can be part of our preparation and participation in all aspects of the meal, seeking the Beloved Community of God rather than assuming we can build it, or that God will automatically do as we desire. Our prayers can avoid making assumptions while still giving thanks for the meal and the Kin-dom that is always coming near.

We Engage in Memorative Practices that Acknowledge Trauma and Celebrate Resistance, Resilience, and Risk (The *Habitus* of Dangerous Memory)

Until now I've been holding off on discussing memory and story as practices of Holy Communion. It's so easy for us to focus on the narratives and on the theological explanations, allowing our attention to be deflected from what we're actually doing. That's why I've made an effort to foreground changes in ritual acts (and some language) more than theological explanations. Still, it's important for us to consider the ways we will go about remembering Jesus, his community, and what happened to them. As Herbert Anderson and Edward Foley make clear in their book *Mighty Stories, Dangerous Rituals: Weaving Together the Human and Divine*, ritual and story need each other.[33] Without narrative (and sometimes narrative that has been reactivated in our imaginations), our rites can become hollow, degenerating into rote gestures. Much of the preceding discussion in this book assumes alternative memorative practices in connection with Holy Communion. The following, then, are areas where such memorative practices might benefit from the same kinds of recovery and reimagining that we have been applying in other ways.

Remembering Resistance

In our prayers, songs, and teaching we can remember that Jesus was the leader of a resistance movement. Prior to his execution, he resisted both oppressive and corrupt systems (political, social, religious) as well

---

32. Grimes, "Ritual," 279–93.

33. "For human beings, narrative and ritual are symbiotic: they have an intimate and mutually beneficial relationship despite their individual identities" (Anderson and Foley, *Mighty*, 25).

as particular people. As we noted in earlier chapters, his meal practices resisted the ordinary ways that meals reinforced social boundaries of class, gender, ethnicity, religion, and more. As he begins to encounter opposition and real danger, Jesus continues his nonviolent resistance, still enacting and proclaiming the Beloved Community of God. More than his suffering, it is this continuing, alternative way of living out justice and compassion that witnesses to God's activity with and through him. The collective memory of Jesus' vow before being arrested ("I will never again drink of the fruit of the vine until that day when I drink it new in the [Kin-dom] of God" [Mark 14:25]) is a memory (constructed or not) of a resistance leader. Jesus continues that resistance to the end, but it is important for our storytelling that we be clear: Jesus' resistance, his refusal to collude with the ruling powers of his day, does not cause his death. He does not choose death by choosing to resist. That is the victim-blaming narrative of the empire, which says that resistance always equals death.[34] It is the narrative of the abusive husband who says, "Don't make me hurt you" (or worse, "If I can't have you, nobody will.").[35] Sometimes it is also the narrative of coping: "I guess it had to be this way. He gave his life by being faithful to his calling." Neither of these narratives is true. Whether Jesus is wholly innocent or not,[36] our stories need to be clear that his death is caused first and foremost by the choices made by government and religious leaders. We may see those choices as typical or even likely, but they were not the only possible outcome. Leaders could have chosen otherwise, as in Jer 26:24, where Jeremiah predicts the destruction of Jerusalem, but is not put to death because he knows the right people in power. Jesus' death is neither inevitable nor necessary.[37] His resistance

34 The following sentences may be a trigger for survivors of domestic violence.

35. As Marjorie Procter-Smith (*Praying*, 103) says, "Women need an alternative to the narrative that says women who engage in resistance and seek fuller lives should expect death."

36. For helpful discussions of the risks involved in overemphasizing the innocence of victims, see Brock, "Ending."

37. I realize this is a sticking point because it challenges the atonement theory that has been so central to much of Christian theology. The perspective I am working from here is that Jesus' crucifixion wasn't necessary because God wasn't somehow limited to that option; it wasn't necessary to reveal the truth about God or the way of the Beloved Community of God. Nor was Jesus' crucifixion necessary to reveal humanity's often less-than-enthusiastic reaction to his way of living, or to reveal God's resilience in the face of human violence. All of this—the truth about God, the way of the Beloved Community, humanity's disappointing response, even God's resilience—was revealed in Jesus' ministry. The fact that Jesus persisted in his work even while suffering, even

for the sake of justice and compassion, on the other hand, is absolutely critical.

We can also remember Jesus' disciples as a community of resistance. Before the crucifixion, as Rita Nakshima Brock points out, the women and men around Jesus functioned as a crucial community of solidarity and resistance that helped to make his ministry possible.[38] He depended on them at times, for hospitality, support, and counsel. They also healed people, fed them, and traveled from town to town at great risk. They were a resistance movement. Because the way of life Jesus sought to embody was a social one, it *required* others whose empowered participation mirrored his own in order to become a reality. It couldn't have happened without them. Thus, Jesus did not simply provide a vision beyond personal, social, and spiritual brokenness that was written down and passed on.[39] He was part of a group of women and men who actually lived in ways that began to subvert systematic and personal oppression. They began to live as if that oppression were not the only possibility. The lived reality of their collective resistance is integral to the good news of the gospel.

After the crucifixion, people whom Jesus has loved, healed, and trained, groups of women and men who have labored and suffered with him in his ministry, continue to resist. By the grace of God and their own courage, they reconnect with one another.[40] They dare to meet, in spite

when it meant risking death, does not mean that the suffering itself accomplished anything crucial. As the disciples persist, the crucifixion and its trauma become less important than the larger project of revealing an alternative wisdom, an alternative order, an alternative politics to, among other things, violent surrogacy. Despite humiliation, Jesus continues, with, in, and through those who follow him, participating in the Beloved Community coming near.

38. "The Gospel narratives give us glimpses of the mutuality of Jesus' relationships in their pictures of Capernaum, a place to which Jesus repeatedly returns for support and nurturing, and in the settings of the stories in which Jesus is visiting the houses of his friends for conversation and physical comfort. Even during his most active ministry, he rarely goes anywhere alone; one of the first acts of that ministry is to call others to participate in creating the *basileia,* the community of God/dess." (Brock, *Journeys,* 66).

39. Where Delores Williams focuses on Jesus' ministerial vision in *Sisters,* I would say yes, *and,* beyond his value as a visionary teacher and role model, Jesus, along with the women and men who followed him, enacted an alternative social/political/economic/spiritual reality of Kin-dom ministry. This lived, social reality is something that existed concretely in the world and has not ceased down to today. It was praxis, and it was forged in community.

40. It is important for our purposes here that human resilience *is,* in one sense,

of the ongoing danger and the trauma inflicted on them by his execution. With a particular kind of defiance, they pray and eat as they had before, and when they do, they find that the Beloved Community of God continues to come near. Jesus' ministry is resilient, not only as a sacred memory,[41] but as an ongoing, life-giving politics of resistance, a way of living creatively and resistantly with evil. While Jesus has not conquered sin and evil in any dramatic, triumphalistic way, neither has he been conquered. He is, as Darby Ray says, "neither the Conquering Christ nor the Conquered Christ, but the One who liberates through resistance to evil and compassion for the suffering."[42] Resistance—and beyond resistance, living as if the Beloved Community of God can still come near despite the intractability of evil—is revealed as a critical characteristic of the disciples' ongoing practice, and a persistent locus of God's activity.

This brings us naturally to the memory of God's resistance. From this perspective, the resurrection is evidence of God's ongoing resistance to human evil and the violence of the cross. Rather than being primarily a sign or a message, however, the resurrection can be remembered as God's practical, collaborative activity within the communities of Jesus' followers so that their work (and Jesus' work) for the Beloved Community can continue. As we've seen, resurrection does not redeem the violence or undo the trauma associated with it. There is always "after the storm" in the collective memory of the early church. The suffering of Jesus, and loss of him as he was before, remain.[43] The torture and deaths of Jesus' followers only compound this. Yet, that violence and its effects are not the final word. The Spirit continues to draw the disciples together and inspire them. Because of God's persistent activity in the world (in resurrection and the power of the Holy Spirit), the way of Jesus, that is, the project of helping the Beloved Community to come near, is resistant even to death.

God's grace, while not overshadowing human agency. Otherwise, what we call the grace of resilience can easily collapse into a wholly human reality and *grace* can lose its transcendent content.

41. "In this challenge that is life, the story of Jesus' refusal to be inscribed by the forces of evil surrounding him becomes for us a sacred memory that keeps the possibility and hope alive, reminding us that because a praxis of resistance was actualized 'once upon a time,' it can be yet again" (Ray, *Deceiving*, 137).

42. Ray, *Deceiving*, 87.

43. "The resurrected body did not erase the suffering endured: Jesus' scars remain as evidence that the crucifixion was real. No future hope or restoration negates the reality of past injury. The hope is real nonetheless: Christ is alive among those who had followed and befriended him" (Keshgegian, *Redeeming*, 175).

Our memorative practices, then, can focus less on obedience as a virtue of discipleship and more on resistance as a celebration of God's resilience in Jesus.

Remembering Trauma

We can speak plainly about the suffering and death of Jesus—as well as the later torture and deaths of his followers—while acknowledging the ways that trauma may have shaped the early church's stories. This might apply particularly to any warrant (here meaning a story that provides authorization for ongoing practice) or words of institution during the meal. It may also apply to other parts of our prayers and to songs.

Behind the valorization of suffering and martyrdom, behind the characterization of Jesus' agony as the pinnacle of virtue and the key to our salvation, is another story. It's the story of how Jesus' suffering and death disrupted all meaning for his community, of how their terror and grief blotted out all rational explanations. Jesus' bleeding and dying are not primarily noble or purposeful or efficacious here. They are primarily horrific and traumatic. In this story no one has come up with any salvific accomplishments for his death yet. The death itself accomplishes nothing other than what government leaders intend: the disruption and atomization of resistance.

Behind the spiritualization of Jesus' death, which presents events as occurring "according to the definite plan and foreknowledge of God" (Acts 2:26), is a story at once smaller, more banal, and more similar to the stories of thousands of people killed senselessly and carelessly by governments and warlords around the world. In this story there is typically some kind of public show of resistance to oppression, an arrest out of the public view, and a very public body displayed as a warning. Without legions of angels at his command (Matt 25:53), we glimpse the terrifying possibility that, after his arrest, Jesus was not actually able to choose or control the violence done to him. Without being drenched in meaning at the moment of his death,[44] Jesus comes much closer to a solidarity of circumstance with all those who are tortured or abused.[45] Here the

44. In "The Displaced Body of Jesus Christ," for example, Graham Ward speaks of the *iconicity* of Jesus' body (understood here as a socially constructed body) overwhelming the *physicality* of his body after the crucifixion, "drenching it with significance." See Ward, "Displaced," 170.

45. By "solidarity of circumstance" I mean to counter the tendency of the privileged

traumatic memory of crucifixion is of one who dies less like the savior of the world and more like a Guatemalan schoolteacher who disappears suddenly and shows up one morning in a ditch. The disciples are left to try to understand, theologizing as best they can.

Behind the insistence that Jesus died in fulfillment of the Scriptures is a story of bereft and grieving disciples, searching the Jewish Scriptures for ways to give meaning to Jesus' death, as well as the more recent executions of their family and friends. Behind the insistence that his death was inevitable and necessary is the heartrending reality that it could have been otherwise had those in authority been more just and made different choices. Behind the coping stories that shift blame to Jesus (who chose his path) or to all of sinful humanity (who made it necessary) or worse yet to the Jews ("His blood be upon us and on our children!" [Matt 27:25]) is a much more difficult and out-of-control story, in which, after a point, neither Jesus nor the crowds nor the disciples had any control at all.[46!] Like the survivor of childhood abuse who struggles to accept the terrifying narrative in which it couldn't have been her fault because she couldn't actually control what happened to her, we can struggle to tell the story of Jesus and his community so that the trauma is remembered *as trauma*. As difficult as that may be, as much as it may rub against our own personal and communal wounds, these stories are important for the process of recovery and the resilience of Jesus' ministry.

The first response to these stories might well be mourning. Contemporary memorative meal practices that acknowledge the trauma of the cross and the traumatized texts of Jesus' persecuted followers can invite us to grieve. They can make space for us to feel the loss of Jesus without turning his death into a site of meaning making—that is, without trying to make it into something good as well as bad. They can invite us to stand in the shadow that is Good Friday, saying only, "Were you there when they crucified my Lord?" without short-circuiting the loss, or avoiding the grief.

We can also respond by honoring what Jesus' followers said and did in order to cope, and survive. That doesn't necessarily mean we accept those early memorative practices as they are, or that we continue to use them in the same way we traditionally have. It means that the struggle of

to construe solidarity as always being something that is chosen. Often, for example, solidarity among the poor is partly chosen and partly imposed by entrapment within exploitative systems.

46 [Possible trigger for survivors of violence.]

our ancestors in faith becomes part of our memorative practices. Recovery from trauma often includes honoring what one did to survive while acknowledging that those strategies are sometimes no longer needed or effective. Looking back, behaviors that might seem dysfunctional or even immoral may ultimately be claimed as the assertion of a will to survive under terrible conditions. These behaviors can then be honored for the purpose they served, at the same time freeing up the survivor to begin the work of rehabituating or reprogramming particular behaviors or responses.[47] In light of our work in earlier chapters, we might call it inscribing new *habitus*.

Our memorative practices in worship can do the same. We can honor the biblical narratives as an important means of coping for New Testament communities, without necessarily feeling obligated to continue telling the stories the same way in our liturgies. Modern biblical scholarship, for example, rarely suggests today that passages from Psalms and Isaiah were really about Jesus. Instead, scholars generally honor the attempts of New Testament writers to interpret the life and death of Jesus through the existing scriptures of that time, while not imposing their later interpretations upon the original authors.

Remembering Resilience

Perhaps most importantly, we can remember the grace of resilience. We can remember how the community around Jesus was resilient in the face of violence and loss. We can give thanks that when the disciples came out of hiding and found one another again, the Beloved Community of God continued to come near, and in some mystical way Jesus himself was resilient. The matrix of community gave rise to the experience of resurrection, and in turn God was revealed to have been at work all along. We can pray and sing and dance our joy that God was and is resilient in spite of human brokenness and in the face of systems of violent oppression. The crucifixion, which was supposed to drive Jesus' community apart and end his movement, was not enough to prevent the continuation of meals of resistance, justice, and compassion. God is resilient. Our deeper communion remains. The way of Jesus persists.

47. "Claiming these as survival techniques, once useful but no longer effective, the survivor begins to see and know her own agency and power" (Keshgegian, *Redeeming*, 54).

This is the memory that is most dangerous to empire: the memory of resistance that survived. It is the memory most threatening to the totalizing narrative of Caesar or Pharaoh (or the Borg: "Resistance is futile."[48]) It is the memory most disruptive of cultures of discrimination or disparity. Yes, the memory of Jesus' suffering is also a dangerous memory, in that it disrupts the empire's narrative that everything is fine.[49] But as William Cavanaugh points out in *Torture and Eucharist,* the memory of suffering at the hands of the empire also serves to shore up the dominant powers, because it perpetuates, even spreads, the memory of violent repression.[50] It reminds us of what the empire is capable of, simultaneously reinforcing the dominant narrative. The most dangerous memory, then, is the memory of an alternative politics, an alternative economics, an alternative mode of faith, *an alternative empire,* that wouldn't go away. When the meals of Jesus' ministry continue, when the healing and the welcoming continue, they undermine what was supposed to be the final word: "I will strike the shepherd, / and the sheep will be scattered" (Mark 14:27; cf. Zech 13:7; Matt 26:31). Because God, community, and practice are all resilient, Jesus rises again among the people.[51] In this way, the memory of resilience reveals the ongoing work of God in the world, alongside the intractability of evil. The memory of resilience invites us to continue in the way of Jesus, regardless of what comes, because we remember that resilient generations before us have continued to collaborate with God, tasting the surpassing joy of the Beloved Community.

48. The Borg are a fictional race of aliens who conquer other planets and races by assimilating them (through the use of cybernetic implants) in the television series *Star Trek: The Next Generation* and *Star Trek Voyager,* and from the movie *Star Trek: First Contact.* The best-known phrase used by the Borg is, "Resistance is futile." In popular culture the Borg sometimes signify colonialist ideology.

49. See Bruce Morrill's discussion (in Morrill, *Anamnesis*) of Johannes Metz and the concept of dangerous memory in relation to the Eucharist.

50. Cavanaugh (*Torture,* 55–56) quotes Michael Taussig as saying, "The State's interest is in keeping memory of public political protest, and the memory of the sadistic and cruel violence unleashed against it, alive! . . . It feeds nightmares, crippling the capacity for public protest and spirited, intelligent opposition."

51. Bishop Oscar Romero famously said, "I have often been threatened with death. I must tell you, as a Christian, I do not believe in a death without resurrection. If am killed, I shall arise in the Salvadoran people" (Quoted in Brockman, *Romero,* 248).

Remembering Risk

"Let us also go," says Thomas to the other disciples in John 11:16, "that we may die with him." Jesus has just told the disciples that he is going back to Bethany, just miles from Jerusalem, where Jesus had almost been stoned to death recently. There's an odd moment of bravado here, in which Thomas is trying to rally the disciples by calling them to join him in death, in solidarity with Jesus. It's odd because Thomas's heroic speech, even if hyperbolic, seems to miss the point. His words make it sound like dying is the purpose of the trip—and Jesus isn't going to Bethany in order to die. Yes, the risks are real, as they all know. They really could all wind up dead. But that's not the point—that's not why Jesus is going. He's going for the sake of healing—both of the living and of the dead. He's going because he *loves Lazarus*, and Martha and Mary, as the Gospel text says (John 11:5). And so, he's going back into danger for them, and for the same work of healing that he has always done. Thomas looks toward Bethany and all he can see is death looming, but Jesus has no intention of dying. Jesus sees his friends, along with all the wonderful possibilities for resurrection and abundant life, and decides it's worth the risk.

I've found this story quite helpful in thinking about Jesus' final confrontation with authorities in Jerusalem, and how we go about re-membering risk at Holy Communion. A crucial distinction surfaces here between what Sharon Welch would call an "ethic of risk," and intentional self-sacrifice (or hyperbolic speeches that valorize it). An ethic of risk, Welch suggests, "begins with the recognition that we cannot guarantee decisive changes in the near future or even in our lifetime." It is propelled by "the equally vital recognition that to stop resisting, even when success is unimaginable, is to die," in more than one sense.[52] An ethic of risk, from Welch's perspective, involves risk that is strategic, grounded in community, and rather than being focused on controlling the outcome (because the outcome can't always be foreseen) aims at the creation of a matrix of conditions needed for change to occur. It is a wise-as-serpents approach that lets go the need for one's own actions to win the day, focusing more on calculated risk for the long term and for community, when one does not have the luxury of giving up. This is a crucial distinction because we have so often conflated risk and self-sacrifice in remembering Jesus' suffering and death, following the lead of the traumatized texts of the New Testament as they increasingly insist that Jesus was in control.

52. Welch, *Feminist*, 20.

Two stories will help to illustrate the subtle distinction we're trying to see. The first is historical, the second from this week's news. In early 1940, Rabbi Yithack Nissenbaum was among some four hundred thousand Jews confined to the Warsaw Ghetto (an area of about 1.3 square miles) by Germany's occupying forces. There, within months, he realized that the tradition of *kiddush ha-Shem* or "sanctification of the Name" (meaning "sanctification of G*d"), whereby Jews often chose martyrdom rather than surrendering their faith, was not, by itself, adequate to a situation in which the Third Reich sought the utter destruction of the entire Jewish community. So, Nissenbaum began teaching and writing about the *kiddush ha-hayyim,* or the sanctification of life. "This is a time for *kiddush ha-hayyim*, the sanctification of life," he wrote, "and not for *kiddush ha-Shem*, the holiness of martyrdom."[53] Food and medicine were smuggled into the Ghetto in the name of the sanctification of life, but occupants also gathered at great risk for secret concerts, lectures, and prayer. They did so for the experience of beauty and of their own humanity in a dehumanizing and genocidal situation. "Many performed the *mitzvah* of *kiddush ha-hayyim* by enhancing, defending, or even just barely clinging to life," writes Emil Fackenheim. "Some could sanctify life only by choosing death."[54] Martyrdom was sometimes necessary, but it was no longer the point, nor even the highest virtue, in this context.[55] The goal of resistance was life, dignity, survival. The useful concept of *kiddush ha-hayyim* spread widely in the camps and Ghettos as the war continued.[56]

This week, as I've been pondering and writing about risk, a man named Charles Kinsey was shot by police in North Miami, Florida. Mr. Kinsey is a behavior therapist in a group home. One of his clients, a man with autism, ran away from the home and was sitting in the street, very distraught. Mr. Kinsey ran after him, and was trying to calm him down when police arrived. A local resident had called the police, reporting that a man with a gun was out in the street, threatening suicide. Video taken

---

53. Fackenheim, "Spectrum," 127.

54. Fackenheim, "Spectrum," 128.

55. I recognize that there are differences between Jesus' situation and the Warsaw Ghetto. The Romans were not seeking the same kind of final solution. The point is not that the circumstances were identical, but that in Jesus' life and ministry we can see, through the lens of trauma theory, a story in which the affirmation and sanctification of life is central, not the pursuit of martyrdom.

56 The following paragraphs may be a trigger for survivors of traumatic violence.

by a bystander shows that when police arrived, guns drawn, Mr. Kinsey, an African American male, lay down on the ground as directed, with his hands in the air. You can hear him repeatedly trying to convince his client to lie down. You can also hear him yelling, "I am a behavior therapist! All he has in his hands is a toy truck! A toy truck! There's no need for guns!" The autistic man would not comply with police commands, and suddenly an officer fired three shots, hitting Mr. Kinsey once in the leg.

Mr. Kinsey was then handcuffed and left facedown and bleeding on the hot summer pavement for twenty minutes until an ambulance arrived, but he survived. So this is not a martyrdom story. His unjust suffering is important, and the officer involved was eventually found guilty of culpable negligence, but for Mr. Kinsey, that was not the point. He was focused on his client. His intention was not to give his life or to sacrifice himself in order to be faithful to his ideals. His intention was to resolve the situation and go home to his family.[57]

He could have chosen otherwise. After all, a number of highly publicized police shootings of unarmed African Americans have happened over the last few years—and a couple of police have been shot by African Americans acting alone. Tensions are high. Mr. Kinsey could have fled as the police cars approached. He could have distanced himself from his client physically, to clarify that he was not the "problem." In spite of the danger, in spite of the fact that Mr. Kinsey was an African American man in a confrontation with police, he stayed with his client. He knew that encounters between people with autism and law enforcement too often end tragically. So he took the risk, and in so doing probably saved the young man's life.

Jesus and his disciples took tremendous risks. They touched people who carried biological and social contagions, breached Sabbath conventions, associated with all sorts of marginalized people, and engaged in public resistance to authorities. They continued to do so when they met with repression, and even when their initial efforts failed (e.g., Luke 4:29). In spite of the crucifixion, the community continued to take risks, gathering publicly and continuing the ministry they had started together.

They were not simply naïve. They knew the dangers from experience. Several stories describe their run-ins with angry crowds, and John the Baptizer had been arrested and executed early on, perhaps even at the beginning of Jesus' public ministry (Mark 1:14). It's not incidental that

---

57. Chokshi, "North Miami."

the New Testament writers remember Jesus saying that he was sending his followers out like sheep or lambs into the midst of wolves (Matt 7:15; Luke 10:3). We underestimate Jesus and his disciples if we assume that they were just blundering their way toward Jerusalem, taking for granted that God would protect them.

If we can bear to face a story of Jesus' death in which he is not controlling everything, and in which even so he and his disciples choose to speak and act anyway, then we may be able to see their courage and their intent more clearly. Despite the stories of theological bravado that portray Jesus as moving purposefully toward his death, we may begin to discern something closer to the *Kiddush ha-hayyim* and the solidarity with the marginalized of Mr. Kinsey in the way Jesus and his followers are remembered. They may have entered Jerusalem willing to risk being martyred, even resigned to the possibility, as Martin Luther King Jr. and Oscar Romero were. But that still doesn't mean that death was the point or that they chose it. From the perspective we have been working to discern here, it's more likely that the point was always to help the Beloved Community of God come near, again and again, by embodying a particular way of living with God and others. Jesus looked toward Jerusalem, knowing the volatility of his occupied country and the brutality of the authorities, and decided it was worth the risk. Real risk means that sometimes the outcome may not be what we want or expect. An ethic of risk emerges here that is, as Welch might say, neither the path of the intentional martyr nor that of the pragmatist who only acts when the outcome is assured.[58] Jesus did not give his life, as Matt 20:28 says. He risked his life, not knowing the outcome, and his life was taken from him by the authorities.

This is not to deny the virtue of people who actually choose dying for the sake of others. In some cases people make a conscious choice to help or defend, knowing that they will not survive. But when we paint all altruistic suffering and death with that same broad brush, we do not tell the truth. We deceive ourselves, and in the process we miss realities of risk-taking that are crucial to the life of discipleship, and to Holy Communion, in this world where it's not always given to us to know the outcome of our actions.

58. Welch (*Feminist*, 78) says of the ethic of risk, "While the consequences of actions are taken into account so that one does not risk death over every offense, the approach is not narrowly pragmatic, acting only when one is sure of the consequences of that action."

In our memorative practices, then, we can lift up with thanksgiving the ethic of risk embodied by Jesus and his disciples, who were willing to put their bodies on the line. We can do this without lapsing into stories that assume Jesus' death was something he intended. We can lift up the value of risk, but also of survival, and of resisting evil wisely. We can pray and sing in ways that invite us all to embrace an ethic of risk for the sake of the Beloved Community of God.

Remembering Community

Already we've talked about the importance of Jesus' community as an indispensable context for his ministry: their resistance, their resilience, their risk. The community around Jesus is the necessary matrix for his resurrection. When we gather for Holy Communion, then, we can remember the community around Jesus, and not just Jesus himself. If anamnesis is about drawing a past reality into the present moment, our anamnetic labors can help to connect that early community with our own. We can celebrate and affirm our ongoing resistance and resilience in continuity with theirs.

As an important aspect of that communal focus, we can make a point to remember women who were part of Jesus' community, lifting up their names alongside the names of men. Mary of Magdala, Mary the Mother of Jesus, Mary and Martha of Bethany—these and others were undoubtedly present for many of the meals of Jesus' ministry. If the meal stories do not mention their names (or the names of male disciples) specifically, we can still include them, broadening the sense of community and its leadership in our remembrance.

Remembering the Larger Story

If we can allow the trauma of the crucifixion to shrink to size, as Flora Keshgegian says, if we can allow it to take its place in the larger narrative of Jesus and his community, then our remembrance can present a very different perspective.[59] Other meals and other themes can come more clearly into view. We can recount all of the meals of Jesus' ministry as the basis for our meal. We can tell the stories of healing and reconciliation that took place in connection with Jesus' meals. We can frame

59. See Keshgegian, *Redeeming Memories*, 184.

our acts of eating and drinking with the whole incarnational/anastasial mystery: Jesus' birth, life, crucifixion, and resurrection.[60] Beyond that, we can remember and give thanks for God's work in the many meals of the First Testament that informed Jesus' ministry: Abraham and Sarah's meal with angels (Gen 18:1–8), the manna in the wilderness (Exod 16:4–12), the meal on Mount Sinai (Exod 24:11), the bread of the Presence (Exod 25:30), the miraculous sharing of the last loaf among Elijah, the widow of Zeraphath, and her son (1 Kgs 17:8–16), and so on.

We Use Multiple Ritual Forms for the Meal

If we are going to remember more than just the one upper room story, we will most likely need multiple meal formats to go along with the different narratives we use. There is a particular wisdom in this. Early on in my research, I was searching for a single, authoritative alternate format for the meal. At a meeting of the North American Academy of Liturgy, liturgical theologian Jill Crainshaw helpfully pointed out that more than one meal format, more than one ritual logic, would honor the multiple catechetical narratives that shaped meal practices in early communities of the Jesus movement. She also gently suggested that multiple meal formats would be more resistant to the development of a new single, dominating rite that might end up suppressing other early narratives.

Chapter 6 outlined six main catechetical stories I have identified that may have functioned independently, informing the meals of different early communities. Each of these suggests a slightly different ritual logic, with some overlap: (1) water and (new) manna, echoing the exodus story; (2) the feeding of the multitude; (3) the eschatological promise of the upper room; (4) a footwashing-oriented meal; (5) Emmaus; and (6) the breakfast on the beach. My sense at this point is that these six different kinds of meals could complement each other over the course of a liturgical year in the life of a congregation.

Admittedly, an inherent messiness comes when we open up our liturgical life to multiple meal practices. I confess that in my work with students I have more than once found that their experimentation with the meal has triggered a more conserving, "That's not orthodox enough" kind of impulse in me. Through conversation, though, we've been able

---

60. *Anastasial*, meaning "related to the resurrection." See the footnote in chapter 4, note 35 for discussion of *anastasial* versus *paschal*.

to ground our choices (and our disagreements) in Scripture and in our honest sense of what the Holy Spirit may be up to in this meal. Multiple formats may be disorienting in some ways, but with sustained attentiveness to Scripture and the Spirit, we can find our way.

What Would This Look Like Exactly?

If you're like many people who have attended my lectures or read drafts of this project along the way, by this point you're ready (or you've been ready for quite some time) for some example liturgies—concrete services that demonstrate what Holy Communion can look like when the proposals outlined here are lived out in an actual community. For several reasons I've chosen to post some sample liturgies on a website (www. belovedcommunion.org) rather than printing them here. The first is that I've come across a number of books on liturgy that contained good ideas, but the dated style or pedantic tone of the liturgical resources in the appendix undercut the impact of the book. My hope is that the ideas and suggestions laid out here will engage and inspire you on their own. I don't want to include liturgies that page-flippers might easily dismiss (or use!) without deeper engagement with this book.

The second reason is that while I've been experimenting with Communion liturgies for some years now, I haven't yet arrived at something that feels like a destination. Even the services I tried a few years ago now seem to have been "on the way." They are missing an important nuance or are moving too far in a particular direction. By posting the services of Holy Communion to a website, I can keep revising them or can replace them with something completely different. They can continue to change and grow. Others can add to my work—people like you.

The third reason is that I genuinely believe in the value of contextualization, working out meals that will actually function well in your particular setting. I don't want to pretend that I can legislate what will be practical for your community or what will be experienced as authentic. Even before you go look at the website, I encourage you to talk with people in your community about what this approach to Holy Communion might look like where you are.

If it helps to get at least some small idea, here are words of institution I've used with some regularity in more traditional services of Holy Communion, to try to *begin* moving toward the kind of radical meal

RESISTANCE, RESILIENCE, AND RISK   167

practices discussed here. These words of institution can give you at least a sense of the general direction we've been traveling.

> **Presider One:** We remember, Gracious God, that Jesus ate and drank with the poor and the wealthy, with sinful and righteous alike. When he saw the multitude that followed him with nothing to eat, he took some loaves of bread, and a few fish, (*lifting bread*) and after giving thanks to you he divided the bread and gave it to the disciples. And all ate and were filled.

> **Presider Two:** When his arrest seemed near, Jesus sat at table in an upper room, with his closest friends and relatives. As he had done so many times before, he took the bread, (*lifting bread*) and after giving thanks to you he shared it among the disciples, vowing to continue the struggle in spite of the risk. He said, "I will not eat this again until it is fulfilled in the Beloved Community of God."

> **Presider Three:** Likewise after the meal he took a cup, (*lifting cup*) and after giving thanks he gave it to them saying, "Truly I tell you, I will never drink of the fruit of the vine until I drink it new with you in the Beloved Community of God."

> **Presider Four:** For a time it seemed that all was lost. Jesus was executed by the authorities, and his disciples scattered in fear and despair. But at an evening meal in Emmaus, and at a breakfast campfire by the Sea of Galilee, Jesus once more took the bread (*lifting bread*), and after giving thanks to you he divided it and gave it to his disciples, opening their eyes, binding up their wounds, continuing the meal, and revealing plainly that your steadfast love is stronger even than death, and your labor with us continues, for the sake of your realm.

It's not too Hard

One of the reasons that this book has taken so many years to write is that every time I allowed myself to imagine a different way of practicing the sacred meal, every time I considered a new way of seeing the tradition, the same three words have played over and over in my head like an audio loop. *It's too hard.* At times I would step away from this work for weeks at a time, unable to see how anyone would ever attempt such challenging and risky ways of eating and praying together. I still have reservations myself about trying to live out the kind of life this book proposes. I've come to recognize that the difficulty of such practices is part of what made them hard to sustain in the first place. So I acknowledge that many churches will go on performing rites that emphasize sign acts and rhetoric over the difficult work of creating meals radical enough to form people in the *habitus* of the Beloved Community of God. I can't say that I blame them.

Nevertheless, I've also come to see that it's not impossible. People are already trying new ways of celebrating Holy Communion, and some of those experiments are working. We don't have to leap into trying everything at once. You and your community can take small steps. You don't have to throw out your traditions wholesale and organize elaborate, exhilarating, risky meals every week. You can add a new sacramental practice to your community's life that happens every once in a while and go from there. You can try something and then talk about it. You can find what works best in your place. Pay attention and see what blossoms, what bears fruit.

There needs to be room for grace in this. We're human. There will be mistakes. Keep seeking what is holy, and difficult, and real. Eat in ways that surprise you, and that allow God to surprise you. Keep your eyes, ears, and heart open, to sense when the Beloved Community is coming near. Follow that instinct and that longing.

8

Concluding Reflections

Practical Sacramentality
and the Beloved Community of God

Heaven on Earth

What was it was about the meals of Jesus' ministry that caused people to go away believing what Jesus and his disciples proclaimed: that the Beloved Community of God had actually come near to them? People like Zacchaeus, or all those people in Luke 10 that the seventy disciples encountered when they were sent out to heal, eat, and say that the Kindom had come near? As Luke tells it, the seventy returned with joy (Luke 10:17). In addition to the disciples' healing work, the meals of Jesus' ministry themselves clearly had an impact, because they loom so large in both stories and teaching. We don't get a lot of direct reporting about them though. Certainly the meals must have fostered a sense of hospitality and inclusion, but their appeal was deeper than that. Something powerful and sacred in those meals must have drawn people deeper, giving rise to an ongoing tradition of Christian eating, even after Jesus' execution. What was so awe-inspiring and transformative?

My hunch, based on the ideas we've been examining, is that when Jesus and his disciples ate with people or fed them, the experience wasn't just amazing or strikingly different from the norm. It was like heaven.

It was as if heaven had come, for a moment, on earth. I don't mean this merely as a grandiose, figurative way of saying it was beautiful, which I would guess it was; or that it approached some high ideal of community, which I assume it often did. I mean that when people experienced such a radically different way of sitting together and sharing food and connecting with God, it convinced them they'd experienced a different reality: heaven on earth. There, with Jesus and his disciples, around a simple meal with some other guests and maybe the light of a few oil lamps, the Beloved Community of God had come near, on earth as it is in heaven.

This happened not primarily because the correct words were spoken (though prayer was certainly essential). It happened not primarily because of the efficacy of the signs (though naturally the meal carried an important and irreducible signification and symbolism). It happened primarily because when hungry people were actually fed, when real sharing actually happened, when people crossed boundaries and broke rules about who eats with whom, and when it was all bound up together with practices of prayer, the meals had a certain practical sacramentality about them. That is to say, the sacramentality of the meals flowed precisely from their practical effects. They were sacramental not simply because of what their words or gestures signified, but more because the extraordinary, pragmatic outcomes of the particular meal practices awoke participants to something deeper. They were sacramental because they engaged in real resistance to violence, exploitation, and alienation. They were sacramental because they functioned as a counterpolitics and a countereconomics. More than receiving a communicated sign of grace that transformed them, people at table with Jesus were drawn into a different social and spiritual matrix that was eminently practical and sacramental at the same time.[1] It's similar to Robert Hovda's description that we encountered back in chapter 1:

> Good liturgical celebration, like a parable, takes us by the hair of our heads, lifts us momentarily out of the cesspool of injustice we call home, and puts us in the promised and challenging reign of God, where we are treated like we have never been treated anywhere else: where we are bowed to and sprinkled and censed and kissed and touched and where we share equally among all a holy food and drink.[2]

1. It's important to note here that in order to be efficacious, these meal practices had to be ensconced in the messy realities of embodiment and interaction.

2. Hovda, "Vesting," 220.

The heart of those meals wasn't just an ideal that people understood, or an intense personal experience, though it may have included both of those. It was a constellation of practices and relationships that engaged participants holistically and collectively, lifting them, for a time, out of the ordinary, structuring environment of practices that shaped their lives.

When they worked, I suspect the meals of Jesus' ministry were sacramentally efficacious in at least two ways. First, they achieved a kind of open commensality, Sabbath economics, bodily nurture, and welcome into prayer that elicited a holistic (and not narrowly psychological) experience of proximity to something numinous and gracious—a sense that the Beloved Community had come near. If participants gained any awareness of divine agency, it was an embodied sense, a gut sense that they were being drawn into collaboration with God's compassionate, resilient, and creative activity in the world. Second, the meals worked to the extent that people were transformed over time by their participation in that alternate social and spiritual matrix. This transformation came from engaging in practices that called upon people to actually welcome, share with, and seek the divine in the other. The meals were efficacious insofar as they formed people with the *habitus,* the dispositions for behavior, of the Beloved Community of God. For many, these kinds of efficacy will appear paltry and thin. To me they seem to be clear traces of God's grace moving in the world. They seem sacramental in a way that I can wholly embrace.

Over time, the meals appear to have shifted their gravitational center toward symbol, and signification. As eucharistic meals have increasingly substituted practices aimed at both practical effect and signification with practices aimed primarily at signification, Christians have needed to work harder to assert the meal's spiritual efficacy. Theological claims about the meal, our insistence in teaching and in prayer, have gradually become the basis for that efficacy, instead of the meal's practical features and results. We have tried to make the spiritual effects of Holy Communion more reliably repeatable, moving away from radical and risky meal sharing in the process. Grace that had been more a quality or characteristic of practical acts, practical effects, and relationships became reified as a commodity of grace-endowed ritual objects.

In the course of this research, I've come to believe that we need to counter that drift, recovering a more practical sacramental theology. I've become more and more convinced that the practical effects of radical, prayerful meal sharing are a sounder (though less controllable) foundation for any meals that we would call sacramental—or sacraments. If we can recondition ourselves to avoid the eucharistic *habitus* of violent surrogacy and learn instead from the movements of people who are already trying to reintegrate more of the meal practices of Jesus' ministry, we may find that we no longer need to lean as heavily upon strident catechetical insistence that the meal is sacramentally efficacious.

Like an Animal of the Forest

You may have noticed that the Beloved Community of God is a bit odd (or odder than usual) in the approach to Holy Communion toward which we've been moving. For one thing, it's always coming near but it never arrives, certainly not in any durable way. It's only ever approaching, and tends to be fleeting and fragile at that. It draws near in pockets here and there: in flashes of fire, like Jesus at Emmaus, causing our hearts to burn within us but then vanishing, leaving us with a sense of mystery and longing.

Perhaps even odder is that this coming near of the *basileia* of God does not appear to be the initiation of an imminent, enduring empire. While it challenges the established order, and its presence in multiple locations may act as a general leaven of sorts (Matt 13:33; Luke 13:21), it's not the first foothold of a new dispensation spreading inexorably across (read "colonizing") the land. It's not taking over. Evil is not vanquished here: not now and not assuredly in the future. Evil keeps reinventing itself, and in the face of real, lingering trauma the hope of any final, eschatological triumph is muted. Consequently, the Beloved Community of God seems to have an enduring quality of alterity, and a tempered hope for the long haul.[3] It celebrates abundant life here and now, but it retains an element of resistance, and a *mitzvah* (commandment) of *Kiddush ha hayyim* (the sanctification of life).

---

3. In relation to the alterity of the Beloved Community, Victor Turner speaks in a parallel way of the stages of *communitas* of ritual, saying that normative *communitas*, the later stage when people attempt to transform the experience of *communitas* into a "perduring social system," creates a structure that is itself antithetical to *communitas*. "To do this it has to denature itself, for spontaneous communitas is more a matter of 'grace' than 'law,' to use theological language. Its spirit 'bloweth where it listeth'—it cannot be legislated or normalized, since it is the *exception*, not the *law*, the *miracle*, not the *regularity*, primordial freedom, not *anangke*, the causal chain of necessity" (Turner, *From Ritual*, 49).

In keeping with this sense of instability, the Beloved Community of God seems to have an element of performativity about it as well.[4] While grounded in the deep communion we all share and in the work of the Holy Spirit (who is discovered to have been active all along), this Kindom is something we must join in doing in order for it to come near. Unlike more patriarchal ideas of an eternal kingdom irrupting into history, here the Beloved Community of God doesn't always exist. It doesn't perdure in some ontological way (as the Spirit does) while we wander off into bickering or compassion fatigue or deep-seated prejudice. It's more fragile than that and relies upon the alchemy of imperfect human collaboration with the divine. It is only something that is done, and done collaboratively.[5]

Nevertheless, we are not able to *make* it come near. The Spirit blows where it will, and the Beloved Community can't be controlled or reliably produced. There are no formulas, and we cannot create it with the flip of a liturgical switch. It becomes harder to claim that the church is coterminous with the Beloved Community, always and everywhere, as well. Sometimes you play a piece of music and all the notes were there, but you just know somehow that it didn't really "happen." Sometimes you remember all the ingredients and you follow the directions, but the recipe just doesn't turn out.

Next, if it's heaven on earth, the Beloved Community of God is not a naïve image of that. After the crucifixion, and during decades of violent persecution, the Beloved Community itself is shot through with traumatic return—an "after the storm" that is not swallowed up in victory, but remains. Easter is bound up with stories about touching the wounds in Jesus' hands and side. The risen Christ himself evokes the irreversible shatteredness of the person, the community, the way of life that had come before. He remains the Crucified One. Things will never be the same, and if we're honest, it's not all for the good. Yet, the community, the communion, and God are resilient, continuing to reach toward abundant life. This dialectic of trauma and resilience—this fragile, nonlinear movement toward recovery and reengagement—is ultimately revealed to be constitutive of the way the Kin-dom is done.

4. By "performativity" I mean something that has the characteristic of being tenuously constituted in time only by the repetition of acts. For discussion of performativity, see Butler, "Performative," 519–31.

5. If this seems too much like works righteousness, keep in mind that the meal we are pursuing is open to all from the beginning.

The Beloved Community is deeply rooted in the biblical concept of *shalom*: the social, political, economic, even ecological well-being or flourishing of all of creation.[6] *Shalom* shares a close relationship to the New Testament concept of *koinonia*: an active sense of communing with one another (Acts 2:42), communing in the Holy Spirit (Phil 2:1), or even communing with the risen Jesus (1 John 1:6).[7] Lastly, it is rooted in particular contexts. It will look very different in different communities at different times, and what worked before may not work now. This is an irreducible corollary of the fact that the Beloved Community is something that must be done, in particular times and places.

To what, then, shall we compare the Beloved Community of God? It is like an animal of the forest. It comes of its own accord. We cannot make it appear, and no amount of beating the bushes will flush it out. All we can do is prepare the optimal conditions: bringing what we have to share, risking vulnerability to the other, opening ourselves to the Spirit. If we are patient and keep coming back, the creature may come near: standing silently at the edge of the firelight, bringing an awe-inspiring glimpse of a different world, joining our gathering just out of reach. If we don't make any threatening movements, it may share our corner of the world for a while: a tentative, luminous communion. Even then, we cannot capture the creature and display it in a cage whenever we want. That would just wreck it. No set sacred words or gestures will command it to return, either. All we can do is keep coming back to prepare, keep doing our part, knowing that this beautiful, unpredictable creature is out there, somewhere beyond the first line of trees. In this way it is the creature who trains us how to live both *in* and *for* communion.

What Kind of God Is to Be Practiced?

This wonderful question from Sharon Welch has been a guiding star for the journey recorded here.[8] Much of the searching and imagining in this book flows from the question of what kind of God will be enacted through our practices of Holy Communion. The point is not that we are

6. For discussion of the biblical concept of shalom, see Brueggemann, *Living*.

7. I've chosen "communing" here because I believe it comes closer to the active sense of the noun *koinonia*.

8. Mary McClintock Fulkerson (*Changing*, 20) writes, "The crucial inquiry of a liberation theological epistemology, as Sharon Welch says, is not, Does God exist?, but What kind of God is to be practiced?"

somehow able to control the ontological nature of God by how we choose to act. Rather, from a liberation theology perspective, the point is that, given our limited human grasp of the divine, we are called to discern and choose the kind of God we will practice, knowing that the impact of our choices matters to God and to the world. The practical impact of our sacramental practices for all of creation, and especially those who are oppressed, wounded, or most vulnerable, matters to God because of God's overarching work for *shalom* on the earth. That impact matters for us as well, because we ourselves are bound up together in the web of relationships that is the great communion of being. Not only do our choices about the kind of God we practice in Holy Communion help to shape the character of God that is enacted in our community of faith more generally, but they also form us with particular *habitus,* shaping how God will be enacted in our daily walk of discipleship.

This perspective moves us toward a liturgical life in which the aim of the sacrament is not revelation or meaning or identity or even a gift of grace in any sense that can be meaningfully (or at least helpfully) distinguished from a holistic mode of practice. Neither is praxis our sacramental aim, in which we work to stitch back together reflection and action that have been divided by our own analysis. Rather, this liturgical life comes closer to clothing ourselves in a seamless garment of practice, of living into our communion with God and others because we have found that our way of knowing God is more performative than conceptual, and our living in communion with God is more joining in, moving in time together, than cognitive grasping or achieving a certain state of being.

So, what kind of God will be practiced in our sacramental meals? My hope and prayer is that you and your community will find both new and ancient ways to practice a God who is resilient. I hope the God you practice can bear the pain and anger of the traumatic return but still always be reaching beyond it toward recovery, not bound in the same loop or trapped in the same violent, repetitive logic. I hope that you will find ways to practice a God who is doggedly resistant to violent technologies of the body, a God who continually subverts the logic of surrogacy and the totalizing narrative of empire. I hope the God you practice moves with wisdom and patience among the horrors that linger and those that are yet to come, weaving and reweaving solidarity for the struggle. I pray that your sacramental meals will practice a God who carries a deep and abiding longing for communion, drawing us out toward the risk of meeting God in the face of those who are other to us.

Imagine for a moment Holy Communion as it can be in your community of faith. Imagine that it is not only a "countersign to the devaluation and violence directed toward the exploited, despised Black body," as M. Shawn Copeland says,[9] but also a counterpractice, a eucharistic solidarity that is actually able to counter the fragmenting, isolating violence of White supremacy. Imagine the sacrament does not just signify that Black bodies are beloved of God but enacts that truth in practical ways, treating people like they have never been treated anywhere else. What would that meal look like in your circle?

Or imagine that a young woman comes to your faith community for Communion, and that she is a survivor of human trafficking. Now, imagine how she might be gently invited into practices that both proclaim and treat her as a sacred *Thou*. She doesn't have to touch or hug if she doesn't want to. She is not asked to perform her assent to the commodification of Jesus' body, made available to others. Instead, she is given respect in an embodied way. She is offered agency, solidarity, and love. Imagine that the meal is so healing and empowering for her that she is able to come away with astonishing words on her lips for anyone who would exploit her: "This is my body. It's not for you."

Then imagine a middle-aged man who comes in and sits in the back pew or chair. He's a refugee, a survivor of war and of torture. He can't even sit with the rest of the group at first. You can tell that he wants to participate but is struggling with all that he can't unsee, unfeel, or unlearn. He's not going to be "all better" soon, or maybe ever. Imagine him eventually able to participate in a sacrament that refuses to valorize suffering. Imagine that it focuses instead on imitation of the disciples, who came together in spite of all that had been done to Jesus, and to them. Imagine a meal that helps him to mourn, and to know in his body the feel of community again. Would not God be at work there?

Holy Communion is so important. It's been such a central part of the Christian faith down through the centuries. It is worth struggling for, encumbered as it may be with distorted meanings and gestures that have come unmoored from practical effects. The ministry of Jesus and his community still invite us to collaborate with the Holy Spirit's work of helping pockets of the Beloved Community of God to come near, again and again. May God bless your community's ongoing efforts to practice sacred meals in the way of Jesus. May more and more of the situations in

9. Copeland, *Enfleshing*, 127.

your life reveal themselves as thin places. May you move with purpose toward constant communion. And may blessing and honor, glory and power, be unto God.

Find liturgical examples and join the conversation at:
www.belovedcommunion.org.

Bibliography

Allen, James, et al. *Without Sanctuary: Lynching Photography in America*. Santa Fe: Twin Palms, 2000.

Anderson, C. A., et al. "Violent Video Game Effects on Aggression, Empathy, and Prosocial Behavior in Eastern and Western Countries: a Meta-analytic Review." *Psychological Bulletin* 136/2 (2010) 151–73. https://www.ncbi.nlm.nih.gov/pubmed/20192553.

Anderson, Herbert, and Edward Foley. *Mighty Stories, Dangerous Rituals: Weaving Together the Human and Divine*. San Francisco: Jossey-Bass, 1998.

Bell, Catherine. *Ritual Theory, Ritual Practice*. New York: Oxford University Press, 1992.

Boihem, Harold, dir. *The Ad and the Ego*. DVD. Santa Monica, CA: Parallax Pictures, 1997.

Bourdieu, Pierre. *Outline of a Theory of Practice*. Cambridge Studies in Social Anthropology 16. Cambridge: Cambridge University Press, 1977.

Bradshaw, Paul F. *Eucharistic Origins*. 2004. Reprint, Eugene, OR: Wipf & Stock, 2012.

———. *The Search for the Origins of Christian Worship: Sources and Methods for the Study of Early Liturgy*. 2nd ed. New York: Oxford University Press, 2002.

Brock, Rita Nakashima. "Ending Innocence and Nurturing Willfulness." In *Violence against Women and Children: A Christian Theological Sourcebook*, edited by Carol J. Adams and Marie M. Fortune, 71–84. New York: Continuum, 1998.

———. *Journeys by Heart: A Christology of Erotic Power*. New York: Crossroad, 1988.

Brock, Rita Nakashima, and Rebecca Ann Parker. *Proverbs of Ashes: Violence, Redemptive Suffering, and the Search for What Saves Us*. Boston: Beacon, 2001.

———. *Saving Paradise: How Christianity Traded Love of This World for Crucifixion and Empire*. Boston: Beacon, 2008.

Brockman, James. *Romero: A Life*. Maryknoll, NY: Orbis, 1989.

Brown, Raymond E. *The Gospel according to John I–XII*. Anchor Bible 29. Garden City, NY: Doubleday, 1966.

Brueggemann, Walter. *Living toward a Vision: Biblical Reflections on Shalom*. Shalom Resource. New York: United Church Press, 1982.

Buber, Martin. *I and Thou*. Translated by Walter Kaufman. New York: Scribner, 1970.

Butler, Judith. *Bodies That Matter: On the Discursive Limits of "Sex."* New York: Routledge, 1993.

———. "Performative Acts and Gender Constitution: An Essay in Phenomenology and Feminist Theory." *Theatre Journal* 40 (1988) 519–31.

179

Cameron, Jane and Günter Stampf, dirs. *Der Kannibale von Rotenburg: Interview with a Cannibal*. Starring Armin Meiwes. Produced by Stampfwerk Medienproduktions und vermarktungs et al. 2 DVDs. Germany: n.p., 2007.

Carroll, James. *Constantine's Sword: The Church and the Jews: A History*. Boston: Houghton Mifflin, 2001.

Caruth, Cathy. *Unclaimed Experience: Trauma, Narrative, and History*. Baltimore: Johns Hopkins University Press, 1996.

Cavanaugh, William. *Torture and Eucharist: Theology, Politics, and the Body of Christ*. Challenges in Contemporary Theology. Oxford: Blackwell, 1998.

Central Intelligence Agency. *The World Factbook* (website). Washington, DC: Central Intelligence Agency. https://www.cia.gov/library/publications/the-world-factbook/geos/xx.html.

Chauvet, Louis-Marie. *Symbol and Sacrament: A Sacramental Reinterpretation of Christian Existence*. Collegeville, MN: Liturgical, 1995.

Chokshi, Niraj. "North Miami Police Officers Shoot Man Aiding Patient With Autism." *New York Times*, July 21, 2016. https://www.nytimes.com/2016/07/22/us/north-miami-police-officers-shoot-man-aiding-patient-with-autism.html.

Coleman, Monica A. *The Dinah Project: A Handbook for Congregational Response to Sexual Violence*. Cleveland: Pilgrim, 2004.

Collins, Mary. *Worship: Renewal to Practice*. Washington, DC: Pastoral Press, 1987.

Combs-Schilling, M. Elaine. "Etching Patriarchal Rule: Ritual Dye, Erotic Potency, and the Moroccan Monarchy." In *Readings in Ritual Studies*, edited by Ronald L. Grimes, 104–18. Upper Saddle River, NJ: Prentice Hall, 1996.

Cone, James H. *The Cross and the Lynching Tree*. Maryknoll, NY: Orbis, 2017.

Connerton, Paul. *How Societies Remember*. Themes in the Social Sciences. New York: Cambridge University Press, 1989.

Cooper-White, Pamela. *The Cry of Tamar: Violence against Women and the Church's Response*. 2nd ed. Minneapolis: Fortress, 2012.

Copeland, M. Shawn. *Enfleshing Freedom: Body, Race, and Being*. Innovations. Minneapolis: Fortress, 2010.

Crossan, John Dominic. *The Birth of Christianity: Discovering What Happened in the Years Immediately after the Execution of Jesus*. San Francisco: HarperSanFrancisco, 1998.

———. *Jesus: A Revolutionary Biography*. San Francisco: HarperSanFrancisco, 1994.

Crossan, John Dominic, and Jonathan Reed. *In Search of Paul: How Jesus's Apostle Opposed Rome's Empire with God's Kingdom*. San Francisco: HarperSanFrancisco, 2004.

Daly, Mary. *Beyond God the Father: Toward a Philosophy of Women's Liberation*. Beacon Paperback. Boston: Beacon, 1985.

Derrida, Jacques. "Form and Meaning: A Note on the Phenomenology of Language." In *Speech and Phenomena, and Other Essays on Husserl's Theory of Sign*, 107–60. Northwestern University Studies in Phenomenology & Existential Philosophy. Evanston, IL: Northwestern University Press, 1973.

———. *The Gift of Death*. Translated by David Wills. Religion and Post-modernism. Chicago: University of Chicago Press, 1995.

Dix, Gregory. *The Shape of the Liturgy*. London: Continuum, 2001.

Douglas, Mary. *Purity and Danger: An Analysis of Concepts of Pollution and Taboo*. London: Penguin, 1970.

Driver, Tom F. *Liberating Rites: Understanding the Transformative Power of Ritual.* Boulder, CO: Westview, 1998.

Eiesland, Nancy L. *The Disabled God: Toward a Liberatory Theology of Disability.* Nashville: Abingdon, 1994.

Eliot, T. S. "Little Gidding." In *Four Quartets,* 49–61. New York: Mariner, 1968.

Episcopal Church. *The Book of Common Prayer.* New York: Church Publishing, 1979.

Evangelical Lutheran Church in America. "Care for Returning Veterans." PowerPoint presentation. https://www.elca.org/Resources/Federal-Chaplains/.

Evans, Rachel Held. "Is Your Church too Cool?" RELEVANT Magazine, June 29, 2011. https://relevantmagazine.com/god/your-church-too-cool//.

Fackenheim, Emil. "The Spectrum of Resistance during the Holocaust: An Essay in Definition and Description." *Modern Judaism* 2/2 (1982) 113–30.

Feuillet, André. *La Christ sagesse de Dieu: d'apres les epitres pauliniennes.* Etudes bibliques. Paris: Gebalda, 1966.

Fitzmyer, Joseph A. *The Gospel according to Luke: Introduction, Translation, and Notes X–XXIV.* Anchor Bible 28A. Garden City, NY: Doubleday, 1985.

Fitzpatrick, Andrea. "The Movement of Vulnerability: Images of Falling and September 11." *Art Journal* 64 (2007) 84–102.

———. "Reconsidering the Dead in Andres Serrano's *The Morgue:* Identity, Agency, Subjectivity." *Canadian Art Review* 33/1–2 (2008) 28–42.

Fortune, Marie M., and James Poling. "Calling to Accountability: The Church's Response to Abusers." In *Violence against Women and Children: A Theological Sourcebook,* edited by Carol J. Adams and Marie M. Fortune, 451–63. New York: Continuum, 1995.

Foucault, Michel. *Discipline and Punish: The Birth of the Prison.* Translated by Alan Sheridan. New York: Pantheon, 1977.

———. "Two Lectures." In *Power/Knowledge: Selected Interviews and Other Writings, 1972–1977,* edited by Colin Gordon, 78–108. New York: Pantheon, 1980.

Fulkerson, Mary McClintock. *Changing the Subject: Women's Discourses and Feminist Theologies.* Minneapolis: Fortress, 1994.

García-Rivera, Alejandro. *The Community of the Beautiful: A Theological Aesthetics.* Collegeville, MN: Liturgical, 1999.

Girard, René. *Things Hidden since the Foundation of the World.* Translated by Stephan Bann and Michael Metteer. Stanford: Stanford University Press, 1987.

———. "The Uniqueness of the Gospels." In *I See Satan Fall Like Lightning,* 121–36. Translated, with a foreword, by James G. Williams. Maryknoll, NY: Orbis, 2001.

Goudey, June Christine. *The Feast of Our Lives: Re-imagining Communion.* Cleveland: Pilgrim, 2002.

Grimes, Ronald L. *Deeply into the Bone: Re-inventing Rites of Passage.* Life Passages. Berkeley: University of California Press, 2000.

———. "Ritual Criticism and Infelicitous Performances." In *Readings in Ritual Studies,* 279–92. Upper Saddle River, NJ: Prentice Hall, 1996.

Gutschenritter, Jackie. Personal correspondence with the author, October 2016.

Haldeman, Scott. "The Welcome Table: Worship That Does Justice and Makes Peace." *Liturgy: Worship with Justice* (Journal of the Liturgical Conference) 17/1 (2001) 3–13.

Hays, Richard B. *First Corinthians.* Interpretation. Louisville: Westminster John Knox, 1997.

Herbert, T. Walter. *Sexual Violence and American Manhood.* Cambridge: Harvard University Press, 2002.

Herman, Judith Lewis. *Trauma and Recovery: The Aftermath of Violence—from Domestic Abuse to Political Terror.* New York: Basic Books, 1997.

Hiers, Richard H., and Charles A. Kennedy. "The Bread and Fish Eucharist in the Gospels and Early Christian Art." *Perspectives in Religious Studies* 3/1 (1976) 20–47.

Hope [pseudonym]. "And the Truth Will Make You Free." In *Victim to Survivor: Women Recovering from Clergy Sexual Abuse,* edited by Nancy Werking Poling, 61–78. Cleveland: United Church Press, 1999.

Hovda, Robert. "Vesting the Liturgical Ministers." In *Robert Hovda: The Amen Corner,* edited by John Baldovin, 213–33. Collegeville, MN: Liturgical, 1994.

Isasi-Díaz, Ada María. *En La Lucha/In the Struggle: A Hispanic Women's Liberation Theology.* Minneapolis: Fortress, 1993.

Jackson, Jesse. Keynote for Dr. Martin Luther King Jr. Day Observance. Speech presented at Northwestern University, January 15, 2001.

Jasper, R. C. D., and G. J. Cuming, trans. and eds. *Prayers of the Eucharist: Early and Reformed.* 3rd rev. enl. ed. Collegeville, MN: Liturgical, 1990.

Johnson, Maxwell E. *The Rites of Christian Initiation: Their Evolution and Interpretation.* Rev. and exp. ed. Collegeville, MN: Liturgical, 2007.

Kaufman, Michael. "The Construction of Masculinity and the Triad of Men's Violence." In *Men's Lives,* edited by Michael S. Kimmel and Michael A. Messner, 4–17. 4th ed. Boston: Allyn & Bacon, 1998.

Kennedy, William Bean. "The Ideological Captivity of the Non-Poor." In *Pedagogies for the Non-Poor,* edited by Alice Frazer Evans et al., 232–56. Maryknoll, NY: Orbis, 1987.

Keshgegian, Flora A. *Redeeming Memories: A Theology of Healing and Transformation.* Nashville: Abingdon, 2000.

———. "The Crucifixion as Trauma: A Reading of Jesus' Death and Its Significance." Paper presented at the Annual Meeting of the American Academy of Religion, Denver, CO, November 2001.

Kilborne, Jean. "Killing Us Softly 4." Northhampton, MA: Media Education Foundation, 2010. https://youtu.be/xnAY6S4_m5I/.

King, Martin Luther, Jr. "I've Been to the Mountaintop." Speech delivered April 3, 1968, Memphis, Tennessee. *American Rhetoric* (website), *Top 100 Speeches.* http://www.americanrhetoric.com/speeches/mlkivebeentothemountaintop.htm/.

Kittel, Gerhard, ed. *Theological Dictionary of the New Testament.* Vol. 3. Translated and edited by Geoffrey W. Bromley. Grand Rapids: Eerdmans, 1965.

Lakoff, George. *Women, Fire, and Dangerous Things: What Categories Reveal about the Mind.* Chicago: University of Chicago Press, 1987.

Landler, Mark. "Eating People Is Wrong! But Is It Homicide? Court to Rule." Kassel Journal. *New York Times,* December 26, 2003. https://www.nytimes.com/2003/12/26/world/kassel-journal-eating-people-is-wrong-but-is-it-homicide-court-to-rule.html/.

LaVerdiere, Eugene. *The Eucharist in the New Testament and the Early Church.* Collegeville, MN: Liturgical, 1996.

Levinas, Emmanuel. *Entre Nous: On Thinking-of-the-Other.* Translated from the French by Michael B. Smith and Barbara Harshav. European Perspectives. New York: Columbia University Press, 1998.

————. *Totality and Infinity: An Essay on Exteriority.* Translated by Alphonso Lingis. Duquesne Studies. Philosophical Series 24. Pittsburgh: Duquesne University Press, 1969.

Le Guin, Ursula K. *The Ones Who Walk Away from Omelas.* Creative Short Story. Mankato, MN: Creative Education Inc., 1993.

Leonard, John K., and Nathan Mitchell. *The Postures of the Assembly during the Eucharistic Prayer.* Chicago: Liturgical Training, 1994.

Lietzmann, Hans. *Mass and the Lord's Supper: A Study in the History of the Liturgy.* Translated by Dorothea H.G. Reeve. Leiden: Brill, 1979.

Macy, Gary. *The Banquet's Wisdom: A Short History of the Theologies of the Lord's Supper.* Akron, OH: OSL Publications, 2005.

Mallory, Chaone. "Acts of Objectification and the Repudiation of Dominance: Leopold, Ecofeminism, and the Ecological Narrative." *Ethics and the Environment* 6/2 (2001) 59–89.

Marxsen, Willi. *The Lord's Supper as a Christological Problem.* Translated by Lorenz Nieting. Facet Books: Biblical Series 25. Philadelphia: Fortress, 1970.

Maudlin, Michael G. "God's Contractor: How Millard Fuller Persuaded Corporate America to Do Kingdom Work." *Christianity Today* (June 14, 1999) 44–47. https://www.christianitytoday.com/ct/1999/june14/9t7044.html/.

Mazza, Enrico. *The Celebration of the Eucharist: The Origin of the Rite and the Development of Its Interpretation.* Translated by Matthew J. O'Connell. Collegeville, MN: Liturgical, 1999.

————. *The Origins of the Eucharistic Prayer.* Translated by Ronald E. Lane. Collegeville, MN: Liturgical, 1995.

McGowan, Andrew B. *Ancient Christian Worship.* Grand Rapids: Baker Academic, 2014.

————. *Ascetic Eucharists: Food and Drink in Early Christian Ritual Meals.* Oxford Early Christian Studies. Oxford: Clarendon, 1999.

————. "'Is There a Liturgical Text in This Gospel?' The Institution Narratives and Their Early Interpretive Communities." *Journal of Biblical Literature* 118 (1999) 73–87.

McKirdy, Euan. "The Crux of the Matter: The Filipinos Crucified on Good Friday." https://www.cnn.com/2016/03/25/asia/philippines-easter-good-friday-crucifixion/index.html.

McLaren, Brian. "Light Fires, Issue Permission Slips, Invite Others into the Interpretive Community." Speech given at the Festival of Homiletics in Minneapolis on May 21, 2014. https://www.slideshare.net/brianmclaren/festival-of-homiletics-2014-lecture.

Min, Hahnshik. "Beginning Thoughts on Rituals for Male Abusers." In *Understanding Male Violence: Pastoral Care Issues,* edited by James Newton Poling, 195–204. St. Louis: Chalice, 2003.

Mitchell, Nathan D. "The Impact of Twentieth-Century Approaches to Scripture for Understanding the Connections between Jesus and Eucharist." *Liturgy Digest* 4/2 (1997) 41–86.

Momartin, Shakeh, and Mariano Coello. "Self-Harming Behaviour and Dissociation in Complex PTSD: Case Study of a Male Tortured Refugee." *Torture* 16/1 (2006) 20–29.

Morrill, Bruce T. *Anamnesis as Dangerous Memory: Political and Liturgical Theology in Dialogue.* Peublo Book. Collegeville, MN: Liturgical, 2000.

Morrison, Toni. *Beloved*. With an introduction by A. S. Byatt. New York: Everyman's Library, 2006.

Mulvey, Laura. "Visual Pleasure and Narrative Cinema." *Screen* 16/3 (1975) 6–18.

Myers, Ched. *The Biblical Vision of Sabbath Economics*. Washington, DC: Tell the Word, Church of the Savior, 2001.

"NCTTP Member Centers." *National Consortium of Torture Treatment Programs* (website). http://www.ncttp.org/members.html/.

Niederwimmer, Kurt. *The Didache: A Commentary*. Translated by Linda M. Maloney. Hermeneia. Minneapolis: Fortress, 1998.

Nussbaum, Martha. "Objectification." *Philosophy & Public Affairs* 24 (1995) 249–91.

Ortner, Sherry B. *Making Gender: The Politics and Erotics of Culture*. Boston: Beacon, 1996.

Patterson, Stephen J. *Beyond the Passion: Rethinking the Death and Life of Jesus*. Minneapolis: Fortress, 2004.

———. *The Lost Way: How Two Forgotten Gospels Are Rewriting the Story of Christian Origins*. New York: HarperOne, 2014.

———. "Paul and the Jesus Tradition: It Is Time for Another Look." *Harvard Theological Review* 84 (1991) 23–41.

Peres, Julio F. P., et al. "Spirituality and Resilience in Trauma Victims." *Journal of Religion and Health* 46 (2007) 343–50.

Perry, John M. "The Evolution of the Johannine Eucharist." *New Testament Studies* 39 (1993) 22–35.

Poling, James Newton. *The Abuse of Power: A Theological Problem*. Nashville: Abingdon, 1991.

Power, David N. *Sacrament: The Language of God's Giving*. New York: Crossroad, 1999.

Presbyterian Church (U.S.A.). *The Book of Common Worship*. Prepared by the Theology and Worship Ministry Unit for the Presbyterian Church (U.S.A.) and the Cumberland Presbyterian Church. Louisville: Westminster John Knox, 1993.

Procter-Smith, Marjorie. *In Her Own Rite: Constructing Feminist Liturgical Tradition*. Nashville: Abingdon, 1990

———. *Praying with Our Eyes Open: Engendering Feminist Liturgical Prayer*. Nashville: Abingdon, 1995.

———. "The Whole Loaf: Holy Communion and Survival." In *Violence against Women and Children: A Theological Sourcebook*, edited by Carol J. Adams and Marie M. Fortune, 464–79. New York: Continuum, 1995.

Rambo, Shelly. *Spirit and Trauma: A Theology of Remaining*. Louisville: Westminster John Knox, 2010.

Ray, Darby Kathleen. *Deceiving the Devil: Atonement, Abuse, and Ransom*. Cleveland: Pilgrim, 1998.

Reuther, Rosemary Radford. *Sexism and God Talk: Toward a Feminist Theology*. With a new introduction. Boston: Beacon, 1993.

———. *Women and Redemption: A Theological History*. Minneapolis: Fortress, 1998.

Rich, Adrienne. "Diving into the Wreck." In *Diving into the Wreck: Poems, 1971–1972*, 22–24. New York: Norton, 1973.

Riggs, John W. "From Gracious Table to Sacramental Elements: The Tradition-History of *Didache* 9 and 10." *Second Century* 4 (1984) 83–101.

Rohr, Richard. *The Naked Now: Learning to See as the Mystics See*. New York: Crossroad, 2009.

Rouillard, Philippe. "From Human Meal to Christian Eucharist." *Worship* 53/1 (1979) 40–56.

Schwartz, Regina M. *The Curse of Cain: The Violent Legacy of Monotheism.* Chicago: University of Chicago Press, 1997.

Schwiebert, Jonathan. *Knowledge and the Coming Kingdom: The Didache's Meal Ritual and Its Place in Early Christianity.* Library of New Testament Studies 373. London: T. & T. Clark, 2008.

Shaw-Thornburg, Angela. "This Is a Trigger Warning." *Chronicle of Higher Education: The Chronicle Review,* June 24, 2014. https://www.chronicle.com/article/This-Is-a-Trigger-Warning/147031/.

Sloyan, Gerard S. *John.* Interpretation. Atlanta: John Knox, 1988.

Smith, Dennis E., and Hal E. Taussig. *Many Tables: The Eucharist in the New Testament and Liturgy Today.* 1990. Reprint, Eugene, OR: Wipf & Stock, 2001.

Star-Ledger Continuous News Desk. "FBI Arrests 16 in N.J. as Part of National Child Prostitution Crackdown." November 9, 2010. https://www.nj.com/news/2010/11/fbi_arrests_16_in_nj_prostitut.html.

Stookey, Laurence Hull. *Eucharist: Christ's Feast with the Church.* Nashville: Abingdon, 1993.

Tabor, James D. *Paul and Jesus: How the Apostle Transformed Christianity.* New York: Simon & Schuster, 2013.

Taussig, Hal. *In The Beginning Was the Meal: Social Experimentation & Early Christian Identity.* Minneapolis: Fortress, 2009.

Taylor, Mark Lewis. "American Torture and the Body of Christ." In *Cross Examinations: Readings on the Meaning of the Cross Today,* edited by Marit Trelstad, 264–77. Minneapolis: Augsburg Fortress, 2006.

Terr, Lenore. *Too Scared to Cry: Psychic Trauma in Childhood.* New York: Harper & Row, 1990.

Terrell, JoAnne Marie. *Power in the Blood? The Cross in the African American Experience.* The Bishop Henry McNeal Turner/Sojourner Truth Series in Black Religion 15. Maryknoll, NY: Orbis, 1998.

Thurston, Herbert. "Washing of Feet and Hands." In *Catholic Encyclopedia.* Vol. 15. 1913. http://en.wikisource.org/wiki/Catholic_Encyclopedia_(1913)/Washing_of_Feet_and_Hands.

Turner, Victor. *From Ritual to Theatre: The Human Seriousness of Play.* Performance Studies Series 1. New York: Performing Arts Journal Publications, 1982.

United Church of Christ. *Book of Worship.* New York: United Church of Christ Office for Church Life and Leadership, 1986.

United Methodist Church (U.S.). "Service of Word and Table I." In *The United Methodist Book of Worship,* 33–39. Nashville: United Methodist Publishing House, 1992.

Ward, Graham. "The Displaced Body of Jesus Christ." In *Radical Orthodoxy,* edited by John Milbank et al., 163–81. London: Routledge, 1999.

Wainwright, Geoffrey. *Eucharist and Eschatology.* London: Epworth, 1971.

Welch, Sharon D. *A Feminist Ethic of Risk.* Minneapolis: Fortress, 1990.

West, Traci C. *Disruptive Christian Ethics: When Racism and Women's Lives Matter.* Louisville: Westminster John Knox, 2006.

White, James. *Sacraments as God's Self Giving: Sacramental Practice and Faith.* With a response by Edward J. Kilmartin. Nashville: Abingdon, 1983.

Williams, Delores S. *Sisters in the Wilderness: The Challenge of Womanist God-Talk.* Maryknoll, NY: Orbis, 1993.

Zagajewski, Adam. "Try to Praise the Mutilated World." Translated by Clare Cavanagh. *New Yorker*, September 24, 2001, back page (not numbered). https://www. newyorker.com/magazine/2001/09/24/try-to-praise-the-mutilated-world.

Zapor, Patricia. "At Border Mass, Bishops Call for Compassion, Immigration Reform." Justice. Politics. *National Catholic Reporter*, April 2, 2014. https://www.ncronline. org/news/justice/border-mass-bishops-call-compassion-immigration-reform.

Subject Index

Scripture Index

Name Index